D0065115

The Urban Scene in the Seventies

Proceedings of a Conference
on Public Policy
for Urban Minorities and the Poor
in the 1970s

The Urban Scene

in the Seventies

Edited by

James F. Blumstein
and
Eddie J. Martin

1974

VANDERBILT UNIVERSITY PRESS
Nashville, Tennessee

Library of Congress Cataloguing-in-Publication Data

Conference on Public Policy for Urban Minorities and
the Poor in the 1970s, Nashville, 1972.
The urban scene in the seventies; proceedings.

Includes bibliographies.
1. Cities and towns—United States—Congresses.
2. United States—Economic policy—1971–
—Congresses. 3. Cities and towns—Planning—United
States—Congresses. I. Blumstein, James F., 1945–
ed. II. Martin, Eddie J., 1943–   ed. III. Title.
HT123.C26 1972   301.36′3′0973   74–3452
ISBN 0–8265–1196–1

Printed in the United States of America

John Wesley [signature]

Contents

Contents

Preface

THIS conference represented a co-operative effort between the Vanderbilt Urban and Regional Development Center and the Fisk Urban Affairs Institute. In giving a basic support grant to the Urban and Regional Development Center, the Ford Foundation specified that a significant portion of the moneys awarded be spent on programs that would foster institutional co-operation between Vanderbilt and Fisk universities. The impetus provided by the Ford grant has led Vanderbilt, a predominantly white institution, and Fisk, a predominantly black institution, to constructive interaction in developing their urban studies and public policy programs. Overcoming a historically rooted mutual distrust has not been an easy task—and the goal is far from completely achieved—but the programs of co-operation spawned by the Ford Foundation grant have helped to contribute to a close and cordial working relationship between the Urban and Regional Development Center and the Urban Affairs Institute. The success of the conference marked an important step in the direction of more harmonious and productive institutional bonds.

The papers presented in this book are slightly modified versions of the pieces actually prepared for and delivered at the conference, which took place in Nashville, Tennessee, on April 5–7, 1972. We have done some editing, but we have exercised the self-restraint that all too infrequently characterizes the editorial process. In the very few cases where there has been disagreement, the editors have deferred to the authors.

In order to maintain the conference flavor and to retain fidelity to the content of the conference itself, we have not sought to fill in possible substantive gaps in the material by soliciting additional articles or seeking to reprint pieces published elsewhere. Obviously, there is a cost in terms of incompleteness, both because of the limitations imposed by the conference format and also because of the lapse in time between the conference and the appearance of the published proceedings. Despite these inherent limitations and the occurrence of terribly important events in the interim—the New Federalism and revenue sharing being the most significant—we felt that publication of the conference proceedings would make an important contribution to the literature as an indication of what some of the nation's foremost experts were saying at a single moment in history.

Since the conference was held in the spring of 1972, it has become apparent that bold initiatives still must be taken in the area of urban policy. Imaginative programs must be formulated and nurtured, and this will require a heavy dose of commitment by government, the private sector, citizens, and institutions of higher education, such as Fisk and Vanderbilt. This will require an increasingly greater willingness on the part of universities to play an aggressive role in dealing with problems faced by urban communities in this country. Fisk, through its Urban Affairs Institute, and Vanderbilt, through its Urban and Regional Development Center, are committed to mobilizing all of the available resources to address and solve problems on the urban scene. The concerns of these universities must include not only policy analysis but also policy formulation. They must provide thought and spawn action and welcome the activist as well as the technician.

Fisk and Vanderbilt, as institutions of higher learning, working together jointly and in co-operation independently, have a vast storehouse of expertise that has not been fully utilized in the past and should be tapped more completely in the future. A great challenge lies ahead for government, foundations, and private industry to move with dispatch to mobilize and support the efforts of institutions of higher learning such as Fisk and Vanderbilt in their work in urban affairs and public policy. Only through co-ordinated efforts and pooling of complementary resources of expertise will there develop a climate conducive to change that is so necessary for policy implementation.

The book is organized in three parts. In the first section, the articles seek to define the problems that public policy should be addressing. The papers in the second section evaluate past programs in terms of focus and effectiveness, while the pieces in the final section discuss policy formulation for the future. It should be self-evident that centers of learning, primarily the universities, will have an important role in developing tools for refining techniques of problem analysis and policy evaluation. Moreover, it is clear that both the private and public sectors will continue to rely on the resources of the academy in formulating policy strategies and alternatives in the future. The programs at Vanderbilt and Fisk are committed to assisting in this process.

JAMES F. BLUMSTEIN
EDDIE J. MARTIN

Nashville, Tennessee
December 1973

ACKNOWLEDGMENTS

The idea for this conference arose in a meeting among Cecil Butler, then of the Fisk University Urban Affairs Institute, William Yancey, then director of the Vanderbilt Urban and Regional Development Center, and James Blumstein, then Associate Director of the Vanderbilt Urban and Regional Development Center. Subsequently, John Archibald was engaged to serve as co-ordinator of the project, in close collaboration with Mr. Butler and Mr. Yancey. To them goes the bulk of the credit for making the conference and this book a reality.

Norma Weaver was instrumental in seeing the manuscript through from the conference-paper stage to the end product; her contribution has been invaluable. Eleanor Phillips has provided assistance in reference research, and her important role is gratefully acknowledged. Finally, appreciation must be expressed to Carole Lampley and Marilyn Richardson, who typed the manuscript through the various stages of the editorial process.

Of course, none of this project would have been possible without the generous support of the Ford Foundation, to whose munificence we shall remain everlastingly indebted. We should also like to acknowledge the financial assistance of the U.S. Department of Health, Education, and Welfare, which also helped to make this program possible.

The Urban Scene in the Seventies

Political Power
for Minorities

THIS month of April is only six days old and yet it marks the death of two great Americans. One of them, of course, is Dr. Martin Luther King, Jr., who died April 4, 1968. But Americans generally, and black people particularly, permitted the death of Adam Clayton Powell yesterday—April 4, 1972—to go virtually unobserved. There were relatively few reactions and nothing of a national nature at all. It may be that many of you here were too young to have known about Clayton Powell, or that in acquainting yourself about him, you relied so very heavily upon the white news media that was part of his downfall, part of the disgraceful exhibition which saw the man ousted from the Congress to which his people not only elected him but had re-elected him. There is a lesson in that for you who engage in rhetoric. Adam Clayton Powell emphasized power and paid the price.

Whom did he hurt, running around with girls? Whom did he hurt, driving a Jaguar? If they could have proven that he ever embezzled money from the United States government, don't you know he would have been in the penitentiary? He passed the most powerful legislation to aid and assist urban communities for the poor and black people that has ever been passed in any comparable period in the history of the United States. No white man is ever going to have the insistence that Powell had, and the power to deliver, and the willingness to do it.

Adam was never able to tell in his own words what he gave to this country. But black people ought to know and find out about him because he was a hero, he was a great big man. The things that he did "wrong" are the things that you talk about all the time—and that is,

3

he exercised raw negative power. The way that this country emasculated him ought to make you wiser as you go about learning, first,
what power is; second, how to obtain it; third, how to use it wisely
and effectively; and, finally, how to maintain your life, reputation,
and your ability so as to remain in a position where you can do
things for people.

Now let me talk about cities, the urban core, and political power,
and about what, if anything, can be done about the country today and
its problems. I'm not sure that the picture I am going to draw is one
that you are really ready to deal with. I don't profess to have the
answers; all I have are the opinions and the experiences which have
served me. They may not serve for you. I myself have often thought
how very much better it would be if every one of the folks I know
would only agree with me; but since they will not, then the best
way to make the world look bright is never mind what others say,
just go ahead and do what you think is right.

I am going to focus on the issue of education. I am going to
illustrate, by painting a picture of urban education, the nature of
urban problems. Many people want a separate school system, control
of the schools, the educational system, and the classroom. For all of
you who want to control the cities it is a well-documented fact that
probably by 1980 most large cities, industrial cities, will be *black,*
and *brown,* and *bankrupt.* To the people who look forward with
relish and anticipation to presiding over the cage that embraces you
with alienation, helplessness, and powerlessness, continue absorbing
yourself in fiction about what it is to control cities in the condition in
which they are today. Our cities have concentrated families on welfare. The National Social Security Administration established that the
minimum poverty level a family of four can live on is $3,968. In the
cities of our country are concentrated 45 million people who all fall
below that poverty-level line. People with jobs, people with income,
bring life to a city; people without jobs, people without sufficient
income, bring destruction. One thing you are going to have exclusive
control over is poverty. One out of every five people in New York
City is on Welfare Row, one out of six in Boston, one out of eight in
Cleveland. Another 46 million Americans earn less than $6,000 a
year. You not only have the poor, but you also have people who
literally work forty hours a week and more and cannot earn a decent
living. Of these people in the great cities of our country, some 11
percent have no private use of a kitchen, 24 percent live in houses
with no hot or cold running water, 22 percent have no private bedroom of their own, 48 percent (in the last six months) have been

unable to afford milk for their children, and another 18 percent are children who are unable to attend school because of lack of clothing. In the metropolitan areas where black kids are concentrated, a black begins the first grade with a lower achievement score than a white child. By the time they get to the sixth grade, blacks are two grades behind; by the time they get to the twelfth grade, they are 3.3 grades behind. Three times as many of these young black students drop out of school as do whites. In some of our cities, 70 percent of the teen-agers are without jobs.

Those who say that they want a separate black school have their wish. It isn't a question of whether you have a separate black school, it is a fact. What city is it that you know of that doesn't have almost all-black schools? Cleveland, Pittsburgh, New York, Boston, Los Angeles, Chicago—you tell me how many of your schools are inte-grated. In the city of Cleveland, 97 percent of all the black people live on the east side; the schools which they attend are virtually all black. Go to Washington, D.C. How much more separate can you get, with 97 percent black school population? Go to Chicago, where, in order to make sure you stay in the black schools, they set up those little wagons, or whatever they are, by the schools to put the black kids in. What do you mean, you want separate black schools? You have them. The question is, do you enjoy them?

I suggest that, as you study the urban condition, just deal with these facts. In Chicago, for example, the ten lowest-ranking schools all happen to be black. That's lowest-ranking by any of the criteria used to judge academic caliber of the school. In those schools, 63 percent of the teachers have had less than three years' experience, and some 70 percent of them are not even fully certified. In the city of Detroit, in 1967, you had the grandest riot of all time: estimated destruction anywhere in the neighborhood of 40 million to 100 million dollars' worth. All the schools in that area are almost entirely black. Thirty of those schools were dedicated during the administration of President Ulysses S. Grant. That's what you want to preside over, that's what you want to have control over.

Schools are run with money. Schools have no more money than cities do. Not only is there less money available for urban education but what is available has to be spent on *noneducational purposes* in the city schools more than in the suburban schools. You start out getting fewer dollars, usually less than half that of suburban schools, and then of that amount some 69 percent of it must be spent on things like maintenance, administration, and secretarial personnel, just to keep up with the duties that have been given to the city schools.

The problem is exacerbated because almost all of the school systems in this country draw their money primarily from property taxes, usually some 60 to 70 percent. The federal government has contributed less than 8 percent of the educational costs in this country. The urban school must be financed by the property tax which must be approved by the voters. Well, you know what has happened in the cities. The black has concentrated in the cities of the country while the white man has moved out. The remaining white persons are consistently voting down school bond issues and school tax levies because they are the only ones who have any property. Now that you have control over a predominantly black city, your next problem is where to get the money. What has happened without the money? In Youngstown, Ohio, they just closed the schools for six weeks because they couldn't pass a school bond issue or tax levy. In Gary, Indiana, presided over by a black man, they had to have a special night legislature to keep the schools opened. Was it because they had a black mayor? No. They have a white mayor in New Rochelle, New York, where they had to close schools. In the great city of Philadelphia last year, they were paying schoolteachers off in scrip. I haven't heard of anything like that since the depression.

In the city of Houston, Texas, the voters by a two-to-one majority defeated a 5-million-dollar tax levy and a 20-million-dollar bond issue. In Los Angeles, they defeated school bond issues three times. As a result they had to eliminate services. Services to whom? To the black people. Who else is basically and generally in that system, and the system in Philadelphia and in Cleveland? I am trying to send a message, and I want it to be perfectly clear. Do not listen to those who say that you should have a separate black school system and that they ought not to be integrated, that there ought not to be busing. Don't cripple these black boys and girls any more than they are already crippled by the isolated life they are living in this segregated, separatist society of ours. You are doing nothing but aiding and assisting everything and every person who believes that money is the easiest way. Everybody condemns the apartheid in South Africa. What is different about apartheid in South Africa and separatism in Chicago? Isn't the effect the same? Aren't you kept out of the system and deprived of the basic socio-economic benefits? Twenty years ago black Americans were segregated in this country. Twenty years ago you could not sit down at a lunch counter and have an ice cream soda in the capital of the United States. And you say you want separatism; they had it, you've had it, in spades. In the southern states in this country, the black people had to rise above it. From the back of buses and streetcars. In sixteen states and in the capital, black children were not permitted to go to school with white children in public schools. All these people who lost their lives in Tennessee, Georgia, Alabama, and Mississippi, did so to open up the doors for people to have some participation in this country, to be able to live decently, to have a decent home, to be able to clothe their children adequately and to send their children to good schools, and now look at you. What is this, this theory of separatism sweeping us up and placing us back in a condition and a state of mind that seems, at least to me, to be inconsistent with yourself?

Let me go ahead and tell you some more about the cities. National unemployment right now is some 6.2 percent. Now, that's everybody in the country. An official unemployment rate for black adults is 10.3 percent. Now, that's a pity. And when I say official, it means 10 percent of all the employable adults, male and female, who have been in the job market. There is well over another 10 percent of black adults, both male and female, who have never been on the job market so they cannot even be counted. We live in cities where you don't have a decent hospital for this great concentration of the poor. When I was growing up in Cleveland thirty years ago, we had to go all the way over to the west side to get medical treatment. Thirty years later, the poor in Cleveland still have to go to the west side to Metropolitan General Hospital.

The houses are old. We built 5,280 housing units for those on low income and for the elderly in the city of Cleveland in two years, but we have 50,000 substandard dwellings in the city. Fifty thousand! One year we put 5,000 hard-core unemployed people to work; but in the same year 4,000 kids dropped out of school and began looking for jobs. Another 1,700 employed persons were displaced by automation. We couldn't even hold the line. There isn't even money in most of these cities to demolish the old and substandard structures that stand there, as rattraps and places for the drug addicts, perverted bums, and what-not to hang around in. We don't have the money to destroy, let alone to build.

There isn't a city in the country that hasn't cut back on services. Those of you who are black, or white and poor, know that the area in which you live has always had the least amount of service from city administration. This is just a fact of life. The poor, the powerless, the minority get whatever's left after those who have some, the middle class, the politically powerful have had their needs taken care of. Then the administration gets to your area. So now what's happening in every big city? They are laying off garbage workers, they're laying off recreational employees, they're laying off medical personnel and technicians. This means that in the area where you already have the minimum health care in the first place, they are closing the health centers, closing the venereal disease centers, closing the tuberculosis treatment centers. It means that some boys and girls who are poor in the city go as far as the fourth or fifth grade before they ever receive a vaccination against various communicable diseases. It means that every year in these cities the number of infants who die at birth keeps getting larger because their mothers never saw a doctor until they were on the delivery table. You can double that number for those who die within the first year because of lack of any kind of postnatal care. Many students are bored in school, not because they don't have the intellectual ability, but in many instances because they really aren't being worked. Ear and eye defects are never discovered because they happen to live in a neighborhood where people don't have opportunities to go in and have examinations of their children.

In these cities there is a great concentration of automobile traffic. Pollution from traffic fills the air. When they say that the air is poison, those aren't just words. There is literally lead in the air. When you go into any of the central city neighborhoods and check any of the children in the neighborhood, you find a high incidence of lead poisoning just from breathing the air and a high incidence of pulmonary infection that's specific to air. And you know what, *there isn't anything a mayor can do about it* to any great degree because the cities have also had to rely on that same property tax that the schools draw from for most of their income. But as these cities have gotten older, the value of the property has declined, so you get less revenue. The rallying cry of everybody is, "Let's clean up the slums." But clean up means clear out. So they go in and they clear out the slums. It's right to do it, but I want to tell you also that those old derelict buildings were homes—not good homes, but they provided shelter. Cleaning up and clearing out means shifting one neighborhood and overcrowding the next one.

We need academic facilities in our cities. The colleges and universities have for too long been built out in the country. And with this great concentration of people now in the urban areas, we must have more colleges and universities inside the cities. Yet even in doing this you undermine the tax base. Have you ever thought what happens when they build a college or university? Whatever was formerly on that land was a tax-producing facility. When you build that college or university, it's *tax exempt*, but the city has to be *responsible for it.* So you lose the dollars originally coming in and replace them with a tax-exempt facility and add a new responsibility for the city that has to be taken care of by a diminished tax base.

Cities are beginning to have a black complexion. The reason is fairly simple. White people move out of the city because people who improve their economic status move. This is not new to mankind. Although the media talk about the whites leaving the cities, they cannot explain it. People have always moved away. For example, by the time it became an official city, all but three of the original settlers of the city of Cleveland had moved out. Rockefeller began in the city of Cleveland, lived on 22nd Street; this was back at the turn of the century. Then he moved from 22nd down to 40th Street, and then he made more money and finally moved outside of the city. If you look at any city, you can draw circles around it. You can see that the farther away from the old, decayed part of the city where the industry and business is located, the higher up is the income bracket of families. So they have always moved out, but because of racial situations in America, white people have been able to move out of the cities in numbers and at income levels that we have never seen before. This movement has received support and aid from the FHA mortgage-guaranteed-loan program. The federal government has specifically and clearly excluded black people from participating. So it means that with a two- or three-hundred-dollar down payment and middle income, whites move out of the city. Historically it would have probably taken two generations before they would have enough money to move into the higher cost of living in the suburbs outside the central city. But it is a fact that our great cities such as Atlanta and Baltimore are rapidly becoming black-majority cities now.

I have talked with the mayors, and every one of them has had to explain the plight of his city. The cities by 1980 will literally be bankrupt. Services are being reduced. There's only so far down that you can go before all that you have left to provide is some kind of minimum police and fire protection and a most inadequate garbage and rubbish service. All of the other things that people, particularly the poor, look to the government for today, the city will not be able to provide.

The havoc of American society is documented in the Kerner Commission Report. This country happens to be two nations, one white and one black, separate and unequal. The racial hostility in this nation is worse today than it ever was. The chances of a young black boy or girl getting a decent education are less today than they were ten years ago. The prospects of the black unemployed adult getting a job get weaker every day.

I paint that picture for you because it just happens to be a fact. If you don't believe me, ask Mayor Richard Hatcher in Gary, Indiana, where last week, by his own official statement, he counted 39 percent unemployed in Gary. Is that what you want to preside over? Well, those are the facts.

What is it that has to happen? Well, I happen to know only one way that a minority group has conditionally restored its image: Get control of its own destiny and effect some kind of personal economic self-sufficiency. There are only two ways of participation in the life of this nation, the economic system and the political system. But you cannot get into economics unless you have some money. I don't know how you can talk about having your own separate existence and at the same time expect The Man to finance you. I don't know how you do it. I wouldn't want to do it. You say, as a minority, all you need is to have enough money to really make yourself self-sufficient. I don't believe it; I haven't seen it happen. When people talk to me about black capitalism, I don't know what they mean. This is no country for small businessmen, white or black. The important thing about the ITT case is that ITT is a conglomerate. That means this company that originally started out in the business of communication today manufactures paper towels. It manufactures and sells refrigerators and all kinds of household goods. It is in almost every area of endeavor in this country: one company that has literally just absorbed dozens of small industries and businesses. When they merge with your business, it means that you go out of business. It means that, if you have a grocery store, you cannot compete with A & P and with Kroger. You cannot buy in sufficiently large stock to make your price competitive with these chain stores. This business of operating a grocery store—you might as well give up and forget about it. I don't know any car dealer that buys his cars from a black automobile manufacturer, I don't even know a black manufacturer of cars. Well, where is the business going to come from, where is the self-sufficiency going to come from?

I'm just painting a picture of our country as it exists today. Concentration of high crime; drugs that are crippling our children; young people victimized in every way; higher juvenile delinquency rate; even basically dual systems of justice. The more that you permit those who are powerless, helpless, and weak to concentrate in one place, the less you make it possible for them to gain any kind of strength—whether political or economic.

Conc.

For those who argue that revolutions are led by a minority, I want to say to you that I don't know of any successful revolutions in history that did not have either the participation or at least neutrality of the army or the police force of that country. If there is one of you in this auditorium that happens to know anything to the contrary, then you educate me on it. And if you believe that the police in this country are going to let you carry on a successful revolution, then you really are indulging in fantasy.

I want you to understand me, now, about the police because I want to get the notion of violence out of your mind. Not because I'm nonviolent, because I'm not. If you come up here and hit me in the mouth, you're going to get the damnedest fight you ever had. I am not Martin Luther King, Jr., I am not Gandhi, but neither am I going to commit suicide, and I don't want you to commit suicide for me. That's why I want to take time to tell those of you who fantasize about civil revolution in this country not to do it. I wouldn't mind if they would take only you, but when they come after you, they're going to come after me, too. And I don't want to go.

The police in this country are armed and trained far beyond anything you can imagine. There is not a big city in this country that does not have some form of armored car owned by the police. The police have every kind of automatic weapon you can dream of; bulletproof vests. Hundreds of millions of dollars are going, not to educate police to be better policemen, but rather to arm policemen better. So when you go out, have in mind that you are dealing with a force that understands how to deal with violence. They understand how to deal with violence and have no compunction against using violence. I don't know whether you need more positive evidence of the readiness of the police in this country to cope with black physical violence.

If you happen to think that it just relates to black people, it doesn't. It relates to anything that threatens. Don't think about 1941 as being ancient history; that was only thirty or so years ago. They put American Japanese in concentration camps. Do you know they still have those concentration camps? I'm not talking about what America might do; I'm talking about what America has to do; they've got to get rid of these concentration camps. They are there, maintained, ready to go.

I want you to think a little bit about another thing. In the Second World War, I was over there driving those trucks. I was trained in the infantry just like most black folks were, but when we got overseas, we were put in trucks, laundry companies, things like that. I knew about the Jews being massacred there, but you know what, it never really reached inside of me. I knew that white folks were fighting white folks—it was their war. White newspapers all through the United States carried on a crusade to get the black soldiers to get in the front lines. When they came to my company and told us that all the men who wanted to go to the front line should step forward, nobody moved. Let the white folks do it, we understood that. There was another part of this that black soldiers needed to understand and black soldiers today need to take a lesson from. They kill Germans, right. Germans killed six million people. Six million people, and do you know what they were? They were mayors, judges, upholsterers, schoolteachers, educators, social workers, students, new-born babies. The whole issue of this is, is that something that only Germany would do to Jews? Why? Prejudice happens to have been associated with the discrimination against Jews. The potential of that happening in America is now and always present. If that is true, how are we going to carry on the political revolution that's necessary to correct some of the acknowledged problems that all of us either know by living with them or know intellectually? There is one way. We must take all who have common interests at stake and together form a coalition of interests.

Now is this a new idea? Of course not. The most recent historical evidence of it was President Roosevelt's New Deal. He pulled together people who had traditionally not been Democrats but who were suffering in common from the extensive unemployment that the depression brought.

So what do we have to do in this country? Well, if we look around we find out that there happen to be, besides 22 million black Americans, 17 million Spanish-speaking people and 20 million senior citizens—persons over the age of 60 who are trapped in this poverty- and crime-ridden deteriorated central city. Then there's the poor white who no longer is out there on the farm like he used to be. Now 74 percent of all Americans live on less than 2½ percent of the land. Poor whites are in that city just like we are. I had to teach the poor whites in Cleveland that they should be in the coalition with Carl Stokes. That's the only way I got elected. Cleveland is not a black city. Cleveland is 63 percent white, and I went to the whites, the unemployed, the blue-collar worker, the middle and southern Europeans—Bulgarian, Romanian, Polish people, Italians—people in competition with the black man in the economic role, where the tenseness and the hostility are greater. But I went to the poor white in our city and I showed him how he suffered from lack of good schools in his area, how the services weren't any better in his area than in the black area, how the police beat him up just like they beat us, the blacks. How they didn't have medical care centers in their neighborhood, any more than they had them in the black neighborhood. And I used to tell them about a story illustrating how some white people regard other white people. When I was a prosecutor, two white squadsmen came in and asked me for a warrant on a lady. They didn't call her a lady. I asked them, "What are you so upset about?" They proceeded to tell me that they had gotten a call. This woman was over at a bar trying to sell some of her that nobody wanted to buy. She got upset and started calling people some bad names. So they went over and tried to get her to leave, but she wouldn't leave. So they called the wagon. It took four of them to put her in the wagon. I said, "Was she white or black?" The squadsman said, "Neither one; she was a hillbilly." He knew that that lady wasn't black, and he wasn't going to let her be white, so he made her something else. And that's how the poor white lives in the cities. The unfortunate thing is that they keep these two classes that have every reason to work together in constant conflict with one another.

Let no one tell you that the problems are not solvable. The problems of education are solvable. Money may not be everything, but it is far ahead of whatever is second. And as you approach these problems, money is the first criterion that you have to have. So let's just quickly review what it is that you have to do by way of getting the money for these different people acting in coalition. Obviously you are going to have to get this nation to reorder its priorities. You cannot continue to spend 30 million dollars in Indochina when your schools and houses are in a shameful condition here at home. It means that you cannot spend 5.5 billion dollars on the space shuttle when every morning from seven to nine o'clock and every afternoon from four to six-thirty you have a massive traffic jam in every city in this country. We have to get out of this disastrous massive war involvement in Indochina. You cannot fight a war and also provide for needs at home. Then you must educate this country of ours, sensitize this country of ours, to secure revenue-sharing for the cities. Revenue-sharing is a simple proposition. While the local level has been raising our taxes some 436 percent in the last twenty years, the federal government has been cutting its taxes. You may not realize it, but just last year, the federal government reduced your income tax. On the local level someone, either the mayor, the school system, the county or somebody is trying to raise taxes, while the federal government is cutting taxes. Great wealth, great growth each year, so what you have to do is cut the *arbitrary forces* 1½ percent and 2 percent and dedicate that money back to the city so that we can build the schools, build the houses, provide food and clothing. And then finally you must have re-distribution of income. Income redistribution has to come. Twenty percent of the people of this country possess over 80 percent of the wealth. There have to be things such as the Family Assistance Program that is presently before the Congress. It must be approved. America happens to be the only industrial country in the world that does not have some guaranteed income. There is presently a bill that Congress has failed to pass, to guarantee health care. Every other industrial country in the world has that, with the exception of ours.

Those are the things which I see as constituting the facts of America, of urban life and the dilemma we are in, the traps which we have placed ourselves in.

PART I

Defining the Problems in Their Institutional Settings

Chapter 1 ANDREW BILLINGSLEY

American Values and the Urban Crisis: Federal Welfare Policy

J OHN KILLENS, faculty member at Howard University and one
of the nation's outstanding writers, has observed that America
will be the first nation in history to move from barbarism to decadence
without going through civilization. It is an apt commentary on the
status of our society as we go about our daily lives bombarded on all
sides by slogans like "urban crisis," "black ghetto," "welfare mess,"
"busing," "black illegitimacy," and "population explosion." All these
slogans are designed and utilized to mask the complex realities we
face in this society. At the heart of those realities is urbanism, and at
the heart of urbanism is black people, and both the nature of our
society and the nature of black people are tremendously distorted,
not only by the mass media, but by our finest and most enlightened
social scientists, intellectuals, politicians, and educators.

A first priority, then, if we are to understand the nature of our
urban situation and if we are to design more enlightened federal
social policies, is to understand, describe and analyze the true nature
of American society.

John Gardner and the American promise. In the area of federal
policy, urban affairs, and the general welfare, no voice in the American
establishment is saner, more persistent, more informed, and more
committed to the common good than that of John Gardner. The dual
themes of individual freedom and striving for excellence, coupled
with his belief that our present society can renew itself through a
commitment to basic American values, run throughout Gardner's
writings and are expressed in his life and work as well. He knows, and
says very well, that the society is in trouble; it is in crisis; it is

decadent. He earnestly believes, however, that the society may be renewed on the basis of the values in which he believes, and he believes
that most white Americans share his basic values and beliefs, which
he assumes to be American beliefs, and the American practice. He is
a most remarkable American fighting for what he truly believes in.
Thus, whether he is functioning as an educator, a foundation executive,
a high government official, or a public protest leader, he symbolizes
the finest in leadership qualities and social analysis that exists today
among white men of intelligence, ability, and influence. As we have
indicated elsewhere, John Gardner is truly a credit to his race. The
problem is that he does not truly represent his race, and he is not a
real leader because he has no substantial following among his people.

Unfortunately, Gardner, like Gunnar Myrdal before him, has an
essentially false conception of American society. Myrdal thought, for
example, that the American dilemma consisted essentially of a conflict
between the basic values in which Americans believe, including
freedom, democracy, and equality on the one hand, and the practice
of Americans toward black people which represents the antithesis of
these basic values. Americans are, therefore, according to his view, in a
quandary, a dilemma. They are torn between their basic beliefs and
their actions. Gardner believes similarly that Americans have a basic
value commitment to justice, freedom, equality, and that the problem
is: How can America practice the individual achievement and commitment to excellence, which the society needs to renew itself, and
at the same time hold onto these basic values? Gardner is somewhat
more optimistic than Myrdal. He thinks that the solution to the
dilemma can be found within the values themselves. Thus, his task
and that of other reformers is to arouse the American people to a
reassertion and re-evaluation of and recommitment to the true nature
of their values and beliefs.

The trouble with this analysis is that it is based on a faulty
premise. The fact is that Americans do not have a dilemma; they do
not truly believe in equality or democracy or any of the other widely
accepted views about basic American values. Most scholars know
what Gardner should also know, that the best way to find out the
values of a people is to observe their behavior over time. One of the
least accurate ways of finding out the values of a people is to ask them
to tell you, or to read what they write about their values in books or
what they say in speeches or how they answer questionnaires. Sometimes, as one listens to the eloquent pleadings of John Gardner's
speeches, one gets the sense that he knows this, that he senses the
mythical basis on which his ministry is built. Little wonder, then, that

he is a lonely, frustrated man crying out in a modern wilderness trying to arouse his fellowman to regain what was never truly there—a commitment to the common good. For it must be clear to the careful observer of our society and particularly our nation that whatever common good has emerged is a by-product of something else which Americans consider much more important, and that something else is much more closely related to self-centeredness, ethnocentrism, greed, power, death, and destruction than it is to any commitment to co-operation, to life, and the common welfare.

Basic American values: violence. What then are the basic values and characteristics of the American people which help us understand the true nature of this society? First is violence. We are coming increasingly to understand that the American people are a violent people. This is a violent nation and the government, following the basic values of the people and interpreting them quite correctly, is therefore one of the greatest perpetrators of violence the world has ever known. It is much easier to get the support of American citizens for a war against people than it is to get their support for a war against poverty. The federal budget has reflected this value pattern by allocating vast sums to fight the Vietnam war, while giving relatively peripheral priority to programs designed to solve the problems of the inner cities (Clark, 1967:39).

Another indication of the basic commitment to violence on the part of Americans is reflected in our most important cultural expressions. Thus, violence on television, in movies, in literature, and on the stage is at the heart of American culture and American values. The massive five-volume report prepared by the U.S. Surgeon General, issued in January of 1972, provides considerable support for the connection between violence on television and damage to children. The problem, however, does not lie with television, for television programming is, in our view, a reflection of the violence in the American character structure rather than a cause of it. Consider, for example, how difficult it is to establish reasonable controls on the manufacture, sale, purchase, and use of guns. It has been estimated that in this country alone there have been at least 750,000 firearms fatalities. This includes murders, suicides, and accidental deaths. Yet politicians who support firearms control legislation do so at considerable political peril.

The major American pastimes might be ranked as follows: (1) engaging in violent behavior; (2) engaging in putting down violent behavior on the part of others; (3) observing violent behavior directly and indirectly; and (4) talking about violence and the reactions of other people to it. Why such preoccupation with violence? In my own view, it is because our society is dominated by a people whose essential greed can most easily be satisfied by their tremendous capacity for destruction. In a new book called *The American Way of Violence*, (1972) Professor Alphonso Pinkney has observed that American society actively nurtures coercion and cruelty and that the economic system of the country requires systematic slaughter in this country and overseas. Of course, those people and groups who benefit most from such organized and mass violence are likely to be the most critical of individual reaction to violence on the part of poor, powerless people at the bottom of society.

Racism. While violence is at the heart of the collective American national character, racism in all its individual, institutional, and collective forms is an important second characteristic. One of the earliest analyses of racism in America was contained in Hamilton and Carmichael's book, *Black Power* (1967:4):

Racism is both overt and covert. It takes two, closely related forms: individual whites acting against individual blacks, and acts by the total community against the black community. We call these individual racism and institutional racism.

The theme was given national attention in the work of the Kerner Commission report (National Advisory Commission on Civil Disorders, 1968:203): "White racism is essentially responsible for the explosive mixture which has been accumulating in our cities since the end of World War II." In a new book, *Children of the Storm* (Billingsley and Giovannoni, 1972:8), we have defined racism as follows:

Racism, in our view, is a set of attitudes and/or behaviors exhibited by members of one racial group (white people) toward members of another racial group (black people) which are negative, unfavorable, and detrimental to the well-being of the latter and functional for the well-being of the former. Racism, then, is the systematic negation, exploitation, and oppression of one racial group by another. Evidence abounds of the systematic negation, exploitation, and oppression of black people in this country. Thus, we speak of white racism. It is hard to find examples of systematic oppression of white people by black people. It is, therefore, misleading to speak of black racism, as some would want to do. . . .

These attitudes and behaviors we call racism may be held and exhibited by individuals, or shared in groups, or embodied in the policies and procedures of organizations and institutions.

A further distinctive feature of racism is that it may exist and operate at the covert level where it may be said to be latent. Or it may exist and operate out in the open and in an overt or manifest manner. This is true of individual, collective, and institutional racism.

The commitment to violence and the commitment to racism are often combined and sustain each other when the society deals with black people individually or collectively. One can see this in the oppression suffered by blacks in the system of justice as exemplified by the courts and the police. Herbert O. Reid, Professor of Law at Howard University, served as Staff Director of the Commission of Inquiry which found that the police in Chicago spearheaded a reign of terror against the Black Panthers, and in all probability murdered Fred Hampton and Mark Clark in their raid on Panther Headquarters in Chicago in 1969. The New York *Times* article that described the Commission's report quoted it as saying that the raid was a "search and destroy mission aimed at the leaders of the Illinois chapter of the Black Panther Party." The report said that the police fired first, that there was no resistance by the Panthers and, indeed, that they cried to the police to stop firing to no avail. The report concluded:

The conception and planning of the raid, the sequence of events inside the apartment, the volume of police gunfire, and the toll of deaths and injuries do not particularly lend themselves to the characterization of these events as a "police-Panther shoot-out"; they could equally well lead to characterizations of events as slaughter, and summary execution (New York *Times,* 17 March 1972:17).

In commenting on that report, Professor Reid has observed that there is a tremendous increase in arrests in the urban ghetto.

One of the tragic things about it is that you're talking about blacks and the poor, and they are not having one damn bit on input in how they are to be put in jail and kept in jail. . . . A kind of repressive period is upon us and gaining momentum. . . . After a while, these people [the police, prosecutors] begin to approach their task with a missionary zeal. They begin to feel as though they are about God's business. You get the feeling that they would try any method, fair or foul, with the notion that if we don't get you today, we'll get you tomorrow (New York *Times,* 1 August 1971).

Professor Reid is referring to a deep-seated cultural value in American society reflected in the administration of criminal justice.

Ramsey Clark, former Attorney General of the United States and author of a perceptive book entitled *Crime in America* has observed that, "We cultivate crime, breed it, nourish it. Little wonder we have so much (1970:66)." He continues:

Perhaps the greatest reflection on our character is that we were relatively unconcerned for decades while crime festered in the slums. Thousands of heroin addicts died annually there and we barely noted it. Our concern arose when new social dynamics and population movements brought crime and addiction out of the slums and inflicted it on or threatened our powerful and well-to-do.

Nor is the confluence of violence and racism confined to the prosecution and persecution of persons found guilty of crimes. Despite the fiction in American law that one is entitled to a speedy trial by a jury of one's peers, and that one is innocent until proven guilty, just the opposite is the reality that black people face. Indeed, a large number of black youths who are presently incarcerated have never been found guilty of any crime. Much of the agony expressed by prisoners comes from men who have been imprisoned without trial. A recent study shows that when prisoners in New York City jails rioted in 1970, their priority demand was for a speedy trial, a right theoretically guaranteed them by the Constitution.

Ethnocentrism. Still a third characteristic of our society is ethnocentrism by the dominant groups and longing to be like them on the part of minority groups. In *Black Families in White America* (1968: 156), we refer to this as the Anglo-conformity doctrine, which gives rise to a series of illusions of white grandeur. This configuration includes the illusion that white people of Anglo-European heritage are superior to black people of African heritage in every major respect (more stable, more beautiful, wiser, more competent, more moral, more normal, more powerful, and the like). Of particular harm to the advancement of blacks is that many black people hold the same illusion of white superiority. Perhaps it is a natural human characteristic to define one's worth in terms sanctioned by the most powerful persons in society, but this illusion is crippling to the cause of black progress.

Individualism. This discussion of basic American values cannot close without some reference to individualism which gives rise to individual greed and personal advancement at the expense of the common good. How else can we explain that 112 Americans who had earnings of more than $200,000 dollars last year paid not a single cent of federal income tax (New York *Times*, 3 January 1972)? Or that the Governor of California, a very wealthy man, paid not a cent of state income tax? Or that dozens of millionaires paid no income tax? You would think that these upstanding citizens who benefit so much from the resources of the country would be eager to contribute to the federal treasury for the common well-being of their less privileged countrymen, or even for the support of other government functions. Not only does the system allow and indeed encourage these men to exercise such selfish greed, but it rewards, honors, and applauds them for doing so, and other Americans are only envious that they cannot do the same. There is no basic commitment in the collective American national character toward the common good except where it serves a selfish interest. Little wonder that programs of social welfare are so easily sacrificed to other priorities.

This, then, is the value context out of which American society functions—violence, racism, enthnocentrism, and individualism. These basic values have helped to build a strong country. At the same time, however, they help to account for the inability of this society to come to grips with its social problems. And this value constellation is mainly responsible for the nation's rapid decline. It largely accounts for the fact that the black man in America and black people as a people, when they are not being oppressed, are largely ignored. Benjamin Quarles, an outstanding historian, observed a few years ago, "When we pick up a social science book, we look in the index and under 'Negro,' it will read, 'See Slavery,' 'See Crime,' 'See Juvenile Delinquency,' perhaps 'See Commission of Civil Disorders'; perhaps see anything except the Negro. So when we try to get a perspective on the Negro, we get a distorted perspective (1967:32)."

Black perspective. And this brings us to the matter of perspective, for clearly if we are to understand the nature of the urban crisis, which is not so much a crisis as a chronic condition for black people, and if we are to design federal policies and programs to deal adequately with the urban condition, we must see that condition from the perspective of black people. That is the only way to see it correctly and truthfully for, as we must have learned by now from Lerone Bennett and Frantz Fanon and Jean-Paul Sartre, truth is the perspective of the truly disinherited. Black people in the urban areas of our country are truly disinherited, and if we do not see the urban condition from the perspective of black people, we will continue to misperceive it and will continue to fashion solutions which don't work.

Thus, if the first priority in understanding the urban situation and the development of more effective federal policies is to understand the true nature of American society, including its value base, the second priority is to understand the realities and complexities of the black

community, including the true nature of childhood and family life in
the black community. Our concept of that life is developed in *Children
of the Storm* (1972) and may be summarized here. Contrary to what
others have written about us, the family is by far the strongest institution in the black community. It continues to be the primary
component of our efforts toward survival and liberation, and it is the
key element in our struggle for positive human development. We
know that when we think of family in the black community, we do
not confine our thinking to husband and wife and two children living
together in splendid isolation in their own house. We are a more
complex and humane people than that. And so the extended family
and a multiple variety of nuclear, extended, and augmented family
forms are an intricate part of what we mean by family. And it must be
clear to all of us, as a basis for all we attempt to say and do in the
interest of human development, that were it not for the strength,
endurance, adaptability, and resilience of family life in the black
community, we would not have survived as a people. We cannot, then,
allow others to lead us to discard what is most valuable to our own
struggle. Nor can we allow the problems we face to obscure our
ability to use the strength of our institutions to improve the quality
of our lives and inform our demands on the larger society.

If the family in all its variety and complexity is the cornerstone of
our existence, survival, and development as a people, the value system
underlying our concept of family, which is in its essence a communal
value system deeply imbedded in our African heritage, has been the
soil on which the foundation of our existence has been laid. It is this
sense of community, our commitment to it, longing for it, and willingness to pursue it which is a most valuable and grossly under-
appreciated aspect of our heritage and our promise as a people. Our
goal is to pursue the personal and social development of black people
by mastering, controlling, utilizing, and transforming these systems in
order to create new systems of organization which will be more
compatible with our conception of human development. We recognize
that this is a struggle which is not likely to respond to quick-cure
solutions or easy victories. Our very experience as a people and the
eloquent expressions of Frederick Douglass teach us that.

The black individual, whether child or adult, does not exist in
isolation but is part of family life, whether past, present, or future.
Similarly, the black family does not exist as an isolated unit but is
intricately bound up with the black community and the various
institutions, processes, problems, and opportunities represented
therein. In like manner, the black community itself is a component of

a larger society which must be related to, mastered, and transformed in order that black families may function adequately.

We are particularly concerned that black children receive during the first five crucial years of life the kind of nurture, care, love, and physical and emotional support that will fortify them to run the race in later years as they begin to encounter the formal institutions of society.

Four problems plague the black man in America and reach their zenith in the urban centers of our cities: racist exclusion from the systems and rewards of the larger society; economic insecurity; political disenfranchisement; and cultural oppression. These problems have not responded to federal policies so far, in large measure because the policies have not been designed from the perspective of people who live in the cities.

Let us consider briefly the matter of economic insecurity, a problem which is at the center of the present concern about welfare reform. One of the most imaginative and far-reaching federal programs designed to deal with this problem is represented in the omnibus welfare reform bill vetoed by the President earlier this year. The President's own proposal for a Family Assistance Plan as a concept in its own right, shorn of some of the negative features accompanying it, is also a concept which represents progressive thinking at the federal level. Even so, however, these proposals are so far from the reality of the problem they are designed to attack that the ordinary man in the street must question the competence as well as the commitment of those experts who give advice to the President and the Congress. For how can a program of guaranteed minimum income of $2,400 for a family of four be considered a serious attack on the problem of economic insecurity in the 1970s? As Gunnar Myrdal said at a symposium at the University of California in 1964, the greatest cause of poverty is the absence of money, and the most potent solution to the problem is the access to money on the part of poor people who don't have it. By the government's own standards, $2,400 is not enough to move a family of four out of poverty. Indeed, it is less than half enough. A more realistic approach has been taken by the National Welfare Rights Organization under the dynamic leadership of George Wiley. They have called for a minimum income of $6,500 a year, a position which has also been unanimously supported by the Congressional Black Caucus. A simple test of how close the President's proposals come to reality as compared with those of the National Welfare Rights Organization and the Black Caucus may be observed by reference to the following data. According to a Gallup

Poll conducted in 1970, a national sample of Americans estimated
that the minimum income necessary to support a family of four was
$126 a week. In a similar poll conducted in 1971, the estimate was
$127 a week. The federal government's own Bureau of Labor Statistics
estimated in 1970 that a minimum of $136 a week was necessary for
a family of four in metropolitan areas to maintain a minimum level of
health and safety.

As we may observe, then, the National Welfare Rights Organization
demand for a minimum income of $6,500 is much closer to the
minimum needs of families for health and safe living conditions than
the proposals of the President or the Congress. Moreover, if we
consider the aspiration of families to live beyond the level of minimal
existence, we may be informed by another study done by the Bureau
of Labor Statistics which indicates that in 1970 in New York and New
Jersey it took a gross income of $12,134 to maintain a family of four at
a moderate standard of living. The Bureau published what it calls a
lower budget which requires $7,183 a year, an intermediate budget
which refers to the $12,134 and a higher budget which requires
$18,545 a year for a family of four to live well. Table 1 (New York
Times, 21 December 1970) shows the proportion of these funds which
families have to pay for food, housing, transportation, medical care,
taxes, etc.

It must be clear from the previous discussion that none of the
above proposals for federal welfare policies comes even close to
approaching the real needs of the people who live outside the
American dream. It is our view that such policies are not likely to be
formed or supported nationally until there is some basic change in the
fundamental value constellation of the collective American character.
The question, then, becomes not so much which specific programs
should be recommended as how to change the basic American values
toward a collective concern for the common good.

What must be recognized and incorporated into federal policy is
that the economic situation of black people in urban areas is getting
increasingly worse rather than better or staying the same. In a very
critical analysis of the predicament of black people in the country
today entitled, *Who Needs the Negro?,* Sidney M. Willhelm has observed that the interaction between racism and economic motives have
combined to worsen the economic stability of black Americans. The
crux of his argument is stated as follows:

The arrival of automation eliminates the need for black labor, and racism
values call for the Negro's removal from the American scene. The present

TABLE 1

Where the Dollar Goes
New York—Northwestern New Jersey
Urban 4-Person Family, Three Budgets, Spring 1970

	Food	Housing	Transportation	Clothing & Personal Care	Medical Care	Taxes	All Other
				Percent of Annual Income Spent for			
Higher Budget $18,545	19.1%	25.7%	7.0%	9.2%	3.4%	24.1%	11.6%
Intermediate Budget $12,134	23.0%	25.3%	7.1%	9.5%	4.9%	19.6%	10.5%
Lower Budget $7,183	29.1%	19.3%	6.0%	11.3%	8.3%	15.9%	10.1%

SOURCE: The New York Times, December 21, 1970. Copyright © 1970 by the New York Times Company. Reprinted by permission.

situation is but the final culmination of what has always been the substance of black-white relations: racism expanded to the limits established by economic values (1971:332).

The central problem facing the black community is an increasingly severe economic depression which has existed in the black community since the end of World War II with a slight improvement during the Korean War. The hard fact is that, despite the prosperity in the general society, the economic situation in the black community is getting worse rather than better in relationship to the rest of the society.

Andrew Brimmer, member of the Federal Reserve Board, has repeatedly called for a dual approach to the problem, involving strong, consistent, fair, and effective controls on wages and prices to curb inflation and, simultaneously, massive public expenditures for public services to stem the rising unemployment which is more than 50 percent in many black communities. The fact is, however, that neither of these measures has been seriously undertaken. The wage-price guidelines are in a state of disarray. Public service spending is minimal for the reasons we have already discussed.

While public outlays of funds have increased significantly in recent years, Brimmer has pointed out that inflation is the major cause. Government spending more than tripled between 1955 and 1969, according to Brimmer, from 39 billion dollars to 132 billion dollars, but inflation accounted for well over 40 percent of the increase.

The Washington *Post* (20 March 1972: D7) reported on the worsening economic plight of black people as confirmed by a recent study prepared for Congress by two Massachusetts Institute of Technology economists and released by Senator Proxmire, Chairman of the Joint Economic Committee. The *Post* stated that, in spite of substantial growth in real income in the last two decades, the spread between the poorest and richest categories has widened. In 1949 the gap between the poorest one-fifth and the richest one-fifth was $10,565; twenty years later it was $19,971. The two economists said most techniques for reducing inflation make the poor worse off and that conditions for the poor in American society cannot be changed by concentrating only on education and training. Instead they suggested using government wage and job structures to stimulate increases in private wages, concentrating manpower programs in order to improve income distribution, and adopting minority job quotas.

In its massive *Counterbudget* the National Urban Coalition has developed a blueprint for changing national priorities between 1971 and 1976. In its view the major problem with the country is what it considers "our paralysis of spirit and will." In delineating six major specific goals for the country between now and 1976, they give the highest priority to economic development:

1. Achieve full employment with a high level of economic growth and reasonable price stability—all of our other policy goals depend upon it.
2. Provide all citizens with an equal opportunity to participate in American society and in the shaping of government decisions affecting their lives.
3. Guarantee that no American will go without the basic necessities: food, shelter, health care, a healthy environment, personal safety, and an adequate income.
4. Rectify the imbalance in revenues between the federal government and state and local governments.
5. Assure adequate national security against military threats from abroad.
6. Meet our obligations to assist in the economic development of the world's less-developed nations (p. xiv).

Conclusion. In order to close this discussion on the assumption that change is possible, and to indicate the most fruitful directions such change should take, I would like to advance the following propositions: Economic development of the black community, as a community, both internally and externally, is a basic requirement for transforming the present dysfunctional system into one which serves the needs of black people. This is a first step in the direction of abolishing present welfare programs. The Congressional Black Caucus, the National Black Political Convention and a group of ten black economists have all made earnest recommendations to this effect. Chief among the means of such economic empowerment is the concept of reparations which we have recommended as a type of welfare reform in *Children of the Storm*.

A second idea closely related to the idea of reparations has been advanced convincingly and eloquently by Professor Frank Davis, Chairman of the Department of Economics at Howard University (1972). It is the idea of a national undertaking which he calls Ghetto Enterprises, Inc. The idea has been endorsed by the National Black Political Convention as follows:

That an independent, non-profit publicly funded national black development agency be established under black leadership and control for the purpose of facilitating black ownership and/or control of the full range of business and service enterprises now serving ghetto communities, including public transportation and communication systems, day care and health centers, housing, educational, and commercial and financial institutions. Local community development corporations would be the implementing agencies. This effort should be awarded multi-year funding with a budget of $5 million for its first year (1972:5).

The political empowerment of the black community is an indispensable concomitant of economic empowerment. Sometimes it will be a cause, sometimes an effect, and sometimes a concomitant of economic development. Again, the National Black Political Convention spoke of a new politics of social transformation. It established a national mechanism for independent black political advocacy. Pending the outcome of such drastic reform, they have recommended the following:

The establishment of black Congressional representation in proportion to our presence in the national population. We are at least 15 percent of the population. Through Constitutional amendment—or any other means necessary—we ought to have a minimum of 66 representatives and 15 senators; that until such time as the House and the Senate represent black people fairly, our due seats are to be filled by persons elected at-large by the national black community. The same principle shall obtain for state and local governments (1972:4).

In our own view, the key concept in political empowerment has to do with the ability of black people to control all of the programs which operate in the black community, and to have an equitable share of input into the policies and programs which operate at the national level and in all communities.

Next to economic empowerment and political empowerment, and sometimes as a basis for each of these, is the increasingly strongly felt necessity for black cultural hegemony over the values and life-styles of our own people. It is only as we are freed of the constraints imposed upon us by an oppressive society, and as we insist on defining ourselves and our behavior, that we will be able to make an independent contribution to the basic value system and character structure of American society.

In the realm of values, it may well be that black youth are the nation's vanguard. Black youth see the nature of the reality we face much more clearly than any other segment of our population. Whether they are locked into the inner city, locked in jails and prisons, locked into the armed forces by a combination of oppression and selective opportunity, or whether they are in fact pursuing higher education, black youth are on the cutting edge of the contradictions in our society. They have come of age in a time when it is not possible to avoid these contradictions, and their heritage allows them to feel and sense the decadence of our society and to call a spade a spade and tell it "like it is." Thus, while some people can earnestly denounce violence and praise the name of Martin Luther King while actively pursuing war and oppression and still keep a straight face, we are not likely to hear such nonsense emanating from the organized black youth movement. And while some people, even some of their leaders, argue that our real mission as a people is to integrate into the society as it is and get a piece of the action, the blind-alley nature of that philosophy is much clearer to them.

The section of the Report of the President's Commission on Campus Unrest dealing with the black student movement aptly captures this sense of reality and determination on the part of youth.

Integration, as currently defined and carried out, appears to many young Blacks to be a doctrine and practice of white supremacy. In their view, integration means the destruction of all things black and the exaltation of all things white, and thus perpetuates the notion that only what is white-controlled, white-determined, and white-led has validity and significance in American society (U.S. Office of the President, 1970:115).

In a sense, what these young people advocate is nothing less than the transformation and strengthening of the total society.

Ultimately, the goal of black activism and of black student leadership is to transform America into a society characterized by justice, equity, freedom, and the fraternity for all Americans (U.S. Office of the President, 1970:116).

The intricate relationship between economic development, political development, and cultural development has been masterfully essayed in the works of Harold Cruse (1967), and eloquently expressed in the poetry of Don L. Lee:

We'll become owners of the New World
the New World.
will run it as unowners
for
we will live in it too

& will want to be remembered
as realpeople.[1]

These young people are the cultural vanguard of the New World
which Don L. Lee speaks about and represents in "We Walk the Way
of the New World."

REFERENCES

Billingsley, Andrew.
    1968   *Black Families in White America.* Englewood Cliffs, N.J.: Prentice-
            Hall, Inc.
Billingsley, Andrew, and Jeanne M. Giovannoni.
    1972   *Children of the Storm: Black Children in Need of Parents.* New York:
            Harcourt, Brace & Jovanovich.
Clark, Kenneth.
    1967   "Sick Cities—and the Search for a Cure." *Transaction* IV, No. 10
            (October 1967):34–54.
Clark, Ramsey.
    1970   *Crime in America: Observations on its Nature, Causes, Prevention and
            Control.* New York: Simon & Shuster.
Cruse, Harold.
    1967   *The Crisis of the Negro Intellectual.* New York: William Morrow &
            Co., Inc.
Davis, Frank.
    1972   *The Economics of Black Community Development.* Chicago: Markham
            Publishing Company.
Hamilton, Charles, and Stokely Carmichael.
    1967   *Black Power: The Politics of Liberation in America.* New York: Vin-
            tage Books.
———.
    1972   National Black Political Agenda. Presented to the National Black
            Political Convention, Gary, Indiana, March 11, 1972.
National Advisory Commission on Civil Disorders.
    1968   *Report.* New York: Bantam Books.
National Urban Coalition.
    1971   *Counterbudget: A Blueprint for Changing National Priorities, 1971–
            1976.* New York: Praeger Publishers.
New York *Times*
    December 21, 1970
    August 1, 1971
    January 3, 1972
    March 17, 1972.

    1. From Don Lee, *Directionscore: Selected and New Poems* (Detroit: Broad-
side Press, 1967), p. 188. Reprinted by permission of the author

Pinkney, Alphonso.
1972 *The American Way of Violence.* New York: Random House.
Quarles, Benjamin.
1967 *Jet* Magazine XXXIII, No. 12 (December 28, 1967).
U.S. Office of the President.
1970 *Report of the President's Commission on Campus Unrest.* Washington,
D.C.: U.S. Government Printing Office.
Washington *Post.*
March 20, 1972.
Willhelm, Sidney M.
1971 *Who Needs the Negro?* Garden City, N.Y.: Anchor Books.

Chapter *2*   DUNBAR S. MCLAURIN*

Economic Policy and Poverty

LET us begin by examining my own interpretation of each segment of the topic "Economic Policy and Poverty." When we speak of economic policy, what exactly do we mean? Do we mean economic policy as set by the people, by local governments, national governments, national goals, businessmen, lawyers, financiers, or just whom?

And when we speak of *poverty*, just what do we mean by that term? Is it not true that this, the richest nation that this planet has ever known, has no poverty? Is poverty not something which exists only in far-off lands, like India, Bangladesh, and the primitive societies of Africa? Can poverty really exist in a nation that has 80 percent of the world's telephones, 90 percent of its television sets, and more plumbing fixtures than the rest of the world combined?

I would answer these questions by indicating that, when I speak of "economic policy," I mean policy which is set by those persons who run America, the power structure. I shall endeavor to refresh your recollection that this power structure, while maintaining a fluidity of roles from government to industry, and leisure to religious activity, nevertheless is the same. We refer to the people who run America and, to a large extent, who run the world, irrespective of the particular roles which they themselves choose to play at a given moment or to which they may assign their lackeys or subordinates.

Poverty needs no definition; but it does need clarification. It is a shock to me and to many people to learn that, in this great land of ours, poverty is not only abundant, but rampant. It was only a few

* Deceased, July 1973.

short years ago, in 1964, that President Lyndon Johnson startled the
nation and the world by suddenly announcing his "War on Poverty."
This phrase was immediately interpreted by some as a cynical, vote-
getting measure, a catch-all phrase designed to give to the President
some distinctive program of his own, separate from that of his
predecessors such as Kennedy, Roosevelt, and others who had promised "a new frontier," "a new deal," etc. In fact, it was considered by
most Americans to be almost completely treasonable to think that
there existed genuine poverty in this, the most prosperous nation in
the world. As a matter of fact, if poverty did exist, and if there were
poor people in the United States, most Americans considered those
persons to be black, shiftless white trash, hillbillies, or the dregs of
humanity who were poor simply because they chose to be so.

In the short eight years since the war on poverty was declared,
however, Americans have witnessed a shocking revelation. Most
Americans are poor, including you and me. It has come as a shock to
the Archie Bunkers and to the so-called insulated white middle class,
that only a very thin line separates them from even the poorest of
Americans. It has come as a further shock to learn from statisticians
how severely and seriously concentrated the wealth of America
really is.

There are several definitions of poverty, and the most common one
has been based on income. Families whose earnings are less than
$3,000 to $4,000 per year, with three or more dependents, are considered to be in the so-called poverty level. As such, they are considered for charity and welfare and considered poor. This, however,
is not the definition I would use for the poor. Those persons may be
destitute, but there are many more of us than we care to admit who
are in all actuality and reality poor. I, for one, would adopt a definition set forth in the recent bestseller, *The Rich and the Super-Rich,*
by Ferdinand Lundberg. In his work, Lundberg says, "I would say
that anyone who does not own a fairly substantial amount of income-
producing property or does not receive an earned income sufficiently
large to make substantial regular savings or does not hold a well-paid,
secure-tenured job, is poor. He may be healthy, handsome, and a
delight to his friends, but he is poor" (1968:28). By this standard at
least 70 percent of Americans are poor, though not all are destitute.
Now this comes as a shock to most of us to realize that basically we
have no financial security. I had a recent meeting with what were
billed as substantial businessmen of Chicago, and some of our greatest
businessmen were there; the Reverend Jesse Jackson shocked the
group almost into a trauma when he said, "There is not a person in

this room owning a business who could have a six-month illness without going bankrupt. Take you out of your businesses for six months, and who of you would not have to start all over again?" The real fact is that overnight any of us can become destitute if deprived of our jobs for any prolonged period of time, and many of us who even continue our jobs will find that medical and similar emergencies over a period of time would render us helpless.

The real distinction between poverty and wealth is not in the amount of one's salary, or money which flows through one's hands, but it is in the amount of independent income-producing property which one owns. Employment-derived income is only a hairline away from poverty. Asset-derived income, however, is the most desirable and the most substantial type of income because it removes one from the poverty class to the class of affluence. This type of income involves little or no drain on one's time or energy. One is not chained to a job, and may elect what he wishes to do if, indeed, he elects to do anything at all. It is thus with a sense of humility that we must each review our own assets and ask ourselves how long we could subsist or exist if we ceased working.

It has been said by a wise old wag that there are three ways of earning a living: (1) To have other people working for you; (2) to have money working for you; and (3) to work yourself. Obviously, the last method is the most insecure.

I have dwelt rather lengthily upon the definition of *poverty* to bring reality to many of us who feel that we are rather secure, and particularly those of us who are black. The *illusion* of security has been created by the wealthy groups in order to keep us as a quiescent, great, gray middle class. Judged by realistic standards, however, it is shocking to realize that the average American owns little more property than do Russian peasants, and by that standard, we also are poor.

Every study which has been made of the distribution of wealth in the United States has shown that it is fantastically lopsided. With such a sophisticated audience it is not necessary to go into these figures in detail, but we are all familiar with the net results of various studies which show, for instance, that the lowest 10 percent of the population receives less than 1 percent of the gross national product and personal income after federal taxes, whereas the upper half of 1 percent of the affluent families own more than one third of the wealth of this country. This concentration of wealth, moreover, has not been gained by earning power of the individual or by the exertion of some effort, whether legal or illegal, useful or mischievous, but comes

mainly from inheriting wealth. Almost every single wealth-holder of
the upper half of 1 percent achieved his wealth by inheritance.

It goes without saying that blacks and other minorities who were
not allowed to participate in the economy when the great concentrations of wealth were being built by the Vanderbilts, the Fords,
Rockefellers, Whitneys, Mellons, and other such families are almost
completely disinherited and stand practically no chance of achieving
any semblance of real wealth in their lifetimes. The wealthiest black
men and black institutions are marginal, at best, and I am including
the well-known list of so-called wealthy and successful black men
such as Gaston, Parks, the two Johnsons, and even a larger group of
more or less anonymous numbers bankers!

Now that we know that we are all more or less poverty-stricken,
what significance does this have for us? It means that we are also
more or less powerless.

The real power in this country today is exercised by only a few
families. Their power and economic influence far exceed even the
percentage of their investment assets. It is generally accepted that the
ownership of perhaps 5 percent in a large corporation is sufficient in
most cases to give corporate control. This would mean that a man with
only 100 million dollars concentrated in 5 percent of the capital stock
of a corporation capitalized at 2 billion dollars actually has operative
power over 2 billion dollars, not over 100 million dollars. This of
course means that his voice becomes large, not only because of the
political campaign contributions which he can make, but also because
of the rippling effect of the expenditures, purchases, and hiring
policies of the corporation. The 2-billion-dollar corporation dispenses
largesse in terms of legal fees, advertising, political and other re-
tainers, and in many other ways.

One must also reckon with the fact that a man who is worth only
100 million dollars, as we mentioned, is able to exert power far greater
than his proportion to the total of investment assets because he is a
member of the "club." By joining forces with others whose interests
lie with him, he is able to exert powerful influences over such policies
as tariffs, taxes, legislation, and even our foreign relations and involvements. In this way, a relatively small number of wealthy individuals
and corporate officials are able to exert a grossly disproportionate
amount of influence.

The lesson to be learned from the foregoing is simply this: The
great concentration of wealth in this country also means a great
concentration of power. The concentration of power means, then, that
the economic policy of this country is directed toward the interests of

the groups in power, namely those who make the rules. It is time for us to stop talking nonsense about "Black Capitalism" unless we face the reality that we are not going to have any role in this country as blacks or as poor people unless and until we become a part of the power structure. We cannot become a part of the power structure until we become a part of the economic structure and wield some economic power.

The military-industrial complex is a powerful combination that shapes national policy, has involved us in wars, and has had us intervene in foreign countries. This concentration of wealth and power has established inner links and connections all over the world, involving American power in all sorts of unknown activities secretly unless some breakthrough or leak causes the information to surface. The ITT case illustrates the point almost perfectly. Digging to the bottom of this case would require an investigation by some disinterested group such as the United Nations. It has already been brought out that ITT influenced the policy and attempted to influence the election of persons who would be friendly to it in South American governments. Apparently, the president of ITT has held monthly meetings with the heads of a world-scattered division, one held in the United States and one meeting in Brussels each month. It is inconceivable that such powerful corporations do not attempt to influence government policy internationally as well as nationally in their own interest, and what has so far been revealed is surely only the tip of an iceberg. In this respect, the corporate world works almost exactly as does the underworld, or one might reverse the pattern and say that the underworld copied its methods from the corporate world.

We are aware that the heroin found in Harlem comes from poppies grown in Turkey, processed in France, and routed circuitously through the illicit drug markets of the world. One shrimp boat alone was picked up carrying between 200 million dollars' worth and 500 million dollars' worth of pure heroin. The President has just announced a subsidy of some 35 million dollars to be given to the farmers of Turkey not to plant poppy seeds. It is to the credit of Congressman Charles Rangell of Harlem that he was one of the first persons to reveal this worldwide conspiracy.

Reviewing the feats of economic power and the extent and definition of poverty which we have just covered, one is overcome by a sense of utter hopelessness. One realizes that there exists a vast national and international solid fortress of interlaced wealth and power against which the ordinary individual appears to be helpless and hopelessly entangled. One might even go so far as to look at himself and his neighbor, drawing our $15,000-to-$30,000 salaries, and begin to wonder if we are not caught in a mesh and that we ourselves are poverty-stricken.

Having reviewed these factors, I am tempted to end my presentation at this point; but my ingrained ego prompts me to continue, perhaps to my detriment, and make a few suggestions about improving the situation I have described.

In the first place, I would suggest that, as blacks, we must view our positions as at the bottom of the ladder. This is both good and bad; for, while it means that we are the most powerless of the powerless, it also means that we have common allies. This is a formidable fact of which we must take consideration. This was the great truth that Martin Luther King had discovered and was seeking to implement at the time of his untimely murder—namely, the forging of an alliance between the poor, the deprived, and the powerless, whether they be black or white. This combination would have been irresistible, and Martin Luther King had to be killed.

The great danger lies in the great illusion which has been perpetrated upon us—that we are well off, not poverty-stricken, and that our interests lie with the propertied persons. While flattering, we cannot afford to indulge in such a luxury; for if we do so, we fall into the same trap that the politically confused, poor southern white fell into for more than a hundred years, deluding himself into the belief that he was better than the blacks and that his interests lay with the monied whites. Therefore, while attempting to hold the blacks down culturally and economically, he himself was mired in the mud.

The second lesson, it seems to me, is that the great mass of persons in the United States and the world are poor and are kept poor because there is a deliberate economic policy to keep them so. All of the New Deal measures and war-on-poverty measures, such as social security, unemployment insurance, minimum wage laws, welfare, etc., are but a trifle, and they are not really designed to grapple with the problem of an equitable distribution of the wealth for the people of the world and of the United States. Once we have rid ourselves of this illusion, we are well on our way to a solution.

To keep a child out of the way, one distracts him by giving him some senseless task and making him feel that it is an important job. We are all familiar with this tactic known as "busy-work." Its sole merit lies in keeping the youngster out of your way while you do whatever you must.

The world of power has played the same game with the poor, the blacks, and the deprived, not only in the United States but in the world. This economic game is that of giving us "busy money." The doling out of 100 million dollars or even of a billion dollars is just something to keep us "busy" while the propertied and the wealthy preserve their wealth, even if that requires senseless wars or other involvements.

The third lesson to be learned is the enormity of our task so that we can proceed to plan for it.

In the February 21st issue of *Commerce Today,* the official publication of the Department of Commerce, on page 9, Secretary of Commerce Stans, while bowing out of the Department of Commerce, hailed a program of awarding 100 million dollars to stimulate minority enterprise. Turning exactly ten pages farther, one finds, on page 19, another article in which the Secretary predicted that the *growth* in the gross national product for the year 1972 would be 100 billion dollars. Mind you, that is not the GNP, but merely the amount by which he predicted that it would expand in one year. When that figure is compared with what was allocated for minority economic development for two years, we can readily see how insignificant our share of the economy is. If we shared in only 10 percent of the 100-billion-dollar growth, we would have ten billion dollars per year. One percent would equal 1 billion dollars per year; one tenth of 1 percent would be 100 million dollars per year. So, actually, minorities were being allocated less than one half of one tenth of 1 percent of the growth of the economy. We have a long way to go.

Finally, I would say that a lesson to be learned and an optimistic prediction is that we cannot look for our salvation to come from above. Poverty seems sometimes to be a part of the conscious economic policy of the power structure of the United States and of the international world cartel of power dealers. But we have one ace in the hole: the machinery cannot operate without people. Therefore, the poor of the world, and the blacks and poor of the United States, are absolutely necessary for the operation of the power machine. The product made by ITT must be consumed by somebody. The typewriters made by IBM must be typed upon by some black girl. The hosiery and pantyhose made by the International Textile cartel must be purchased and worn by black women and poor whites and poor people throughout the world. We have reached an age in technology wherein the rich cannot enjoy their affluence unless *we* make the machines go. The military-industrial complex could not have operated without the millstones of young boys whose lives were put up as a sacrifice to justify the building of ships and armaments. Therein lies our power. We must recognize that, as the war in Vietnam winds down and it becomes obvious that war as a method of increasing power cannot be used and will only result in the destruction of the assets of the power brokers and power holders, there must be some substitute. That substitute is poverty.

The biggest business in the United States today is "poverty." It is the business of attempting to go through the motions of empowering and disimpoverishing people in the inner cities. One hundred million dollars was just voted for the study of sickle-cell anemia; 2.5 billion dollars for law and order assistance; 8 billion dollars for subsidies for housing by the year 1978. A bureaucracy is building up to "save the poor." The only hitch is that the money never filters down to the poor. Every day, we receive reports such as that in the New York *Times* of March 13th, which reported that a study by the Joint Center for Urban Studies at MIT and Harvard University showed that as much as half of the subsidy money of federally subsidized housing never reached the needy families for whom the funds were intended.

The vast bureaucracy created to distribute welfare money and money to addicts and other impoverished persons has become a business within itself. One of the biggest businesses today is "helping minority businesses get started." Floods of experts, consultants, technicians, and urban affairs officers have taken the cream off the top, and the minority businessmen and entrepreneurs seldom get what is due them. I recently talked with a Texan who frankly admitted to me that he had made $1,200,000 in the past eighteen months building group-practice medical facilities for minority persons.

In other words, helping blacks and the poor has become one of America's biggest businesses. Our task is to find a way that we ourselves can get into the mainstream and not be at the end of the stream. We are damned tired of being the urinal for industrial America!

REFERENCES

Lundberg, Ferdinand.
    1968   *The Rich and the Super-Rich.* New York: Lyle Stuart.

Economic Policy and Poverty: A Comment

IN his talk, Dr. McLaurin seems to have done essentially two things. First, he has made several important (although rather obvious) points about the way things are, as follows:

1. The distribution of income and the ownership of wealth are highly unequal.

2. There are many people who are very poor and almost powerless.

3. There are a few people who are very rich and extremely powerful.

4. Those who are neither very rich nor very poor are doing all right at the moment, but their economic status is insecure, particularly because of the risks of unemployment and bad health.

If I understood him correctly, Dr. McLaurin then says that one possible remedy for these problems is an increase in the amount of income-producing property in the hands of the poor.

Dr. McLaurin's talk has renewed my faith in the urgent need for using economic analysis to confront the problems of policy and inequality. I do not wish to imply that nothing but correct economic analysis and economic policy are going to solve these problems; but I do think that we haven't a prayer unless we use correct economic analysis and policy—because a careful economic analysis of some of the facets of poverty and inequality leads to some important conclusions about economic policy and, for that matter, about the social system. Some go so far as to say that the economic system is the determining factor, the base, on which the social system is built. I would myself go a bit further and say that it also works the other way around; but it is undoubtedly true that the economic system has a powerful effect upon social relationships, and that analysis of the way the economic system works can offer some useful insights into the problems of poverty and inequality.

In what follows I would like to discuss three key economic concepts which, I think, offer important insights for economic policy on poverty: competition, efficiency, and investment in human capital. These concepts may not sound relevant to the problems of poverty and inequality; they are not usually raised in discussions of poverty and inequality. This is, indeed, why I have decided to discuss them rather than economic issues which are more obviously related to poverty and inequality, such as a negative income tax. For the extent of poverty and inequality in a society is intimately related to the workings of its economic system—which in turn is vitally affected by the three factors I have chosen to discuss. Thus, while these three factors may have no direct relevance to poverty and inequality, their ultimate relevance is considerable. In not considering them, we overlook important areas where correct economic policy can do a great deal to reduce poverty and inequality.

After discussing these three topics separately to show what insights they offer for poverty policy, I would then like to examine how these three topics can all be brought to bear on the issue of inflation, which, it is often supposed, is an important problem for poverty policy because inflation is supposed to hit the poor hardest.

I

In many sectors of the economy such as autos, drugs, and steel, a few corporations control output and are able to keep out competitors because they face little or no competition, thanks to such barriers to entry as high advertising expenditures, patents, government regulation on competition from abroad, and so forth. In many sectors of the economy, labor unions also enjoy great power. To some extent, this serves only to counterbalance the power of the corporations; but to some extent, some unions give their members very real power— through, for example, apprenticeship programs and similar restrictions —to keep down competition from other workers. What is the result of such situations? Corporations that share a monopoly in a sector of the economy, such as automobiles, are able to charge consumers a monopoly price and earn abnormally high profits. Unions get high wages for their members; and while this may merely counterbalance the great power of the corporations and have no effect on employment, in some sectors this undoubtedly means that the demand for union workers is reduced. This in turn means that those workers not fortunate enough to get such jobs flood other sectors, so that union wages are high, but wages elsewhere may tend to be low.[1] One example of this effect is the construction industry, which is not (yet) dominated by a few firms but instead by a few rather powerful unions. The basic source of power of the construction unions is a myriad restrictions on entry by would-be workers through apprenticeship programs, tests, and the like. By restricting entry into construction work, the construction unions guarantee that the wage of workers in the construction industry will be high. But only a few workers will find jobs in the construction industry, and many workers will have to look elsewhere—which will push wages elsewhere downwards. (And of course the construction unions are not the only example of how to keep one's wages high and other people's wages low by restricting entry into one's line of work. Doctors and lawyers—and, I might add, to some extent—university teachers practice it too, with varying degrees of success. The point is that, once again, the absence of competition or the reduction of competition increases inequality.)

Thus, one obvious item on the economic policy agenda should be a reduction in the degree of inequality through an increase in the degree of competition in the economy. It is incredible how little has been done in this field. The Justice Department has been contemplating a suit to break up two of the three breakfast cereal manufacturers who, between them, control more than 80 percent of the output of that industry and charge prices which are estimated to be 15 to 25 percent above the levels necessary to earn a normal profit and cover normal costs (New York *Times*, June 21, 1971:13; January 7, 1972:41). But in practically all other respects we have been incredibly timid. A particularly serious restriction on competition is the system of import quotas on many kinds of foods and fuels. These quotas, of course, insulate domestic manufacturers from foreign competition and allow them to charge high prices—high prices which fall disproportionately on the poor, since the poor devote a disproportionately large share of their

1. A useful reference is A. Rees, "The Effects of Unions on Resource Allocation," *Journal of Law and Economics*, 6 (October 1963), 69–78. Rees asserts that "the scanty available evidence suggests that monopsony power by employers in United States labor markets is small but not nonexistent" (p. 78)— from which he appears to conclude that very little union power is "countervailing" in the sense used by J. K. Galbraith (in *The New Industrial State*, revised edition [Boston: Houghton Mifflin, 1971] and *American Capitalism*, revised edition [Boston: Houghton Mifflin, 1956]) and in the sense used above. I must admit I find this hard to accept.

budget to food and fuel. But very little has been done to challenge the basic idea that these quotas should be in effect.[2] Similarly, it seems incredible that the "scandal" in the ITT case concerns whether the Nixon administration improperly accepted an out-of-court settlement to get ITT to divest itself of three of its components, when the real scandal, it seems to me, is why it didn't try to break up ITT entirely.[3]

At any rate, it is vain to hope for a reduction in inequality unless we seek a greater degree of competition—rather than the unequal competition we have at the moment. In particular, the unequal nature of competition in many sectors of the economy may frustrate many attempts to promote and develop black-owned businesses.

A second key concept which economic analysis offers economic policy on poverty is the notion of efficiency which, in a general sense, is simply getting the most results from a given amount of effort. I would like to mention two somewhat obscure areas in the present federal tax system where greater efficiency could do a great deal to reduce poverty. The present tax system is a particularly glaring example of how inefficient attempts to reduce inequality not only do not reduce inequality but may actually aggravate it.

Because it does not tax the interest income which people earn from holding municipal bonds, the federal government in 1969 gave up 2 billion dollars in tax revenue[4] in order to subsidize state and local debt. The ostensible reasoning behind this peculiar provision is that, if the interest earnings on municipal bonds aren't taxable, municipalities won't have to pay interest rates as high as those available on corporate bonds, since the interest earnings on corporate bonds are taxable. But consider the position of a man in the 50-percent tax

2. After this paper was written in 1972, the system of import quotas was drastically modified, largely (it seems to me) as a result of unprecedented consumer unrest about inflation.

3. A few heartening straws have been blowing in the wind since this paper was written: for example, the government is now seeking to break up IBM. A radical slogan in the 1960s was "Two, three, many Vietnams"; perhaps an even more radical slogan in the 1970s will be "Two, three, many General Motors Corporations"!

4. J. Pechman, *Federal Tax Policy*, revised edition (Washington, D.C.: Brookings Institution, 1971), p. 303. An interesting discussion of the ways in which many personal income tax provisions benefit the poor much less than the rich, thereby sharply reducing the nominally progressive structure of the federal income tax, appears in J. Pechman and B. Okner, "Individual Income Tax Erosion by Income Classes," pp. 13–40 in *The Economics of Federal Subsidy Programs*, Part 1, General Study Papers, Joint Economic Committee, U.S. Congress (Washington, D.C.: U.S. Government Printing Office, May 8, 1972).

bracket who is deciding whether to buy a $100-municipal bond bearing 5 percent interest or a $100-corporate bond bearing 8 percent interest. Before taxes, he will receive, per year, $5 on the municipal and $8 on the corporate bond; after taxes, he will get $5 on the municipal and $4 on the corporate bond. Obviously, he will buy the municipal bond and, on balance, come out $1 ahead. The federal government loses $4 in tax revenue. On the other hand, if the interest earnings from both municipal bonds and corporate bonds were taxable, the municipal bond would have to offer 8 percent interest to compete with the corporate bond, and the municipality would have to pay $3 more in interest payments. But under such an arrangement, regardless of whether the investor buys the municipal bond or the corporate bond, he would receive $8 before taxes—but can keep only $4 and must now pay $4 in taxes to the government.

With this $4, the government can completely cover the $3 in added interest costs of the municipality and still have an extra dollar for other purposes. In other words, as this admittedly rather crude example suggests, the nontaxable nature of the interest earnings on municipal bonds works mainly to the advantage of persons in high tax brackets, not to states and municipalities. It is an incredibly inefficient way of dealing with the poverty of our cities.

Another equally inefficient aspect of the tax system is the investment tax credit provision whereby companies can deduct from their tax bill some percentage of the cost of their investments in new machines and so forth. Obviously, this is intended to increase the demand for investment goods by reducing their net cost; and greater demand for investment goods will certainly lead to greater employment of workers to produce these goods, and hence to some reduction in poverty. But it would be difficult to devise a more inefficient system of stimulating investment, because companies may use the tax credit provision not only on the increased investment they are making over and beyond their normal rate, but on all their investment, including the investment they would have made had not tax credit ever been in effect. In short, the irony is that the tax credit is a subsidy to induce companies to undertake *extra* investment, but it is paid to companies on the basis of *all* the investment they make—to the tune of three billion dollars in 1969 (Pechman, 1971:302). And if companies already have plenty of idle machines there is in any case no reason for them to want to buy more—as recent experience with the tax credit has shown—so that the tax credit fails to stimulate any investment at all. The net result, it seems, is that the tax credit on investment either does nothing about inequality or else—by giving companies windfall profits on investments they would have made without the credit—may even aggravate inequality.[5]

Thus efficiency in the "tax expenditure" or subsidy provisions of the tax system—in areas such as municipal bonds and investment credits —would, it seems to me, make a real contribution toward reducing the degree of inequality in the country.

A third key concept of economic analysis which offers some important insights into ways of reducing poverty and inequality is the notion of human capital. Dr. McLaurin seems to feel that physical capital or financial capital is the solution, that the ownership of income-producing property determines wealth, and that asset-derived income is therefore most desirable. Dr. McLaurin draws no explicit conclusions from these observations—which, I hope to show shortly, are somewhat misleading—but there appear to be two implicit conclusions for economic policy: first, that the government's poverty policy efforts should give greater emphasis to increasing the amount of income-producing property in the hands of minorities and the poor; and second, that the government should give greater emphasis to removing the artificial constraints such as discrimination which reduce the return on such capital.

This is certainly an appealing policy prescription in and of itself; but, contrary to Dr. McLaurin's implication, there are two kinds of wealth in which to invest. The first is physical capital, such as a business or a house, or something such as bonds, stocks, or savings accounts which give the owner an equity in physical capital. The second kind of wealth is human capital—the productive capacity of people. Now, human capital is in some cases an unusually profitable kind of investment—the profits from which can be used to acquire still more human capital or to acquire physical capital. As Professor Thomas Sowell has observed, the fact that many countries recovered quickly from World War II despite the widespread devastation of that war, and the fact that "refugees can arrive in the United States with only the clothes on their backs and within a few years be prosperous, while the domestic poor seem trapped in a vicious cycle of poverty," may be explained by human capital—"educational investments worth tens of thousands of dollars, as well as business, professional, and industrial

5. To call this provision a "job-development tax credit," as members of the Nixon administration are wont to do, is more consistent with efforts to use advertising pyrotechnics than sound economic analysis, as members of the Nixon administration are also wont to do. See M. C. Jensen, "Tax Credit Seen as Spur to Profits, Not Jobs," the New York *Times*, April 20, 1971, pp. 39–40.

skills accumulated in high-level positions abroad. Such things are the bulk of the real wealth of most middle-class people. . . . The physical things that they own are worth only a fraction of the value of these intangible assets and are symptoms rather than causes of their earning power" (1971:4). This last phrase, in fact, suggests that investment in human capital reaps profits which can be used to acquire physical capital, and that ownership of physical capital is sometimes not so much a cause as a reflection of the true total wealth of persons. Moreover, in some circumstances it is impossible to manage physical capital without first acquiring human capital. Many underdeveloped countries, for example, are desperately short of physical capital but lack the human capital to use effectively what injections of physical capital they are able to get (Schultz, 1961:7). Similarly, many of the difficulties of black capitalism concern not the problems of acquiring physical capital but the problems of acquiring the human capital necessary for the business.

Human capital also has great significance in the context of income inequality. In 1971, about three fourths of total national income took the form not of income from capital or property but of labor incomes —wages and salaries, and supplements to wages and salaries;[6] and some studies, admittedly imperfect, suggest that perhaps half or even three fourths of the total variation in labor income may be attributed to variations in investment in human capital.[7] Clearly, then, the unequal distribution of ownership of human capital may contribute more to the current inequality of incomes than does the unequal distribution of ownership of nonhuman capital—and although it should be recognized that the ability to invest in human capital is undoubtedly affected powerfully by the ownership of nonhuman capital, the reverse is almost certainly true as well.

For these reasons it is not at all obvious that provision of nonhuman capital to the poor and minorities and efforts to remove the artificial constraints on the returns to this capital should receive priority in

6. (These are preliminary figures from the *Economic Report of the President* [1972], p. 209.) This calculation assumes that "total compensation of employees" is the only category of national income which is labor income. However, some portion of several other categories of national income—"business and professional income" and "income of farm proprietors"—is a return to labor rather than to property; so that the figure cited in the text understates that portion of national income which is a return to labor.

7. A useful survey of this topic is J. Mincer, "The Distribution of Labor Incomes: A Survey with Special Reference to the Human Capital Approach," *Journal of Economic Literature*, 8 (March 1970), 1–26.

efforts to reduce poverty and inequality. Presumably the decision to invest in human or nonhuman capital should depend on the rate of return available on either kind of investment; a number of recent studies have suggested that the return to investment in human capital, such as investment in education, compares quite favorably with the return to investment in physical capital, stocks, bonds, and the like. For example, one study[8] has calculated that, on the average, if a northern white male's initial level of education were eight years and he invested in a college degree, he would earn an estimated 12.4 percent on his investment. The real problem emerges when we consider the return to the same investment made by a comparable nonwhite—the nonwhite would earn a return of only three percent; moreover, given the nature of the study, this latter figure can not be considered significantly different from zero in a statistical sense, i.e., there is a fairly good chance that the rate of return could be zero percent.

Does this suggest that investment in physical capital, rather than human capital, is the rational course for blacks to pursue? Failing government action, it clearly is. But it may also suggest that government efforts to increase black investment in human capital and to remove the artificial constraints on black human capital, such as discrimination, could pay real dividends—quite possibly greater dividends than efforts to promote, and to overcome the constraints on, investment in black physical capital.

II

Competition, efficiency, and human capital are thus separately relevant to problems of poverty and inequality. I would now like to describe the ways in which all three are relevant to the problem of inflation—rising prices—which is often regarded as one of the worst enemies of the poor and of minorities. For example, just before the

8. See G. Hanoch, "An Economic Analysis of Earnings and Schooling," *Journal of Human Resources*, 2 (Summer 1967), 310–329. Such studies are still in their infancy, and contain various statistical and theoretical defects which have yet to be remedied completely. For example, the construction of Hanoch's study is such that some of the returns to education may in fact be returns to postschool training, which may mean that the figures given in the study exaggerate the returns to education *per se*. On the other hand, the study assumes that an individual's geographic mobility in seeking or changing a job—which tends to increase one's earning power—is unaffected by his educational investments; but educational investments may enhance mobility, in which case the figures given in the study understate the returns to education *per se*. The net effect of such biases on the study's estimates is unclear.

1968 elections, the Harris Poll found that proportionately more blacks than whites were concerned about inflation; and it is frequently asserted that inflation hits the poor harder than any other group. Is this true?

To answer this question we must investigate the sources of inflation, which are essentially three. The first kind is sometimes called "cost-push" inflation; it is alleged that prices rise because the powerful unions and companies of which we spoke earlier are sometimes able to increase wages and profits at the expense of the consumer, thanks to their insulation from competition. To the extent that this occurs, how does it affect the poor and minority groups? They are a disproportionately small part of the union members and stockholders of the country, so they get very little of the increased wages and profits; but they are, of course, consumers, and do have to pay the higher prices which accompany them. Consider the construction industry. In 1970, nonwhites constituted about 11.1 percent of the civilian labor force (U.S. Department of Labor, 1971:60) but accounted for only about 8 percent of the skilled trades in the construction industry (Shabecoff 1971:1, 44). Since blacks are underrepresented in this industry, blacks would receive a disproportionately small share of the money-wage gains of a wage-push by construction unions (U.S. Department of Labor, 1964:68–69)—and, since blacks tend to devote a somewhat greater share of their budgets to housing (technically, "shelter," whether rented or owned) than do whites (14.9 percent versus 13.8 percent in 1960–61),[9] the effect of a construction wage-push on housing prices will bear disproportionately on nonwhites. Thus, since such a wage-push would raise money incomes more for whites than for nonwhites, and raise the cost of living less for whites than for nonwhites, the net effect of the wage-push would be to raise white real incomes relative to nonwhite real incomes. In general, then, a wage-push seems unlikely to improve the position of minority groups and the poor.[10]

9. This assumes that the increase in the wage is not offset by sharp reductions in employment, i.e., that the elasticity of demand for construction labor is less than unity—which, given the tactics of construction unions (in particular the restrictions they have imposed on the use of capital), seems a safe assumption to make.

10. This may not always hold, however. In 1964, nonwhites comprised about 18.6 percent of the total employment in hospitals (Bureau of Labor Statistics, U.S. Department of Labor, *The Negroes in the United States: Their Economic and Social Situation,* Bulletin No. 1511 [June 1966], pp. 118–121) but (in 1960–61) devoted 4.3 percent of their budget to medical care versus 6.7 percent

A second kind of inflation, which might be termed "structural" or "bottleneck" inflation, arises when the labor market develops shortages of workers with high educational or skill levels, while, at the same time, there remain widespread surpluses of workers with low levels of skill and educational attainment. In such a situation, wages and salaries of the former group of workers rise rapidly, and hence prices of goods, particularly those with a high skill content, go up. Shortages of such workers may be due both to underinvestment in human capital and to anticompetitive restrictions on entry into high-skill occupations (e.g., medicine, construction); but whatever the cause, workers in these occupations enjoy an improvement in their real incomes relative to the rest of the population. Since the poor and minority groups generally possess less skill and education than the general population, they are unlikely to increase their money incomes as a result of structural inflation, but will have to pay higher prices; their real income will thus deteriorate, both relatively and absolutely. Hence structural inflation, like cost-push inflation, is unlikely to improve the position of minorities or the poor.

The last kind of inflation, "demand-pull" inflation, however, presents a different story. "Demand-pull" inflation is the result not of a shortage of specific groups of workers but rather of the widespread shortage of all workers which develops as the economy approaches full employment. The level of aggregate demand for goods is high, and hence the derived demand for workers is high. Thus employers hire extra workers from the ranks of the unemployed, increase the length of the work week and raise wages to attract workers already employed in other firms—all of which tends to lead to high prices.[11]

How does this affect minorities and the poor? The two-to-one ratio of the nonwhite employment rate to the white employment rate

---

for whites (*Consumer Incomes and Expenditures*, pp. 68–69). ("Medical Care" includes expenditures on medicines and doctors as well as on hospital care *per se*, but the figures are suggestive.) In such circumstances a wage-push in hospitals might raise nonwhite real incomes relative to white real incomes. But union organizing in hospitals is only beginning to make headway (for an interesting account of the efforts of a hospital workers' union which is "led by New York Jews but comprised predominantly of Negroes and Puerto Ricans," see T. L. Ehrich, "Union on the Rise: A Tough Local Presses National Bid to Organize Low-Paid Hospital Help," *The Wall Street Journal*, March 3, 1970, pp. 1, 16).

11. This is, of course, the logic underlying the famous Phillips curve. See A. W. Phillips, "The Relation Between Unemployment and the Rate of Change of Money Wage Rates in the United Kingdom," *Economica*, 25 (November 1958), 283–299.

which has prevailed in the past ten or so years suggests that when, in a "demand-pull" inflation, the white unemployment rate falls by one percentage point, the nonwhite unemployment rate will fall by about two percentage points. Other things being equal, this would, of course, raise the real per capita income of the nonwhite community in relation to that of the white community.[12]

Clearly, then, nonwhites and the poor *can* benefit from a *demand-pull* inflation. As the old saying, "First fired, last hired," would suggest, when the economy runs at full tilt, nonwhites and the poor start to make substantial gains. Now, this is not the only way or even the most efficient way (and efficiency is important!) for the poor and minorities to make gains—in fact, an impressive body of evidence points inescapably to the conclusion that tight labor markets must be accompanied by "greatly expanded governmental programs for education, for retraining, for the elimination of poverty and other forms of investment in human beings" (Killingsworth 1968:12–17) if efforts to attack poverty and unemployment are to have maximum impact. But it should at least be clear that one form of inflation may be the ally, not the enemy, of minorities and the poor.

The *over-all* impact of rising prices on minorities and the poor is simply the sum total of the impacts of these three different kinds of inflation. The government's Consumer Price Index is not useful for the study of this question, since the CPI is constructed on the basis of a "typical" or "average" consumer's market basket—in other words, it is a kind of average of black and white (and poor and nonpoor) market baskets. In order to gauge the rise in the cost of living for different groups in the population, it is thus necessary to construct separate cost-of-living indices for each group. A number of studies have attempted to do so, and they all suggest that prices have gone up slightly faster for the goods in the white and nonpoor consumers' market baskets. My own research suggests that between 1953 and 1970 the cost of living for the average white consumer rose by 45.1 percent, while the cost of living for the average black consumer rose by 44.3 percent. Thus, between 1953 and 1970, the increase in the cost of living was about 1.8 percent greater for whites than for blacks (i.e., 45.1 is about 1.8 percent larger than 44.3). Another study, using the same methodology, found that, between 1947 and 1964, the increase in

12. This is admittedly an oversimplification because other things need not be equal. For example, if white earnings grew much faster than nonwhite earnings during a demand-pull, this factor might offset the influence of lower unemployment, which, as noted, favors nonwhites.

the cost of living was about 4.0 percent greater for whites than blacks (Samli, 1970:70). A third inquiry into the cost of living (Hollister and Palmer, 1972) for various groups found the patterns shown in Table 1.

TABLE 1.

Changes in Cost of Living for Selected Groups, 1953–1967

Group	% increase in cost of living	% increase vs. that for all consumers
All consumers (CPI)	24.8%	—
All poor	22.3%	10.1% smaller
Urban nonwhite poor	21.9%	11.7% smaller

SOURCE: Data from R. G. Hollister and J. L. Palmer, "The Impact of Inflation on the Poor," pp. 240–269 in *Redistribution to the Rich and the Poor,* edited by K. E. Boulding and M. Pfaff (Belmont, Cal.: Wadsworth, 1972).

In short, it is evident that, at least during the postwar period, inflation has meant a smaller increase in the cost of living for blacks and the poor than for whites and the general population—[13] and, in particular, that demand-pull inflation can lead to both relative and absolute improvements in the per-capita incomes of the poor and of minorities.

While competition, efficiency, and investment in human capital might not seem to have much direct relevance to the problems of poverty and inequality, and while inflation might seem to be detrimental rather than beneficial to minorities and the poor, I hope I have shown that economic analysis suggests that the contrary is at

---

13. In view of the spectacular increases in the cost of food which occurred in 1972 and 1973 after this paper was written, the statement that "during the postwar period, inflation has meant a smaller increase in the cost of living for blacks and the poor than for whites and the general population" might have to be modified. Black families and low-income families generally devote a higher proportion of their budgets to food than do white families and upper-income families; therefore, since the cost of food has gone up more rapidly in 1972 and 1973 than the cost of other items, the cost of living for low-income and black families has probably gone up more rapidly in this period than it has for upper-income and white families. However, this kind of inflation is in no sense a "demand-pull" inflation in the usual sense of that term; rather, it is more accurately classified as a kind of "bottleneck" inflation brought about by extremely sluggish growth in supply in the face of ever-increasing demand (for example, the failure of the Russian wheat harvest in 1972 and the mysterious disappearance of anchovies off the Peruvian coast led to shortages of agricultural crops and animal foodstuffs, which in turn sent food prices spiralling upward).

least sometimes the case—and that the ultimate relevance to poverty of factors which seem only indirectly linked to it may be very great indeed. Translating the policy proposals implicit in the above analysis into action will mean a long journey; but awareness of the implications of the analysis is an important first step.

REFERENCES

Hollister, R. G., and J. L. Palmer.
  1972 "The Impact of Inflation on the Poor." In *Redistribution to the Rich and the Poor*, pp. 240–269, edited by K. E. Boulding and M. Pfaff. Belmont, California: Wadsworth.
Killingsworth, C. C.
  1968 "The Continuing Labor Market Twist." *Monthly Labor Review*, 91 (September).
The New York *Times*.
  1971 "Price of Cereals Termed Inflated." June 21.
  1972 "Antitrust Action in Cereal Studied." January 7.
Pechman, J.
  1971 *Federal Tax Policy*, rev. ed. Washington: Brookings Institution, Studies of Government Finance.
Samli, A. C.
  1970 "Comparative Price Indexes for Negroes and Whites." *Mississippi Valley Journal of Business and Economics*, 5 (Winter).
Schultz, T. W.
  1961 "Investment in Human Capital." *American Economic Review*, 51 (March).
Shabecoff, P.
  1971 "Blacks Making Few Gains in the Construction Trades." The New York *Times*, June 27.
Sowell, T.
  1971 "Economics and Black People." *Review of Black Political Economy*, 1 (Winter–Spring).
U.S. Department of Labor.
  1971 *Handbook of Labor Statistics 1971*, Table 15.
U.S. Department of Labor, Bureau of Labor Statistics.
  1964 *Consumer Expenditures and Income: Cross-Classification of Family Characteristics, Urban United States, 1960–61* (Supplement 2, Part A, to BLS Report 237–238), July.

Economic Policy and Poverty: A Comment

IN 1928, President Herbert Hoover asserted that "we are nearer to a final triumph over poverty than ever before . . . The poorhouse is vanishing from among us" (Lyons, 1964:178). President Franklin Delano Roosevelt saw "one third of a nation ill-housed, ill-clad, and ill-nourished" in 1937 (New York *Times,* January 21, 1937: 14). During the presidential campaign of 1960, John F. Kennedy repeatedly expressed concern for the seventeen million Americans who allegedly went to bed hungry every night. On March 16, 1964, President Lyndon Baines Johnson called for a national "war on poverty" and declared that "one fifth of our people . . . have not shared in the abundance which has been granted to most Americans and on whom the gates of opportunity have been closed" (New York *Times,* March 17, 1964:22).

And yet, today, there is throughout the United States of America an economic underworld of poverty and much anxiety over the clear and ever-present danger of economic insecurity. Indeed, the annual population survey of the United States Census Bureau revealed that the number of poor persons in the United States increased by 5 percent in 1970. In that year, there were 25.5 million Americans living in poverty. This represented an increase of 1.2 million more persons than were classified as poor in 1969. It seems significant to note that this 5-percent increase in one year reversed a 10-year trend during which the nation's poverty population declined by 5 percent per annum.

The meaning of poverty. Poverty is such a pervasive phenomenon, and has such widespread ramifications, that it is difficult to define. In

the *Economic Report of the President, 1964,* the President's Council
of Economic Advisers stated that the poor consist of those persons
whose total incomes and asset holdings are inadequate to satisfy their
minimum needs. Therefore, "poverty is the inability to satisfy minimum needs." On the other hand, the United States government de-
fines poverty on a sliding dollar scale. In 1959, it was $2,973; in 1969,
it was $3,743; and $3,968 in 1970. Poverty is a level of living that is
incapable of providing adequately for health and physical efficiency,
for meaningful employment and good education. Therefore, it is a
condition of human adjustment which is usually accompanied by
anxiety, frustration, and tension.

"The underlying masses," as Thorstein Veblen called the poor,
suffer a trying and humiliating experience. Poverty means hunger
and inadequate diet; poor housing and overcrowded rooms; faulty
plumbing; an undesirable physical and social environment, and so
forth. The many-faceted pathological condition creates multiproblem
individuals and families, is responsible for much dysfunctional behavior, and causes considerable mental anguish.

The causes of poverty. The causes of poverty are numerous. They
include low productivity, racial discrimination and other market im-
perfections, and absence from the labor force. Each of these factors
usually results in low income and/or no income. And, from a practical
viewpoint, the primary cause of poverty is low income and/or no
income.

A large majority of the American people depend upon wages and
salaries—amounting to about 70 percent of the national income—for
their livelihood. If it is true that, in general, individual incomes depend on the productivity of the individual worker, other things being
equal, laborers who are poor (and their families) are poor because of
their low productivity. To the extent that individual laborers are paid
about what they are worth, the poor receive less incomes because their
low productivity keeps them from being worth more to profit-seeking
employers.

A primary cause of poverty throughout the United States is racial
discrimination in education, employment, health and medical care,
housing, and in practically all areas of human activity. In 1969, black
families in the United States earned an average of 61 percent of the
incomes of white families. But, in the South in 1969, black families
earned only 57 percent as much income as white families (the Houston
Post, February 14, 1971:12-D). Indeed, it has been suggested that if
Negroes with the same education as whites had received the same

average pay as whites in 1966, the personal income of the nation's Negroes would have been 10 to 13 billion dollars greater (Bach, 1968: 434). Furthermore, since the poor are often characterized by ignorance of employment opportunities, apathy, and immobility, they are frequently unaware of alternative job opportunities and are just as often either unable or unwilling to move elsewhere to obtain employment when informed of available jobs.

The heads of at least half of the poor families in the United States are not in the labor force. Among these absentees from the labor force are many who are elderly, physically handicapped, in ill health, dependent children, and a large and growing number of persons who have become discouraged because they could not find employment and ceased to continue looking for work.

Again, all of these factors lead to low income and set it forth in bold relief as the fundamental cause of poverty. These factors are joined by such poverty-re-enforcing dimensions in our culture as the lack of education and/or poor education; high birth rates among the poor; alienation, inarticulateness, and political apathy; and legal discrimination which tends to keep the poverty population "in their place."

Some indications of the extent of poverty in Tennessee. Poverty in the United States is both widespread and pervasive. However, for clarity and ease of understanding it seems desirable to examine the extent to which it exists on a relatively small scale that is probably typical of the big picture throughout the nation. So, let us look at poverty in the State of Tennessee.

Estimates of per capita personal income in Tennessee for 1970 (Tennessee Statistical Abstract, 1969:395–400) indicate that the per capita income for the state was $2,430. Nevertheless, these same data show that in 60 of the state's 95 counties (63.2 percent), per capita personal income was less than $2,000 in 1970. Moreover, it was less than $1,000 in 27 counties, or more than one fourth of the state's 95 counties (28.4 percent).

Figures published in 1968 (Sales Management, Inc., 1968) estimated that 29.6 percent of the households in Tennessee had cash incomes of less than $3,000 and another 18.3 percent had cash incomes of $3,000 to $4,999. This indicates that 47.9 percent, or almost half, of the households in Tennessee had annual cash incomes of less than $5,000. These same estimates show that 31.5 percent of the households in Knoxville had cash incomes of less than $3,000 and another 20.7 percent had cash incomes of $3,000 to $4,999, or 52.2 percent of the households in Knoxville with cash incomes of less than $5,000. In Chattanooga, 28.5 percent of the households had cash incomes of less than $3,000 and another 18.4 percent had cash incomes of $3,000 to $4,999, or 46.9 percent of the households in Chattanooga with incomes of less than $5,000. In Memphis, 24.9 percent of the households had cash incomes of less than $3,000 and another 18 percent had cash incomes of $3,000 to $4,999, or 42.9 percent of the households in Memphis had incomes of less than $5,000. In Nashville, 24.7 percent of the households had cash incomes of less than $3,000 and another 18.9 percent had incomes of $3,000 to $4,999 or 43.6 percent with cash incomes of less than $5,000.

Although the 1970 census data on housing are just now becoming available from the United States Census Bureau, selected housing statistics for Tennessee counties from that bureau's previous census report showed that 756,503 of the 1,084,340 housing units in the state were sound, but about one fifth, or 226,552 of them, were deteriorating, and almost another tenth, or 101,285, of Tennessee's housing units were dilapidated (Tennessee Statistical Abstract, 1969:126–129).

It seems that almost two fifths (36 to 40 percent) of all poverty-stricken families in Tennessee are headed by persons with eight years of schooling or less. According to statistics published by the Tennessee State Planning Commission (1970:8) the median school years completed by persons 25 years of age and older in Tennessee in 1970 were projected to be 9.1 years. This was 2.4 years less than the national median. When compared with the average educational attainment in both the Southeast and the nation, the population of Tennessee seems to be lagging dangerously behind in terms of years of school completed. The other states in the Southeast seem to have increased the median years of school completed at almost twice the rate of Tennessee. Moreover, the rate of increase of median years of school completed for the United States as a whole is almost triple that for Tennessee.

Since the incidence of poverty in Tennessee and throughout the United States is generally ultimately associated with lack of education and/or poor education, it seems advisable to observe that a statewide study of community needs in Tennessee in 1967 (State Agency for Title I of the Higher Education Act of 1965, 1967:150) revealed that, in "dozens" of the 95 counties in the state, the proportion of schoolteachers with substandard preparation ranged as high as 30 percent. In addition, many local school systems throughout the state and nation are hampered still further in their efficiency by poor facilities, inadequate funds, limited exposure of schoolteachers and administrators to effective schools and school systems, and impoverished curricula. Verily, if public policy is going to generate progress in man's efforts to reduce, ameliorate, and eventually eliminate poverty in state and country, the demand for responsibility, competency, effectiveness, and strict accountability in public education institutions must be insistent and unrelenting.

Programs relating to welfare. The major welfare program in the United States is Aid to Families with Dependent Children (AFDC). A great and growing public controversy has recently developed around this program primarily because of the tremendous increase in the number of welfare aid recipients under its provisions. During the 1950s, the number of families receiving aid under the AFDC program increased by 110,000 families, or only 17 percent. However, during the 1960s, the number of families receiving aid under the AFDC program rose precipitously from 745,000 families to approximately 2,500,000 families by 1970—an increase of more than 225 percent. This is not really surprising to students of economic history who have observed the periodic rise and fall in the volume of relief and welfare caseloads, in response to economic and political forces, during the 300 years since relief programs were started in Western Europe.

Perhaps it should be observed that welfare and relief programs have historically been subordinate to economic arrangements. Their principal task is to regulate labor: (1) by introducing welfare and relief programs for the purpose of assimilating and controlling enough of the involuntary idle to restore order when poverty and mass unemployment precipitate civil strife and turbulence; (2) as the turmoil abates the contraction of the welfare and relief roles eliminates those for whom jobs are available in the labor market from the assistance rolls. More specifically, welfare arrangements are usually initiated and/or expanded during periods of civil disorder resulting from mass unemployment and economic privation and contracted when tranquility returns to the society.

Relief and welfare programs developed slowly in the United States. Whereas relief systems in the Western world began three centuries ago amid the mass disorders that broke out during the transition from feudalism to capitalism, the first major relief crisis in the United States did not arise until about 40 years ago during the Great Depression of 1920 and the 1930s. It appears, however, that the real reason for the federal government's relief program was the political disorder that followed the economic collapse.

As previously indicated, during the 1950s, there was only a 17-

percent increase in national caseloads involving AFDC. Also, during
the 1950s, the number of AFDC families in Los Angeles and New
York City rose only 14 percent and 16 percent respectively, and there
was no increase whatsoever in the South. During the 1960s, the
country's black poor engaged in a series of nationwide civil disorders,
and the welfare rolls increased. Furthermore, during the decade of
the 1960s, several federal ghetto-assistance measures were enacted,
lawyers for the poor and social workers encouraged the needy to
apply for welfare assistance and helped them to get it, and AFDC
caseloads increased by more than 225 percent nationally and by 300
percent in Los Angeles and New York City. In contrast to no increase
whatsoever in AFDC caseloads in the South in the 1950s, the AFDC
roles rose by more than 60 percent in the South in the 1960s. Moreover, more than 80 percent of the increase in AFDC cases were
added to the welfare roles after 1965—the period during which the
recent civil disorders reached a peak. Here again, as during past
periods in human history, the welfare rolls expanded in response to
turmoil and civil disorder.

Conclusions and recommendations. There can be no doubt that
past and prevailing economic policy in the United States has been
used to exploit minorities and the poor. Nevertheless, a nation's
economic policy consists of its economic goals and the means of
achieving them employed by government, institutions, and/or individuals. Although policy shifts as economic goals and the priorities
assigned to them change, economic and/or public policy involves a
people's expectations of the economy and the means by which their
goals are to be accomplished.

It seems desirable to the interests of the American people for the
United States to adopt a public policy—an economic policy—that
embraces all legitimate steps necessary to:

1. Reduce, ameliorate, and as rapidly as possible eliminate the
   conditions and factors that contribute to the existence, expansion,
   and perpetuation of poverty in America.
2. Refine and improve the nation's welfare programs so that all
   who need aid from these programs may receive sufficient assistance, and those who are able to work will receive no un-
   warranted relief.
3. Establish effective job training and retaining programs in order
   to help improve and increase the productivity of the country's
   labor force.

It is recommended that the United States Congress, through moral suasion, the enactment of responsible legislation, the establishment of appropriate guidelines for the use of federal funds, and by other means:

a. Establish and maintain a high level of employment in the United States.
b. Accelerate the nation's rate of economic growth.
c. Improve the productivity of the nation's poor.
d. Eliminate racial and job discrimination.
e. Improve the country's labor markets.

Examination of the massive poverty, low level of educational attainment, low income, and similarly untenable economic and social conditions in the nation indicate clearly that the indispensable requirements of dignity, freedom, and privacy are nonexistent for millions of Americans. Article 22 of the Universal Declaration of Human Rights provides that "everyone as a member of society has the right to social security and is entitled to the realization . . . of economic, social, and cultural rights indispensable for his dignity and the free development of his personality" (United Nations, 1963:37). This principle of Human Rights reflects values embodied in the United States Constitution. Therefore, the United States, as a matter of entitlement, should adopt a public policy that seeks to eliminate poverty and improve the condition of the underprivileged; this policy would insist that the provisions of the Constitution be taken as seriously for the poor as for the privileged. For, ultimately, whatever attack the nation makes on poverty, slums, the problems of welfare, job training, and similar matters will not be so much an attack to rescue the poor as it will be a battle to defend the constitutional values of dignity, equality, and freedom. This is not charity, it is a matter of justice.

REFERENCES

Bach, Leland J.
    1968 *Economics: An Introduction to Analysis and Policy.* Sixth edition. Englewood Cliffs, New Jersey: Prentice-Hall, Inc.
The Houston *Post.*
    February 14, 1971.
Lyons, Eugene.
    1964 *Herbert Hoover: A Biography.* Garden City, New York: Doubleday and Company, Inc.
The New York *Times.*
    January 21, 1937.
    March 17, 1964.

Sales Management, Inc.
  1968 *Sales Management Survey of Buying Power*. Sales Management, Inc.
         June 10, 1968.
Tennessee State Planning Commission.
  1970 *Education in Tennessee*. State Planning Division.
United Nations.
  1963 *The Universal Declaration of Human Rights. A Standard of Achieve-
         ment*. Special 15th Anniversary Edition, 10 December 1963. New
         York: United Nations.
University of Tennessee.
  1967 *The Identification of Community Needs in Tennessee*. State Agency
         for Title I of the Higher Education Act of 1965.
  1969 *Tennessee Statistical Abstract*. Compiled and edited by Mary G. Cur-
         rence, Center for Business and Economic Research.

Influencing
Public Policy

THE theme of influencing public policy suggests that there is a need to bring about some changes. This theme also implies that the present policies may not entirely represent the best interests of a substantial number of our citizens. I, for one, feel that there is a great need to effect changes in both the policies and practices of this nation which some still call "the land of the free and the home of the brave." It is paradoxical that, as a nation, we constitute less than 6 percent of the world's population but consume nearly half of the world's critical resources; yet, millions of our citizens still live, and have lived all their lives, in abject poverty. Far too many are quick to say that we are the greatest nation in the world. What cannot be disputed is that we are certainly the richest and perhaps the most powerful nation that mankind has ever known. It seems to me that the challenge of this potential is to effect positive changes for our nation and for all mankind.

In a simple sense, we can break the business or the process of influencing the policy down, perhaps, to two areas: that which represents collective efforts, and that which represents individual efforts.

Collective action can take place through a variety of forums, often referred to as special interest groups. These include organizations like Common Cause, the Sierra Club, the Urban League, the League of Cities, the Conference of Mayors, the American Civil Liberties Union, and the like. In addition, there are professional organizations which are also extremely effective and which I would encourage all of you to join and support and work within. Examples in this category would include: the American Institute of Planners, the American Institute of Architects, the American Bar Association, and the like.

There are also a variety of public forums that allow individuals to participate in decision-making. At the local level these include governmental bodies and planning commissions which, from time to time, hold public hearings in order to get a lead on what the thinking is within a particular area or jurisdiction. Similar opportunities present themselves at the state level and considerable opportunities, perhaps more than ever before, are now present at the national level. In addition, I would keep in mind that many of the standing committees of the Senate and the House are points of contact.

Aside from the more formal organizations and public forums, there are also a variety of other methods that can be used to affect public policy. These include speeches, writing, organizational publications, newspapers, radio or television talk shows, and so forth. You may find these particular platforms to be very effective in airing those concerns that you have.

Our troubled environment. That we live in troubled times is not something for debate. What is worth discussing, however, is how we can help shape policies to deal substantively with the problems that are at hand. The point of departure is the environment in which we function. I am reminded of the words of economist Barbara Ward who wrote in *Spaceship Earth* (1966:1):

In our world today all the irresistible forces, technological and scientific change, are creating a single vulnerable human community. Yet three great disproportions—of power, of wealth, of ideology—stand in our way when we try to devise functioning world-wide institutions to civilize the vast energies of change. Until we overcome these obstacles, we are likely to be left with the energies in their raw irrational state. And this spells disaster.

It seems to me that Barbara Ward is correctly challenging us to harness the human energies that we need in order to overcome the many problems that exist within this society and, for the most part, I feel that is what this conference must be about. To focus on the domestic side for a moment, I am reminded of the words of an English tourist who once wrote about America:

See what is passing now. Look at the exhausted treasury, the paralyzed government, the desperate contest between north and south; the iron curb and brazing muzzle fastened upon every man who speaks his mind. The stabbings and shootings, the intrusion of the most pitiful mean, malicious, creeping, crawling, sneaking party spirit into all transactions of life. The nation is a body without a head, and the arms and legs are occupied in quarreling with the trunk and each other, and exchanging bruises at random.

If history is destiny, as Napoleon once said, this passage must be of some concern in that it was written more than 125 years ago by the author Charles Dickens. Within the last decade, newspaper headlines have made household names of Watts, Newark, Detroit, Kent State, and Jackson State. In spite of two world wars, international peace has yet to become a reality, and domestic tranquility has certainly not been forthcoming.

Civil liberties.   Needless to say, for those who are concerned with the need to establish peace at home and abroad, there is both the sense of urgency and the conviction that we cannot do without. I feel that we are in serious danger of approaching Nazi Germany during the 1930s. In an attempt to oppress a few, the civil liberties of many are at stake; certainly there has never been a time in our history when the abuse of power has been more prevalent. Let us not take lightly the words of Charles Reich who, in his best-selling book, *Greening of America* (1971:128) stated: "The inapplicability of our Bill of Rights is one of the crucial facts of American life today."

We cannot take lightly the recent imprisonment of author Ralph Ginzburg, the mass arrests that occurred during the protest demonstrations in the nation's capital, and the seemingly regressive legislative initiative at many levels of government, particularly those that deal with the delivery of social and educational services.

There is a need to create a great sense of awareness as to what this country is all about. We cannot, as citizens in this nation, be put in a position where we will be afraid to speak out against the issues; we must not hide the truth about what is wrong in America, regardless of those who say the time is ripe to talk about what is right in America. The truth of the matter is that the imbalance between blacks and whites alone in the delivery of social, educational, employment, and legal services suggests that we as a nation condone the practice of *de facto* genocide. On the positive side, the plight of the poor, the plight of the black, the plight of many, may change, because we are beginning to experience meaningful representation and a new surge of political sophistication among many who heretofore have not enjoyed elected office. In addition, the emerging consciousness about the Third World outside of this nation will force greater changes within this nation because we are not, as a nation, resource-self-reliant. Therefore, because it is necessary for our own survival, we must set a better example in terms of blacks, whites, chicanos, Indians being able to live in racial harmony.

Communications. In these days of mass communication and a 20-billion-dollar-a-year-plus advertising industry, I am distressed by the fact that we as black people do not have reasonable means or access to shape our own image effectively. We are, in effect, subjected to a "white filter" at every turn of the TV dial and in every movie theater. How can we really know what America is all about, when black television station and program managers are virtually nonexistent throughout of this entire nation? Blacks as producers, writers, directors, and executives appear to be selectively excluded from the film industry. FCC Commissioner Nicholas Johnson, on March 22, 1972, labeled the men who run commercial network television "a vicious evil influence." He stated that "the broadcasting industry now stands charged with having molested the minds of our nation's children to serve the cause of corporate profit." Socially responsive leadership within the mass media could help to correct the inequities which affect violence and could also deal with the issues of racism and insensitivity toward our fellowman. In order to shape public policy effectively in the United States, we blacks must enjoy representation in policy-making positions within the over-all communications delivery system and also at the operating level within stations, if these policies are to be carried out.

The bureaucracy. In order to effect change and influence policies, it is essential that we understand our institutions. In particular, I feel the bureaucracy warrants special comment. If you come to the nation's capital, you will see huge buildings, perhaps best described as monolithic megastructures, a final suggestion of permanence in an age of transience. Inside, you will find endless passageways that seem to move by almost as if you were standing still. Within these structures are people whose day-to-day decisions shape the lives of many through the manner in which programs are administered.

All agencies are political. Priority is affected by the special-interest groups more than by the needs of the people at large. The bureaucracy is dysfunctioning. In part, this is because there is a tremendous amount of insensitivity, a lack of professionalism, limited financial resources, and an operating climate which has not been stable. Social psychologist Warren Bennis has predicted the demise of the bureaucracy, considering the volatile state of our domestic situation and the need to adjust rapidly to one crisis after another. In time, the Bennis prediction will come true.

The SWEMM *bias.*   The decision-making process often reflects what I call the SWEMM (Suburban White Economically-advantaged Middle-aged Male) bias. The pattern which exists at cabinet and sub-cabinet levels within the Executive Branch is callously repeated throughout government and industry almost without exception. While I would not want to take anything away from the highly talented and unemotional minds that have been able to weigh the subjective with objectivity, I would argue vigorously that there is a need to involve those who can weigh the objective with subjectivity.

In this regard I find that it is imperative that decision-making bodies be complemented with many who are, in fact, urban oriented, black, economically disadvantaged, young, old, and female.

On professionalism.   I find problems within professional disciplines, as well as problems with the exclusion of some disciplines. In far too many instances, we have failed to respect and involve such disciplines as sociology, anthropology, psychology, and biology. I am particularly concerned with what seems to be a prevailing attitude among many bureaucrats that we are all psychologists, or among whites who feel that all black professionals are sociologists. Of particular note is the fact that, within the entire Department of Housing and Urban Development of approximately 16,000 employees, there are only three sociologists. Undoubtedly, the most favored professional is that of attorney. But competence in judicial proceedings does not necessarily insure an ability to affect the delivery system which must benefit those who have the greatest need.

On cities—a lack of commitment.   I could point to some of the quiet initiatives that are being undertaken to affect communities favorably, but to do this would border on hypocrisy, because they are simply isolated acts of charity. My own experience suggests that this nation is still largely uncommitted to a large segment of this society, namely the poor who happen to represent large numbers of the elderly and the black. Nothing is more reflective of this lack of commitment than the conditions existing within most of our central cities. More than thirty years of suburban-oriented priorities in the development of communities are manifest in the problems of abandonment of central-city residential properties. A nation's worth, more than anything else, is reflected in its cities. During the Golden Age of Greece under Pericles, the Acropolis stood as a symbol of great achievement. The cities of Greece such as Delphi, Sparta, Mistras, Olympia, and Delos also at one time flourished. The Golden Age of Greece has long passed, and with it many of its great cities. I am firmly convinced that, so long as the resident population of our central cities is significantly black, a serious commitment from government and industry will not be forthcoming. Only when it is realized that the fate of white America is inextricably bound to that of black America, and that economic prosperity cannot be enjoyed without social progress, will this assertion not be of questionable validity.

Housing. I don't want to dwell on housing, *per se,* because the real emphasis must be on communities. Housing is, however, an issue that has grown in national prominence since the Congressional Subcommittee on the Welfare of Labor of the Committee of National Defense conducted its investigation during the World War I era. Since that time, there have been plenty of "we understand the problem" types of speeches and plenty of "we are going to do something about it" types of legislation. Some 34 years ago, Public Law 412 was enacted by the 75th Congress to "provide financial assistance to the states and political subdivisions thereof for the elimination of unsafe and unsanitary housing conditions, for the eradication of slums," etc. (U.S. Housing Act, 1937:888). What we have now is a history of an insensitive government that in three decades has failed to house its poor citizens adequately. In short, the congressional mandate, while getting stronger, has not been carried out effectively by the Executive Branch. In addition, the private and public sectors alike have exacerbated problems by misplanning, poor programming, and under-funding. The question at this point is: What must we try to do in making a commitment to the people who live within our cities? I propose the following recommendations as initiatives which must be effected to alleviate some of our domestic problems.

1. Relieve all major cities, particularly those approaching bankruptcy, of their matching requirements in the allocation of federal grants so long as the grant-in-aid system remains.
2. Remove residency requirement restrictions affecting prospective tenants of public housing, so that they can enjoy metropolitan-wide, regionwide, and national mobility.
3. Require that representation on the policy bodies of areawide planning agencies adhere to the one man-one vote principle. This would give an appropriate balance to the central cities in reviewing federal grant applications.
4. Discontinue federal insurance assistance to lending institutions whose policies discriminate against neighborhoods on the basis of race.

5. List as unfair all developers who discriminate on the basis of race in the area of sales, hiring, and in making a reasonable quantitative commitment to house low- and moderate-income families.

6. Require that all professional federal employees who are responsible for the delivery of social services account to the Senate Committee on Government Operations for their productivity every year.

7. Provide free medical assistance to black citizens until the disparities are eliminated relating to whites in the areas of infant mortality, maternal deaths, and life expectancy.

8. Discontinue federal assistance to communities that fail to provide a fair share of housing for low- and moderate-income families, particularly in those metropolitan areas where it is vital to allow some of the population to be absorbed within the mainstream of economic opportunity in the suburban jurisdictions.

9. Require that all executives in the social, economic, and physical delivery systems experience, periodically, the environment within which they are responsible for effecting improvements. What this means is that public housing administrators, from the federal down to the local level, would have to spend some time each year living in those areas that their programs deal with.

The case for leadership. A committed leadership is perhaps the most important single factor beyond determination, and it should be kept in mind. I often get disturbed at the general thrust of what is happening and what has been happening for decades in this country. I find much that is encouraging when I see strong and courageous leaders such as Senator Mondale and Governor Askew on education; Congressmen Ashley and Whalan on housing; the entire Black Congressional Caucus on Civil Rights; Clarence Mitchell of the NAACP on Civil Rights; David Rockefeller of the Chase Manhattan Bank on Housing and Community Development; and the many big-city mayors, especially blacks, who are staying "on the case." In addition, many of the public-interest groups such as Common Cause, the National Urban Coalition, and the Joint Center for Political Studies are working arduously to redress the social problems of this nation.

It was on the third day of April in 1968 that the Reverend Dr. Martin Luther King, Jr., delivered his last address to America at the Mason Temple in Memphis, Tennessee. He said something that night that we must never forget.

[W]e aren't engaged in any negative protest and in any negative arguments with anybody. We are saying that we are determined to be men, we are determined to be people. We are saying that we are God's children, and if we are God's children, we are going to have to live like we are supposed to live. Now what does all this mean in this great period of history? It means that we've got to stay together and maintain unity (Gregory, 1971:339–340).

What the Reverend Dr. Martin Luther King, Jr., said says it all about being and doing when we talk about influencing public policy— in short, a conviction of righteous determination with a fearless commitment to action.

REFERENCES

Gregory, Dick.
  1971   *No More Lies.* New York: Perennial Library, Harper & Row.
Reich, Charles A.
  1971   *The Greening of America.* New York: Bantam Books.
U.S. Congress.
  1937   Housing Act of 1937. Act of September 1, 1937, ch. 896, § 1, 50 Stat.
         888, as amended, 42 U.S.C.A. § 1401 (1970).
Ward, Barbara.
  1966   *Spaceship Earth.* New York: Columbia University Press.

Chapter **6**   MACK H. JONES

Government Structure
and Urban Policy

In brief, most of America's wealth and most of America's domestic problems reside in the metropolitan areas. Why, then, cannot this vast wealth be applied through vigorous social measures to meet the growing problem? *Because the resources exist in one set of jurisdictions within the metropolitan areas and the problems in another.* Through a large part of the country this disparity between needs and resources is the disparity between the central city and its suburbs. [Emphasis added.]

THE statement quoted above, which was taken from a report of the prestigious Advisory Commission on Intergovernmental Relations (1969:1), lists some of the substantive dimensions of the urban crisis (though it makes only a rather obtuse reference to its racial aspects), and suggests that the primary barrier to the development of effective programs for their elimination is structural. The same report goes on to categorize the factors responsible for generating the urban crisis as: (1) fiscal and political fragmentation resulting in mismatch of needs and resources; (2) disorderly, uneconomic and antisocial patterns of urban development and land use; (3) timidity of state government in grasping the urban mettle; (4) unbalanced federal-state-local revenue sources; and (5) growth of functional government. That these structural arrangements would inhibit the implementation of comprehensive programs designed to ameliorate the urban crisis can be accepted without debate. However, the assertion that they are determinant variables in the urban crisis bears investigation.

During the 1950s and '60s when the proliferation and fragmentation of metropolitan governments took place, accompanied by disorderly and uneconomic land use and the virtual disintegration of urban school systems, also taking place was the accelerated migration of the

black population to the cities and the reciprocal white exodus from
the cities. Since 1960, as Tables 1 and 2 show, almost all of the black
population increase (3.2 million of total increase of 3.8 million) occurred in the cities (U.S. Bureau of the Census, 1970:12). On the
other hand, 15.5 million of the total 18.8-million increase in the white
population occurred in suburban America.

Moreover, the concentration of blacks in central cities is even more
pronounced when we control for geographical region and the size of
the city. While 58 percent of the black population lives in central
cities, except for the South, more than 90 percent of the black population lives in metropolitan areas. More than three fourths of blacks in
the North and two thirds in the West live in central cities (U.S. Bureau
of the Census, 1970:14). Also, as Table 3 shows, the increase in black

TABLE 1

*Population Distribution and Change, Inside and Outside Metropolitan Areas:
1950, 1960, and 1970*

(Numbers in millions)

Area	Population					
	Negro			White		
	1950	1960	1970	1950ª	1960	1970
United States	15.0	18.9	22.7	135.1	158.8	177.6
Metropolitan areas	8.8	12.8	16.8	85.1	106.4	121.3
Central cities	6.6	9.9	13.1	46.8	50.1	49.5
Outside central cities	2.2	2.8	3.7	38.3	56.3	71.8
Outside metropolitan areas	6.2	6.1	5.8	50.0	52.5	56.4

	Change, 1960–1970			
	Negro		White	
	Number	Percent	Number	Percent
United States	3.8	20	18.8	12
Metropolitan areas	4.1	32	14.9	14
Central cities	3.2	33	.6	−1
Outside central cities	.8	29	15.5	28
Outside metropolitan areas	−.3	−4	3.9	7

SOURCE: U.S. Department of Commerce, Bureau of the Census. Taken from
The Social and Economic Status of Negroes in The United States, 1970, p. 12.
   ª 1950 data for metropolitan areas not strictly comparable to 1970 definition
of SMSA's.

TABLE 2

Percent Distribution of Population, Inside and Outside Metropolitan Areas: 1950, 1960, and 1970

Area	Negro			White		
	1950	1960	1970	1950[a]	1960	1970
United States (millions) ..	15.0	18.9	22.7	135.1	158.8	177.6
Percent, total	100	100	100	100	100	100
Metropolitan areas	59	68	74	63	67	68
Central cities	44	53	58	35	32	28
Outside central cities ...	15	15	16	28	35	40
Outside metropolitan areas .	41	32	26	37	33	32

SOURCE: U.S. Department of Commerce, Bureau of the Census. Taken from *The Social and Economic Status of Negroes in United States, 1970*, p. 12.
[a] 1950 data from metropolitan areas not strictly comparable to 1970 definition of SMSA's.

TABLE 3

Negroes as a Percent of Total Population, Inside and Outside Metropolitan Areas, by Size of Metropolitan Areas: 1960 and 1970

Type of residence	Percent Negro	
	1960	1970
United States	11	11
Metropolitan areas	11	12
Central cities	16	21
Central cities in metropolitan areas of—		
2,000,000 or more	20	28
1,000,000 to 2,000,000	15	20
500,000 to 1,000,000	16	19
250,000 to 500,000	13	15
Under 250,000	10	11
Suburbs	5	5
Suburbs in metropolitan areas of—		
2,000,000 or more	4	5
1,000,000 to 2,000,000	4	4
500,000 to 1,000,000	5	4
250,000 to 500,000	6	6
Under 250,000	7	6
Outside metropolitan areas	10	9

SOURCE: U.S. Department of Commerce, Bureau of the Census. Taken from *The Social and Economic Status of Negroes in the United States, 1970*, p. 12.

population has been heaviest in the larger cities of 500,000 or more.

Conversely, only four to six percent of suburbia is black, with the percentage of black suburbanites varying little with the size of the metropolitan area. Fifty-six to 75 percent of blacks, depending upon the region, live in the areas afflicted with the array of substantive urban problems, while only 4 to 6 percent live in the areas endowed with the resources necessary for dealing with these problems.

The structural manifestations of the urban crisis—disorderly and uneconomic urban development and land use, unbalanced revenue sources, dysfunctional functional governments, etc.—have become increasingly visible as whites have fled from the central city and from their black compatriots, and governments have done little to improve the situation. As the ACIR report (1969:2) put it:

Specifically, government at all levels has been basically passive in the migrational flow of people, in the concentration of industrial development, and in the forging of urban growth policies. Local government activitiy has been marked by economic competition, exclusionary zoning, and building code anarchy. State governments usually have been indifferent to urban financial and service needs and rarely willing to challenge the local goverment status quo. The federal role has been wholly contradictory. On the one hand, Congress enacts area-wide planning requirements, strengthens representative regional bodies, adopts programs to assist the rehabilitation of central cities. On the other hand, the federal-state highway program, FHA's activities, the failure of a fair and uniform relocation policy, and various location decisions of the Department of Defense and other federal agencies more often than not have collided head-on with long-term urban development needs.
The result of all of this has been to accentuate wrong-way migrational patterns of people and business; to forge a white, middle- and high-income noose around the increasingly black and poor inner city; and to subject much of rural America to a continuing course of gradual erosion.

The question to be raised here is whether this seemingly irrational, crazy-quilt pattern of development, with its attendant proliferation of units of metropolitan government was in fact mindless or the result of a series of contrived purposeful reactions of those in a position to influence the outcomes of public policy. Unless we are convinced that the structural dimensions of the urban problems are functions of mindless, capricious decisions, focusing on "good government" structural reforms as means for dealing with substantive urban problems of the black and poor would seem to be a misallocation of resources.

I am inclined toward the view that the structural aspects of the urban problems came into being as a result of sober, rational, calculated actions by whites to separate themselves from blacks in the central city and to insulate themselves from the serious social problems of American society; or, to put it another way, the structural dimensions of the urban problems represent nothing less than the attempt of those who have benefited most from the U.S. largesse (plunder?) to abdicate their social responsibilities to the larger society. For example, exclusionary zoning is rational in light of the goals of its proponents; reliance on regressive sales tax and opposition to progressive payroll taxes as means for enhancing the solvency of cities is rational in light of the goals of those in power.

Every patch in the crazy quilt was sewn in because it redounded to the benefit of some organized interest. Zoning regulations, building permits, tax concessions, etc., are given or not given as a result of pressures brought to bear and not as a result of fits of mindlessness. Problems in intergovernmental structures may be marginal contributory factors, but they are not the primary cause of urban problems; they are reactions to the problem as it is perceived by whites. It should be clear, then, that in discussing government structure and public policy with particular reference to blacks and the poor it is necessary to rise above antiseptic good government arguments and deal with the underlying political realities, for political realities are more likely to determine the nature of structures and the possibility of structural reforms than vice versa.

In order to understand the political realities of urban problems, it may be useful to indulge in a bit of theorizing. Parenthetically, I am aware that there may be those among us who argue that a position paper such as this should be practical and not engage in idle theorizing. To that, I can only say that the landscape is strewn with the remains of atheoretical good-government reformers who failed to recognize that structures, no matter how inefficient they may appear on their faces, are neither adopted nor maintained unless they serve the political interest of some element. Good-government reformers, unguided by a clear theoretical understanding of politics, have also failed to understand that the definition of what is practical usually turns on the extent to which a particular act is consistent with maintaining the status quo. Reforms which would drastically alter the status quo quite logically engender intense reaction and, as a consequence, are deemed impractical.

So much for that. It is theoretically useful to understand that groups in superordinate positions act toward those in subordinate positions in such a manner as to maintain their position of dominance. It should be taken for granted, therefore, that one of the important dynamics of urban problems is the attempts of whites and the well-to-do to maintain their position of dominance. Given this, primary emphasis must be placed upon political empowerment of the central city residents, the black and the poor. Structural reforms that weaken their incipient political power should not be encouraged, and structural reforms that do not alter power relationships cannot be seen as solutions. It would appear that the only way through which the age-old inequities in the distribution of urban services can be reversed is political empowerment of the dispossessed. For example, I am unaware of any information which suggests that the quality of life for central-city blacks is demonstrably better in those cities with fewer intergovernmental problems—the consolidated cities of Miami, Jacksonville, Nashville, or cities such as Houston and Oklahoma City, which have been able to use annexation advantageously.

This is an argument, then, for decentralization, not necessarily for the administrative advantages it might afford, but because it is the only auspicious avenue to significant black political power within the American federal system. However, as the Committee on Economic Development (1970:17) has warned:

The case for decentralization . . . cannot ignore the economic, technological, and social arrangements which favor a centralized system. Small-unit governments are poorly equipped to take advantage of economies of scale and technological innovations; hence they often find it more difficult to respond to the growing and disparate needs of their citizens. Proponents of centralization argue that the interests of the disadvantaged are best served by a larger rather than a smaller unit of government. They point to the economic weakness of the ghetto, the historic conservatism of America's small communities, and the growing dependence on the federal government for social progress. It is clear from the foregoing that what is needed is a system of government that adequately recognizes *both* forces, centralization and decentralization. Such a system must permit a genuine sharing of power over functions between a larger and smaller unit. It must recognize a larger unit to permit economies of scale, area-wide planning, and equities in finance. It must recognize a smaller unit to permit the exercise of local power over matters which affect the lives of local citizens.

This is not to argue that decentralized government will solve the urban crisis. Political empowerment of the poor must be complemented by an influx of additional resources. As one source put it,

they [decentralized governments] will not solve these problems simply because decentralization of city governmental structure does not insure additional resources. In fact neighborhood government without increased resources might make the redistributive aspect of urban political systems even more difficult by creating a great number of competing interest groups (Shalala, 1971:19).

Decentralization must be tied to some mechanism which gives the central city access to, and control over, external resources. This, of course, would not be a new development in American federalism. Presently, federal aid accounts for 18.2 percent (Shalala, 1971:21) of total state-local revenue. As of 1967, direct state and federal aid supported 27 percent of all expenditures within central cities, 29 percent of those in suburbia, and 37 percent of all local expenditures in the remainder of the country (CED, 1970:35). Moreover, as the CED report points out, "direct federal and state aid is equivalent to only 44 percent of central-city taxes, while comparable figures for suburbia and the rest of the nation are, respectively, 53 and 74 percent." Instances have also been found in which central-city residents actually subsidize wealthy suburban areas. In Atlanta, for example, city residents annually subsidize county schools to the tune of $3,199,111, or 23.8 percent of county local education taxes (Research Atlanta, 1972:77).

Thus, in keeping with the historical practice of transferring resources to points of need, the federal government should take the initiative in providing the financial resources to make central cities economically viable, and its initiative must be complemented by rearrangements of taxing and redistributive systems of state and local governments.

The national government must be persuaded that the "urban crisis" is a part of the racial crisis and that, therefore, it can be dealt with only through means which recognize this truth. Just as cabinet-level departments and subcabinet agencies are set aside to deal with matters such as transportation and ecology, a cabinet-level agency for minority problems must be established. All existing services dealing exclusively or disproportionately with the problems of blacks and other dispossessed people would be consolidated in this department that, working through neighborhood structures, would be responsible for assisting central governments in developing programs to deal with substantive urban ills. Programs approved by the department would be funded by direct grants to the cities. Appropriation levels for this department would be based upon systematic projections made by agencies such as the Black Economic Research Center, Committee on Economic Development, and the Advisory Commission on Intergovernmental Relations.

Central cities would have to conform to area-wide planning review requirements of the Housing and Urban Development Act of 1966, but central-city residents would be given sufficient representation, perhaps through some form of weighted vote on specific-issue categories, so that area-wide land use decisions would not unduly contravene their interests.

The Civil Rights Division of the Justice Department (which should be reorganized, restaffed and transferred to the new department on minority affairs) could be given review over certain classes of area-wide planning decisions in a manner similar to the Department of Justice review of electoral statutes and regulations under the Voting Rights Act of 1965. Review procedures would guard against exclusionary land use decisions which encourage black migration into the central cities while at the same time encouraging industry and commerce to move into the opposite direction and, in the process, locking blacks into the densely populated urban preserves.

State and local tax systems must be redesigned. Present systems actually discriminate against the less well-to-do. The major tax source for local governments is, of course, the property tax, which is regressive and discriminatorily administered. The constant rate discriminates against those of limited means and exemption provisions allow too many to escape the incidence of the tax altogether. Figures of exempt properties are not generally kept, but at least one city, Atlanta, Georgia, exempts an estimated 50 percent (Research Atlanta:85) of the total tax digest. Much more revenue can be obtained from the property tax by increased valuation and fewer exemptions. Some states have already begun to move in this direction (ACIR, 1968:3–7). The 1968 yield of this tax, $29 billion, is twice as much as in 1958 (ACIR, 1968:4).[1]

1. Contrary to popular opinion, increased *ad valorem* tax yield need not place an undue burden on the poor homeowner and the renter who normally absorbs the property tax of the landlord. Wisconsin has developed a circuit-breaker plan which protects such persons. The Advisory Commission on Intergovernmental Relations (1968:5), which enthusiastically recommended the plan to other states, describes it in this way:

> The efficiency of this device is reflected in the remarkable transformation of a highly regressive tax into an essentially proportional levy at relatively modest cost to the state treasury. In 1966, approximately 60,000 beneficiaries were granted property tax relief at the cost of about $5 million— less than one percent of the total property tax take.
>
> Property tax relief is granted by the state to all elderly homeowners on that part of their tax load deemed to be excessive in relation to total household income. The elderly renter is also given relief on the assumption

Property tax reform should be coupled with measures to finance public education by means other than the local property tax. Public education should be financed directly from national and state revenue sources, freeing the property tax for other local services. This would virtually eliminate the financial strain on city governments.

Changing the source of funding for public education, of course, does not lessen the need for revenue. States could improve their tax yield by relying more on business taxes and better use of payroll and sales taxes. Since 1954, although total business tax payments have increased, "their relative importance declines in comparison with personal taxes—falling from 36 to 30 percent of total State, and local tax revenue (ACIR, 1967:31). (Appendix A gives a detailed breakdown of state corporation income tax rates.)

Finally, any program designed to improve urban public policy and delivery of services must also deal with the problem situations which propel blacks toward the central cities. Rural redevelopment legislation is being developed by Nixon strategists and southern senators who have not been especially sensitive to the problems of the black and the poor, rural or urban. It is imperative that this legislation and the structures growing out of it reflect the needs of the black community.

---

that 25 percent of his rental payment to the landlord is in effect payment for property taxes.

Under the Wisconsin procedure, the applicant for homestead tax relief files a statement as a supplement to the Wisconsin state income tax return. After audit by the Wisconsin state Income Tax Department, the eligible beneficiary receives compensation for that part of his property tax payment deemed extraordinary under Wisconsin law. The compensation takes the form of either a direct cash refund or a credit against his state income tax liability. The vast majority of applicants have such low income that they have no state income tax liability—a "negative" tax credit situation—necessitating direct cash refund in about 98 percent of the cases.

The point must be emphasized that this type of highly selective aid does no violence to the local fisc. Because this relief program is financed from state appropriations and administered by the State Tax Department, it neither erodes the local tax base nor interferes in any way with either the local assessment or tax collection process.

To insure that only the truly needy persons would receive property tax relief, the applicants must list all forms of money income, including such sacrosanct items as social security and veterans benefits and railroad retirement payments.

Wisconsin's pioneering effort conclusively demonstrates that it is not necessary to force low-income households through the property tax wringer in order to finance public services.

REFERENCES

Advisory Commission on Intergovernmental Relations (ACIR).
  1967 *State-Local Taxation and Industrial Location; a Commission Report.*
        Washington: Government Printing Office.
  1968 *State and Local Finances, Significant Features, 1966–1969.* Washing-
        ton: Government Printing Office.
  1968 *State and Local Taxes: Significant Features.* Washington: Government
        Printing Office.
  1969 *Urban America and the Federal System.* Washington: Government
        Printing Office.
Committee on Economic Development.
  1970 *Reshaping Government in Metropolitan Areas, 1970.* Washington:
        Government Printing Office.
Research Atlanta.
  1972 *Which Way Atlanta, 1972.* Atlanta: Research Atlanta.
Shalala, Don.
  1971 *Neighborhood Government.* New York: American Jewish Committee.
U.S. Bureau of the Census.
  1970 *The Social and Economic Status of Negroes in the United States, 1970.*
        Washington: Government Printing Office.

APPENDIX A

STATE CORPORATION INCOME TAX RATES, JANUARY 1, 1968

State	Rate (percent)	Federal tax deductible[1]	Related Provisions
Alabama	5	X	Financial institutions, 6%.
Alaska	First $25,000 . . . . .5.4	—	
	Over $25,000 . . . . . .9.36		
Arizona[2]	First $1,000 2	X	Financial institutions, 5%.
	$1,001–$2,000 3		
	$2,001–$3,000 4		
	$3,001–$4,000 5		
	$4,001–$5,000 6		
	$5,001–$6,000 7		
	Over $6,000 8		
Arkansas	First $3,000 1	—	
	$3,001–$6,000 2		
	$6,001–$11,000 . . .3		
	$11,001–$25,000 . . .4		
	Over $25,000 5		
California	7	—	Minimum tax: $100
Colorado	5	—	Banks and financial institutions, 6%.
Connecticut[2]	. . . . .5.25	—	If tax yield is greater, 2⅜ mills per dollar of capital employed in Connecticut. Minimum Tax: $30.
Delaware	5	—	
Georgia	5	—	
Hawaii[2]	First $25,000 . . . . .5.85	—	Capital gains entitled to alternative tax treatment are taxed at 3.08%. Financial institutions, 11.7%.
	Over $25,000 . . . . .6.435		
Idaho	6	—	A $10 filing fee is imposed.
Indiana	2	—	
Iowa	First $25,000 4	X[3]	
	$25,001–$100,000 . .6		
	Over $100,000 8		
Kansas	. . . . .4.5	X	Banks, trust companies and building and loan associations, 5%.
Kentucky	First $25,000 5	X	
	Over $25,000 7		

APPENDIX A (*Continued*)

State	Rate (percent)	Federal tax deductible[1]	Related Provisions
Louisiana	4	X	A specific exemption of $3,000, prorated according to the proportion of total net income taxable in Louisiana, is allowed against net income.
Maryland	....................5.25	—	Domestic corporations are allowed credit for franchise taxes in excess of $25.
Massachusetts[2]	....................6.765[4]	—	Plus $6.15 per $1,000 upon the value of its tangible property not subject to local taxation and situated in Massachusetts on the last day of the taxable year if a tangible property corporation (or its net worth allocable to Massachusetts if an intangible property corporation). Minimum tax $100. Domestic corporations pay a tax of ⅓ of 1% of the value of their interest in ships in interstate or foreign commerce, which value is deducted from the corporate excess.
Michigan	....................5.6	—	Financial institutions, 7%.
Minnesota	....................11.33	X	A credit of $500, deductible from net income, is allowed each corporation. Minimum tax: $10. Banks, 13.64%.
Mississippi	First $5,000 ......2 Over $5,000 3	—	
Missouri	2	X	Banks and financial institutions, 7%.

APPENDIX A (*Continued*)

State	Rate (percent)	Federal tax deductible[1]	Related Provisions
Montana	. . . . .5.5	—	Minimum tax: $10.
Nebraska[2]	2	—	The tax rate is 20% of the rate applicable to individuals. The rate for individuals for 1968 is 10% and is set as a flat percentage by the State Board of Equalization and Assessment on or before November 15 annually for the taxable year beginning during the subsequent calendar year.
New Jersey	. . . . .3.25	—	All corporations pay additional tax on net worth.
New Mexico[2]	3	X	
New York	5.5 percent plus tax of mill per $1 of allocated subsidiary capital.	—	Corporations are subject to the 5½ percent tax on net income or a tax on 3 alternative bases, whichever is greatest. The alternative taxes are: (1) 1 mill on each dollar of business and investment capital; or (2) 5½ percent of 30 percent of net income plus compensation paid to officers and holders of more than 5 percent of capital stock, less $15,000 and any net loss; or (3) $25, whichever is greatest; plus the tax on allocated subsidiary capital. Banks and financial institutions, 4.5%.
North Carolina	6	—	Banks and financial institutions, 4.5%.

APPENDIX A (*Continued*)

State	Rate (percent)	Federal tax deductible[1]	Related Provisions
North Dakota	First $3,000 ......3 $3,001–$8,000 ....4 $8,001–$15,000 ...5 Over $15,000 6	X	Banks and trust companies, 5%. Minimum tax: $50.
Oklahoma[2]	4	X	Banks 4%.
Oregon	6	—	Manufacturers may claim an offset of up to one-third of the tax for Oregon personal property taxes paid on raw materials, goods in process, and finished products. Minimum tax: $10. Banks, national banking associations, financial institutions and production credit associations, 8%.
Pennsylvania[2]	................7[5]	—	
Rhode Island	6	—	Alternative tax: 40 cents per $100 on corporate excess if tax yield is greater. Banks and financial institutions, 6% or $2.50 per $10,000, if tax yield is greater. Manufacturers pay 10% surtax.
South Carolina	5	—	Banks, 4.5%, savings and loan associations, 8%.
South Dakota[6]		—	
Tennessee[2]	5	—	
Utah	6	X	Corporations are subject to 6 percent tax or a tax of $\frac{1}{20}$ of 1 percent of the value of tangible property within the state, whichever is greater. Minimum tax: $10.
Vermont[2]	5	—	Subject to reduction if there is sufficient surplus in general fund. Minimum tax: $25.

APPENDIX A (*Continued*)

State	Rate (percent)	Federal tax deductible[1]	Related Provisions
Virginia	5	—	
West Virginia	6	—	
Wisconsin[2]	First $1,000 2	X[7]	
	$1,001–$2,000 ....2.5		
	$2,001–$3,000 3		
	$3,001–$4,000 4		
	$4,001–$5,000 5		
	$5,001–$6,000 6		
	Over $6,000 7		
Dist. of Col.	5	—	Banks and trust companies, 4%; building and loan associations, 2%.

X Denotes "yes."
— Denotes "no."

1. In general, each state which permits the deduction of federal income taxes limits such deduction to taxes paid on that part of income subject to its own income tax.

2. Allows deduction of state corporation income tax itself in computing state tax liability.

3. Limited to 50% of federal income taxes paid or accrued during the taxable year.

4. The rate shown is for business or manufacturing corporations, utility corporations, 5%. Domestic and foreign security corporations (other than regulated investment or bank holding companies, which are taxed at the rate of ⅓ of 1% of gross income or $100, whichever is greater). Domestic and foreign corporations engaged in interstate commerce and not subject to the corporation excise income tax, 1.075% on that portion of their net income derived from business carried on in the state.

5. Increased to 7.5% beginning January 1, 1969.

6. Tax at 4.5% ($24 minimum) applicable to banks and financial institutions only.

7. Limited to 10% of net income before federal tax.

SOURCE: Advisory Commission on Intergovernmental Relations, *State and Local Taxes: Significant Features* (Washington: Government Printing Office, 1968).

PART II
Evaluating Existing Programs

How Not to Feed the Poor: An Overview of Federal Food Assistance Programs

IN the spring of 1968, the Citizens' Board of Inquiry into Hunger and Malnutrition in the United States reported concrete evidence of chronic hunger and malnutrition in every part of the United States, but most particularly in areas with high levels of poverty. The Board's exposé, entitled *Hunger USA*, documented the existence of suffering by tens of millions of Americans who could not afford an adequate diet.

The response of the nation to this recital of the evidence of human misery was immediate—and negative. Many elected officials, stung by some charts and tables that pinpointed their counties as emergency hunger sites, reacted as if they had been indicted for murder. They refused to acknowledge the food needs of the poor. They sought to distort the issue by inducing hundreds of county health officials to swear that they had never seen any instances of persons starving. They hired FBI agents to harass people who had testified before the Board or sent it pictures. They attacked the television networks whose documentaries underscored the Board's findings. From Lyndon Johnson to Orville Freeman, Secretary of Agriculture (1961–69), to Robert Poage, Democrat, of Texas, Chairman, House Agriculture Committee, to Jamie Whitten, Democrat, of Mississippi, Chairman, House Agricultural Appropriations Subcommittee, they purposefully diverted public attention from the facts and focused concern not upon millions of insufficiently nourished poor, but upon themselves and the manner in which they, the legislators and bureaucrats, were performing their jobs. A typical American political performance.

Since 1969, the tide has changed. Slowly and reluctantly, during the past three years, the public, the President, and the Congress have come to acknowledge the validity of the Board's findings and proceeded to take some steps to alleviate the problem. Hearings have been held *ad nauseam*, messages have been written, pledges made, broken, and remade, bills passed, appropriations allotted.

But everything that has been done to date has been in response to the wrong question: How can we feed the poor? The basic and faulty assumption has always been and remains that the government must be responsible for feeding the poor because the poor, if given money instead of a plethora of food programs, cannot be trusted to feed themselves.

The returns from this misguided paternalism are now in. They constitute the depressing history of food relief for the past four years —a history of millions bypassed and still unserved, and millions more receiving only partial aid despite the creation and refinement of five family food assistance programs and thirty-three child nutrition programs.[1]

This nation has undeniably made some positive attempts to put an end to hunger and malnutrition in America. It has tried to spend more money to guarantee the nutritional well-being of the poor. From actual fiscal year 1967 to budgeted fiscal year 1973, the food program budget has been multiplied by six, from 687 million dollars to 4,053 million dollars. Food stamps have jumped from 105.5 million dollars to a minimum of 2,266 million dollars, an elevenfold increase. School lunch funds earmarked for the poor have gone from 2 million dollars to 587.7 million dollars. In the process, the number of food stamp recipients has more than quadrupled (from 2.5 million to 11.1 million),

1. In child nutrition, the laundry list includes general cash assistance for lunch, special cash assistance for lunch, Section 32 aid for lunch, school breakfast, nonfood assistance (equipment), special food service (day-care centers and summer recreation), and special milk (in each of the above categories there is a separate program for private schools or institutions in 20-plus states which are not permitted to disburse funds to private schools or institutions) as well as federal administrative expenses; state administrative expense, Section G6 commodities, Section 32 commodities, Section 41(g)(6) commodities, Section 709 commodities, surveys, training, special developmental projects, Title I—ESEA, migrant food service, handicapped children's food service, school nutrition demonstration projects, Head Start, Follow Through, Johnson-O'Malley, Model Cities, Emergency Food, and public assistance social services. In family food aid, the five are food stamps, food distribution, supplemental nutrition package, food certificates, and Emergency Food.

the number of children fed a free or reduced-price lunch nearly quadrupled (from a 2.3 million to 8.1 million).

Nevertheless, despite all of the money, all of the glowing departmental press releases, all of the legislative hustle-bustle, hunger and malnutrition still exist in this country and affect the lives of tens of millions of Americans.

There are 25.5 million Americans whose incomes are below the Social Security Administration's poverty guidelines and who, by definition, cannot purchase an adequate diet day in, day out. More than 10.9 million of the poor receive no help whatever from any federal family-feeding program. They are left to eke out a subsistence diet on their own.

As for the 11.1 million who received food stamps in January 1972, the boost in their food-purchasing power that came from the Department of Agriculture was meager, at best. The average per-person federal bonus (the value of stamps over and above what the recipient pays for the stamps) was $13.39 a month, or less than 15 cents a meal. To this, the average recipient added $10.50 from his own pocketbook for a grand total of $24 a month or 26 cents a meal. The "nutritional adequacy" of this sum is dubious. It is being litigated in the federal courts. The Agriculture Department is thinking about raising the $108 monthly allotment for a family of four to $112 by the end of the year, which would amount to an annual 2 percent hike over the past three years, while the wholesale food price index rose 1.8 percent in January 1972, alone.

The Agriculture Department has described the Economy Food Plan, of which $108 is the dollar equivalent for a family of four and which is the basis of the food stamp program, as "not a reasonable measure of basic money needs for a good diet," as being for "temporary or emergency use." In the last nationwide Food Consumption Survey (1965–1966), the Department found that less than 10 percent of the families who spent at the Economy Food Plan level were able to buy their recommended dietary allowances for seven essential nutrients, while more than 50 percent of the same families had poor diets because they could not obtain even two thirds of such allowances. Thus, delivering food-purchasing power equivalent to the Economy Food Plan guarantees only malnutrition. That is all that the current food-stamp program supplies to the poor.

An additional 3.5 million poor people are enrolled in the commodity-distribution program. If each one of them received, stored, and later ate the full paper allotment of distributed foodstuffs, which theoretically amounts to 35 pounds of boxed and canned goods a month, he would obtain 100 percent of the recommended daily allowances of protein and six vitamins and minerals, although only 80 percent of needed calories. In fact, however, the program distributes an average of only 28.2 pounds per person per month, furnishing less than 74 percent of items by weight and 73 percent of items by retail value ($9.50 worth, not the ideal $16). To distribute food to the needy on this limited basis does not come close to eradicating hunger.

Federal efforts to feed the poor have failed to reach a significant portion of the poor or to help those they do reach to any substantial and satisfactory degree. For 43 percent of the poor, the federal government offers nothing at all in the way of food benefits. For another 44 percent, it supplies enough for a temporary, emergency diet at the bare subsistence level, if that. For the remaining 13 percent, it assures less than three fourths of nutritional adequacy. That is clearly not good enough.

Perhaps as disturbing as this country's failure to end hunger and malnutrition is the manner in which it has failed. The attempts of our institutions to overcome hunger have been at the expense of the very people they profess to help. The nonmonetary price we are paying to deliver more stamps, more commodities and more lunches than ever before is the cost of treating poor people like cattle, denying them their humanity in the name of efficient program administration, distributing a quotient of moral disapproval and shame with each package, each coupon book, each meal. That is a cost that cannot be justified. For what does it profit us to save our bodies, if we thereby forfeit our souls?

Two thousand years ago, the satirist Juvenal commented that poverty's greatest curse, much worse than the fact of it, is that it makes men objects of mirth, ridiculed, humbled, embarrassed. In 1972 in the United States, we do much worse than the Romans did. The poor we still have with us. Their humiliation is, if anything, more intense. Their efforts to secure welfare entitlements are labeled an outrage by the President. Scorn is heaped upon them periodically by some of the most powerful governors. Cabinet officials explain away high unemployment rates by referring to the excessive number of women in the job market and then devise mechanisms to compel more millions of poor mothers with school-age children to work. In county after county, officials act out their frustrations by outrightly denying the poor access to programs ostensibly funded to benefit them or else by imposing an obstacle course between them and those benefits.

Meanwhile, the federal government sits on its hands, content that its budget deficit may be reduced.

The results are predictable. The statistics appear to indicate that the plates of the hungry may now be close to half-full. But even that half-full status has been at the recipients' expense as they come to realize how pathetically dependent they have become upon the political self-interest of presidents, secretaries, and senators, upon the Alphonse-and-Gaston gavotte among local, state, and federal governments equally anxious to pass along the responsibility for delivery of food aid, upon the capricious ups and downs of budgetary considerations. The poor now know that their nutritional well-being has been treated as the means to other people's ends. The psychological impact easily offsets the physiological help the programs offer.

Dr. Bruno Bettelheim, an eminent child psychoanalyst, has demonstrated that food in our culture is closely identified with love and that there can be no adequate nurture where the person being fed feels that the supplier is dealing with him either on an impersonal, mechanical basis or else belittling him at the same time as he provides:

Eating and being fed are intimately connected with our deepest feelings. They are the most basic interactions between human beings, on which rest all later evaluations of ourself, of the world, and of our relationship to it. Therefore anything that rubs it in that we are not given food in the right way, with the right emotions, questions on the deepest level our views of ourselves and of those who give it to us. That is why food given by the school without due regard to the child's self-respect poisons his relation to school and learning . . .

When the infant is nursed by an unwilling mother, when he is fed without positive feelings, he becomes flooded with impotent rage, a helpless victim of inner tensions . . . that how one is being fed, and how one eats, has a larger impact on the personality than any other human experience. To convey this message to teachers . . . is neglected in favor of stressing physical hunger, as if our greatest hunger were not for being accepted, for feeling important, worthwhile. If teachers would understand this, the psychological meaning feeding children has, we would not encounter situations where teachers threatened little children with not giving them their meal ticket if they do not behave, or do not finish assigned work on time.

Let me repeat: Eating experiences condition our entire attitude to the world, and again not so much because of how nutritious is the food we are given, but with what feelings and attitudes it is given (1970:15–17).

Dr. Bettelheim is right. It is not only how much, but how. The "how" of the recent history of the administration of food aid for the poor is revealing, for the programs have reflected scant concern for the needs of the consumer and all too much emphasis on the requirements of the producer-provider.

Political bonuses

Federal food-assistance programs have always been viewed by their creators primarily as instruments for achieving political objectives and only secondarily as channels for compassionately feeding the poor. The saga of the programs from 1961 to 1972 is best summarized as "government by promise." Each succeeding President and Secretary of Agriculture has felt it incumbent upon himself to make rather sweeping promises to feed the poor in order either to curry political favor or to forestall political damage. Then, whenever the public remembered, he has been forced to explain away his inability to fulfill those promises.

This "edibility gap" was as true of John F. Kennedy as it is of Richard M. Nixon. President Kennedy's first executive order involved expansion of the number of surplus items included in the commodity distribution program. He justified this as helping to satisfy the need for additional food to supplement the diets of needy persons in areas of chronic unemployment. It was designed with his primary campaign in West Virginia in mind. To repay political obligations, he also established pilot food-stamp projects in heavily Democratic localities in such places as West Virginia, Pennsylvania, Eastern Kentucky, and Detroit. He vowed to strengthen the school lunch program "to make the best possible nutrition available to every school child, regardless of the economic condition of his family or local school district." Nothing happened.

That vow was to be repeated in varying forms over the course of the decade. In October 1966, Secretary Orville Freeman guaranteed to every school child the opportunity to be well-nourished within five years. President Johnson swore to accomplish this by June 1970 when, as one of his last official acts, he presented his 1970 fiscal year budget. President Nixon repeated the June 1970 assurance in opening his White House Conference on December 2, 1969, but then, on Christmas Eve 1969, he postponed the target date to Thanksgiving 1970. Not one of these pledges has ever been redeemed. And the presidents have not taken kindly to those who sought to remind them of those pledges.

The programs aimed at families have been especially good political footballs for the executive branch to play with. President Kennedy used food-stamp projects as a reward for good voting behavior. President Johnson informed a news conference in 1964 that it was very important to pass his food-stamp bill, not only for the consumers of the country, but also for its producers and business people. He appealed as much to self-interest as altruism when he signed the Food Stamp Act in August 1964, commenting that it "weds the best of the humanitarian instincts of the American people with the best of the free-enterprise system." A salient fact was that grocers in food-stamp areas experienced an average rise of 8 percent in their profits.

But when it came time in June of 1968 for President Johnson to support Secretary Freeman's testimony in favor of unlimited authorizations for the food-stamp program, he was furiously opposed, because such a move might endanger his tax-cut bill. Several days later, the President exploded when presented with a memorandum outlining a two-billion-dollar commitment to end serious malnutrition and refused to consider other than a minimal increase, despite his public commitments. To satisfy other political objectives, major food program changes had to be sacrificed.

Hunger and food programs were more of a hot potato than a football for President Nixon, when he came into office. The public interest in hunger had led to the creation, in the Senate, of a Select Committee on Nutrition and Human Needs, of which Senator George McGovern, Democrat of South Dakota, was chairman. By adroit use of the hearing process, Senator McGovern was able to keep hunger in the news and bring it constantly to the President's attention. In a well-publicized meeting of the Urban Affairs Council on March 17, 1969, at which approval of a Council subcommittee proposal for one-billion-dollar reform of the food-stamp program was indefinitely postponed, the President told Agriculture Secretary Clifford Hardin that, in his speeches on the Administration's hunger policy, Hardin "can say that this Administration will have the first complete, far-reaching attack on the problem of hunger in history. Use all the rhetoric, so long as it doesn't cost any money" (Kotz, 1971:200).

The historic message of May 6, 1969, constituted a political reversal of the hardened attitude against major expensive changes flowing from that March meeting. It was not that the President suddenly discovered that a program to end hunger was a moral must. It was simply that Senator McGovern had uncovered the plan that the President had rejected and was prepared to grill various officials about their refusal to implement what a governmental consensus supported. To stave off considerable embarrassment, the President accepted the very proposals he had rejected seven weeks before.

The politics of the hunger issue have been and are as important to the Congress as to the President. The original Food Stamp Act was successfully enacted in 1964 only because Congresswoman Leonor Sullivan, Democrat of Missouri, was astute enough to sense that it could be used as a trade by the urban House members in exchange for farm legislation desired by the farm bloc. She took skillful advantage of her bargaining position to exchange a wheat-cotton program for food stamps. In 1967 and 1968, she repeated her strategy of linking urban support for farm programs with agricultural support for food programs and was able to extend and expand the Act and its authorization level.

By 1970, the farm subsidy had become so suspect in the Congress that no alliance could be forged. Urban liberals, who had been willing in 1969 to log-roll the acceptance of unlimited subsidies for passage of a bill on coal-mine health and safety, were too opposed to continuing such subsidies to accept them in return for any increase in food stamps. Food stamps were thus no longer a political asset to the House Agriculture Committee. In fact, they quickly became a distinct liability, because the hunger lobby and the press mercilessly pilloried Committee Chairman R. W. Poage and ranking Republican Page Belcher of Oklahoma for their lack of sympathy for the poor. The Committee was in danger of becoming a national joke. Food stamps were damaging the Committee's image and undermining its standing in the House.

Accordingly, in an unusual about-face, on February 20, 1971, Poage and Belcher wrote to Chairman of the House Ways and Means Committee, Wilbur Mills, Democrat of Arkansas, and told him that they were willing that the Ways and Means Committee, which was considering the Family Assistance Program which included the payment of cash to needy families, should also take over the shaping of the Food Stamp Program, so that there would be a minimum of conflict or overlapping. Poage and Belcher said that they were not normally eager to reduce the jurisdiction of their committee but they indicated their willingness to sacrifice their turf interests for the sake of program efficiency. Translation: they were tired of being harassed by the hunger lobby and of watching food stamps being converted against their will into general assistance providing little or no aid to farm interests.

This recital of consistent political use and abuse of programs for the needy is by no means overstated. Every advance in the reach and quality of these programs has profited the sponsors as much as the hungry. Against this background, it becomes understandable that many disadvantaged persons, even those who receive food stamps or whose children are fed at school, question our system of providing social justice. They know all too well that the main goal for promoting better nutrition is not their well-being, but the personal welfare of the official-promoters, be they executive or legislative. The realization that they are being manipulated is not assuaged by eating decently. Proper nurture demands that the needs of the person being fed be the chief, although not necessarily sole, concern of the provider. The child who is propped up in a feeding chair with a mechanical arm tilting a bottle toward his mouth, while his mother freely moves about doing what she pleases to satisfy her own desires, can never be well fed.

The closed-circle defensiveness of the bureaucracy

When fulfilling the wants of the poor is treated as a means rather than an end in itself, both the government and the governed invariably suffer. But the government is limited by its bureaucratic perspective. It will not strive to determine what sort of treatment the consumer would like. Instead, it turns a deaf ear to every attempt by the consumer to explain his viewpoint. It does not eagerly search for constructive advice enabling it to perform better. Rather, it becomes angry and defensive when criticized and seeks to suppress the critic and uproot his source of information.

This combination of exclusion of the poor from even the most modest advisory role, coupled with invariable negative reaction to adverse commentary, has had a severely deleterious impact on the attitude of the poor and of officialdom alike. The poor become increasingly alienated; official insensitivity becomes more firmly entrenched.

The unwillingness to invite outsiders to share their powers or, at a minimum, to advise them of the preferred manner of exercising those powers has characterized the administration of food programs from the outset. There was no participation of any sort by any outsider in program direction until, in late 1968, the Department of Agriculture for the first time convened a Food and Nutrition Programs Advisory Group of the Consumer and Marketing Service. Its function ostensibly was to review in advance major policy decisions affecting the direction of food assistance programs. At that time, Rodney Leonard, the chief administrator of the service, explored with the group an expansion of food-stamp programs through increased appropriations by lowering purchase prices as opposed to raising total allotments or extending the distribution of stamps to more counties. This was in advance of any action on the issue by the Department. Unfortunately, that group held its last meeting in May of 1969 (to listen to staff statistical reports) and has been defunct ever since, despite countless public promises to resurrect it.

In 1969, the White House Conference on Food, Nutrition, and Health, in the Task Force Action Statement approved by the entire Conference, called upon the President to permit the poor to run their own programs, because "the provision of food services has too often been thwarted by lack of responsiveness at the State and local government levels." The Conference stated its belief that "maximum dignified participation by recipients is insured by transferring organizations and operational responsibilities to duly constituted, broad-based, local community organizations of the recipients themselves" (1970:305).

The Department responded by rejecting the recommendation because "food programs are best operated through a Federal/State/local government structure that is responsive to the needs of the recipients" (1970:305). Father thinks he knows best.

The Administration purposefully scheduled the follow-up conference at isolated, expensive Williamsburg, Virginia, in order to prevent a recurrence of the unexpected take-over of the 1969 Conference by poor people who made impassioned presentations of their interests and demands. It went so far as to exclude from participation any representatives of the poor and invited only government officials, business leaders, doctors, nutritionists, and a handful of church people. This had been the President's original announced plan in May 1969, for the first conference.

When a nutritionist attempted to organize a rump meeting to express dissatisfaction with the process, the organizer of the Conference ordered erased a notice of that meeting that had been chalked on a blackboard. Everything was done to assure that officials would not be questioned and to suppress any semblance of an impartial inquiry into the status of feeding the poor.

The Agriculture Department has consistently rejected offers to permit representatives of the poor to participate in drafting sessions on proposed school lunch or food-stamp regulations. Public outcry forced it to print its school lunch regulations in proposed form with comments invited rather than issuing them in final form by traditional fiat. The Department cancelled a program on food aid scheduled for its February 1971 Outlook Conference for its extension personnel from all over the country because several poverty groups demanded to be heard. In the spring of 1971, it limited to thirty days the period for poor persons to comment on its proposals drastically to revise the food-stamp program despite Senatorial protests, and then promptly proceeded to give the poultry industry sixty days to analyze regulations on chicken inspection.

This negative attitude, resistant to inviting the poor to have any voice in formulating program content, infects all levels of program operations. Food-stamp and commodity recipients have no formal outlet for making demands for nonstatutory program changes to federal, state, or local officials. Their so-called fair-hearing rights extend only to individual protests about their termination from the programs or reduction in their benefits. The parents of school children have no right to participate in state and local decisions about income eligibility for free lunches or any other issue substantially affecting their sons and daughters.

In light of this foreclosure of the administrative decision-making process to the poor, it is not surprising that they have increasingly turned to the courts for redress of their complaints. Since 1968, more than 100 major lawsuits have been filed by legal services lawyers attacking the programs. It is no wonder that the Department's Office of General Counsel constantly requests increases in its budget for additional attorneys to defend program challenges (16 man-years in 1972), while the attorneys' fees of school boards and county welfare offices are also on the rise. The burden this has placed on the courts could be readily relieved were the Department and its state and local counterparts willing to admit the poor into some form of program partnership and enforce program guidelines effectively. Unless this superinsularity, this bureaucratic self-righteousness, is changed, it is doubtful that dignity and justice will ever accompany the provision of adequate nutrition.

Official unwillingness to listen to the poor and to permit them to advise and consent on the programs to which they are subjected is accompanied as well by fear and rejection of even the most constructive criticism. When Assistant Secretary Richard Lyng appeared before the McGovern Committee on March 2, 1970, to review the accomplishments of the Food and Nutrition Service, he quickly skipped over facts and figures to dwell at length upon his feelings about the hearings held by this Board, the dissenters at the follow-up conference, and prior witnesses before Senator McGovern. Mr. Lyng said that much of the criticism of governmental activity was unfair or inaccurate, and he hoped that the critics would not demoralize government officials. In short, Mr. Lyng's hyperdefensive stance, concerned with the welfare of the bureaucrats running the programs instead of the persons to be served by them, is characteristic of the

providers when the quality of their efforts is in the least bit chal-
lenged.

When *Hunger USA* appeared, House Agriculture Committee Chairman Poage hurriedly sent a letter to the county health officers in each
of the 256 counties designated as places in which the incidence of
hunger and malnutrition was likely to be extremely high, inquiring
if the officers knew of any starvation or serious hunger in their areas
occasioned by the inability of individuals either to buy food or receive
it from public or private aid agencies. Predictably, no instances of
either were reported (that is, the officials contacted reported that
they were doing their job well or else, which was more likely, had no
medical understanding of the issue), but there was evidence of much
malnutrition caused by ignorance as to what constitutes a balanced
diet plus indifference by many who should and do know. The officials routed the blame onto the shoulders of the ignorant or deliberately negligent poor.

Beginning in May 1968, Chairman Jamie Whitten of the House
Agriculture Appropriations Subcommittee employed numerous FBI
agents, in addition to regular committee investigators, to interview
those persons anywhere in the country who talked to the authors of
Hunger USA. The agents grilled and intimidated the poor thoroughly.
They gave the Congress a 108-page report, allegedly on the operation
of federal food programs, but basically seeking to discredit our evidence and our witnesses as well as those who had appeared on the
CBS-TV documentary "Hunger in America."

The President, no matter who he is, has reacted in exactly the same
self-protective fashion, exhibiting his basic lack of concern about what
is or is not being done to the poor. President Johnson shunted aside
every suggestion by his staff and the Department of Agriculture that
he reform food-aid programs. Twelve times he said "no" in order not
to rock the boat in Congress and upset his commitments to Senator
Allen Ellender, Democrat of Louisiana, and Congressmen Poage and
Whitten. Only in his final press conference did he dare admit that
"We are going to be held accountable and we ought to face up to
that problem [i.e., hunger]. It is one of the big problems for this
administration. It is a problem I did not solve. I think we have made
some progress, some headway, but we have not found the answers"
(Weekly Compilation of Presidential Documents, Monday, January
20, 1969:127).

President Nixon moved hastily to present his hunger message to
Congress when word of his Urban Affairs Council report leaked to
the press. When the closing session of the White House Conference in
December 1969 made five strong demands for substantial action, the

President's Special Assistant Daniel Moynihan made certain that the demands would not be formally presented to the President by the delegation of hand-picked community leaders the President had agreed to meet with. Then the President was confronted with these demands at a press conference three days later, he went out of his way to reject, publicly and almost out of hand, the two principal recommendations of the conference. The Task Force Action Statement, which had created this problem, was buried in the back of the Conference's final report and labeled "symbolic significance only, representing essentially an endorsement of principles" (White House, Conference on Food, Nutrition, and Health, 1970:16), not specific approval of any of the particular programs espoused. The overwhelming vote of the conferees was diluted to a "general expression of the groups on order of priorities" (White House, Conference on Food, Nutrition, and Health, 1970:15).

In 1971, Vice-President Agnew went out of his way to resurrect the buried matter of the TV show "Hunger in America" by blasting it as inaccurate on the basis of contentions previously rejected by the Federal Communications Commission. OEO, ostrich-like, immediately withdrew the film from its library and refused to show it to outside groups. Film-burning is in vogue only in connection with hunger.

President Truman's classic comment on politics, "If you can't stand the heat, stay out of the kitchen," has been stood on its head by officials reacting to heat on the hunger issues. They simply try to destroy the stove or oven responsible for the heat. When the findings of a report by the Bureau of the Budget on the social cost of malnutrition in the United States and the need for an incremental investment of approximately three billion dollars to eliminate it were accidentally made public in May 1969, the bureaucracy leaped to prevent the report itself from ever becoming available and sought to stem the leak from whence it flowed. Similar counterespionage activities were undertaken when it was disclosed that the Emergency Food Program was going to be illegally spending $300,000 of its funds restricted to the poor to pay for the hotel and food costs of the entire White House Conference (poor and well-off alike) through a dummy corporation controlled by Republican lawyers.

In the fall of 1971, when Senator Charles Percy, Republican of Illinois, held two days of hearings on the adequacy of the commodity distribution program, Secretary Hardin and Assistant Secretary Lyng privately urged him to fire the staff members who had helped set up the critical hearings, on the grounds that they were embarrassing to Senator Percy's party and the President.

The classic instance of this relentless effort to silence any person

whose work casts an unfavorable light on the activities of other officials is the two-year campaign by persons in the Department of
Health, Education, and Welfare (HEW) to suppress and destroy Dr.
Arnold Schaefer. In December 1967, Dr. Schaefer was appointed to
direct the National Nutrition Survey of the nutritional status of low-
income persons in ten states (Texas, Louisiana, New York, Kentucky,
Michigan, California, Washington, South Carolina, West Virginia
and Massachusetts). *Hunger USA* referred to that study and pointed
out that it could not realistically be expected to be completed before
the close of 1968, at the earliest, although the health legislation that
authorized it had called for its completion within six months of enactment in December 1967. Little did we realize, in April 1968, that in the
Spring of 1972 the survey would still be incomplete and not fully released to the public.

What happened in the intervening three years was that HEW
realized the politically explosive nature of some of the material developed in that survey. When Dr. Schaefer testified in January 1969
about his preliminary findings in Texas and Louisiana, which underscored the widespread existence of malnutrition among the poor, he
was front-page news across the country, and the pressure of the
hunger lobby for bigger food assistance programs received the scientific seal of approval it had previously been lacking. Dr. Schaefer
kept the momentum of his material alive by speaking to numerous
audiences. He paid a high price. He was professionally executed.

In July 1969, Dr. Joseph English, a Democrat who was precariously
head of the Health Services and Mental Health Administration in
HEW, determined to remove the survey from Dr. Schaefer's super-
vision in Washington and relocate it in the Communicable Disease
Center in Atlanta, Georgia, under the direction of a bureaucrat appropriately named Dr. Sencer. Dr. English was well aware that the
move would delay the final report's appearance and muffle its impact
upon the food budget. He made certain that this would be the case
by halting the flow of funds for the survey.

In April 1970, when Dr. Schaefer testified once more in front of the
McGovern Committee, he was under strict orders to state facts without
any interpretation whatsoever. He revealed his unhappiness to news-
men but was constrained by his position. Funds for the survey were
routed to various other purposes; the data on the 70,000 persons
tested came in slowly; the use of computers was confused and restricted. Finally, all of his staff left with the final results untabulated.
Dr. Schaefer sought an outlet for his troubles in Senator Hollings
but was immediately warned that he would be fired before his pension

became effective, should he speak out. Dr. Schaefer is now safely packed off to the Pan-American Health Organization, surveying the state of nutrition in Guyana. Only the dogged persistence of Senators Hollings and McGovern has enabled some scattered results of his survey to see daylight. The final report is likely to become available only when the Administration stops being mesmerized by the fact that it is cheaper in budgetary terms to fight hunger when the public has no firm idea of how extensive hunger really is.

The closed-circuit of the bureaucracy expels an offending part and the circle closes once more, impervious to the advice or complaints proffered by the outsiders it was established to serve. Once again, the bureaucracy functions to further its own interests first.

Budgetary constraint

One of the overriding objectives, if not the dominant one, of any governmental structure is the preservation, not the effective expenditure, of the funds entrusted to it. Whatever sum of money it receives for use to help people is viewed as money belonging to it alone and doled out grudgingly to those for whom the money was intended. Any disbursement is carefully monitored and questioned, any saving readily approved. This is the syndrome of the budgetary constraint of officials who consider public funds to be their private treasury.

This fiscal constipation amounts to a new, unprosecuted but heinous form of embezzlement or diversion of funds to personal nonuse in violation of official duty. It distorts program activities, prevents implementation of otherwise approved projects, and invariably operates to the serious detriment of the poor.

The poor are led to believe that certain benefits will soon be theirs and then are disappointed, time after time, as officials squeeze both the budget requested and the appropriation expended. It is this promise of liberality constantly undermined by the reality of parsimony that has bred the cynicism and distrust of the lower tenth of the society for the rest.

This pattern of behavior is indelibly imprinted in the history of food programs during the previous decade. Nothing could more distinctly illustrate the subservience of the goal of feeding the hungry to the concern with spending as little as possible than the President's own remarks to Secretary Hardin in March of 1969. His predecessors were no different. President Kennedy inveighed against those who cut school lunch funds and had his Secretary of Agriculture declare to the Congress that we had the means to abolish hunger, leaving unanswered the question of whether we possess the humanity to do so. Then, succumbing to the siren song of budget manipulations, he proceeded to return unspent to the United States Treasury, over three years, a total of 260.7 million dollars in customs receipts specifically set aside for feeding needy children and other needy persons. He had not the humanity to do other than waste the means. President Johnson declared war on poverty and then withheld 619 million dollars in such funds for food programs in order to meet budgetary restrictions.

The history of food program revisions in 1971 is even more stark in its insistent repetition of White House and budget gnawing away at each individual program in turn, only to have Congress and the public try to intervene to keep the budgetary wolf away from the door. The calendar tells the tale.

April 1971: The Department, upon White House orders, issued proposed regulations for implementing the 1970 Food Stamp Act that set uniform nationwide income standards for receipt of food stamps either at or slightly above the poverty level, but without regard for the welfare payment levels in any given state. As a result, in states with high assistance standards for aged, blind, or disabled individuals and couples (over $160 per month for one person and $210 for two), elderly persons on welfare who were previously automatically eligible to receive food stamps were to be denied such benefits. The thrust of this change, coupled with resource/asset tests that were more stringent than under some welfare systems, was to eliminate as many as 350,000 participants from food-stamp rolls.

There was much comment from Congress and the public. The final regulations, issued in July, automatically included every welfare recipient as a food-stamp eligible. The annual cost of reincluding the one third of a million persons who receive the smallest possible monthly bonus ($10) was not in excess of $42 million. A cheap bone for the poor.

May 1971: The White House reinforced its year-old determination to phase out supplemental food packages for pregnant and nursing mothers and infants (up to six years of age). The program had been initiated in late 1968 and endorsed by President Nixon in May 1969 as part of his alleged special commitment to the health and welfare of those in the first five years of life. No sooner had the Department begun to arouse interest in county health departments in acting as distributing and certifying agencies for the food than the budget axe fell.

The Department was forced to announce in April 1970 that the program could no longer be extended to any food-stamp areas, that, in commodity areas where the program had begun, children ages one through five would not be allowed to participate, and that, for those women and infants still entitled to receive the packages, the food allotment would be slimmed down by reducing vital sources of vitamins A and C, calcium, protein, and riboflavin (no more instant nonfat dry milk or scrambled-egg mix).

The reasons for the Department's efforts to stifle supplementary food distribution were simple. The program was worthless and expensive on both the federal and local levels. It delivered little of real value. The "target group" understandably did not respond. In the District of Columbia, for example, in December 1969, with 37,000 persons eligible and on the rolls, only 13,000 came to collect their packages. Corn syrup and cereal were not uppermost in their minds. Those who might really have made use of foods—the elderly—were excluded, unless, as the Department finally recognized was the case, after the women toted the 40-pound parcels home, they shared their contents with other members of their families. The cost to local administrators was often as high as 40 percent of the benefit (Washington, D.C. paid $450,000 to pass out 1.2 million dollars worth of commodities).

In December 1971, the supplemental food program made a substantial comeback, not because of any objective reassessment by the Department of the nutritional needs of poor pregnant and nursing women and infants, but because of the political debt Secretary Butz had to pay Senator Robert Griffin, Republican of Michigan. Throughout 1971, and especially during the summer, Detroit's repeated requests for an expanded supplemental feeding program to fill the gaps left by inadequate food-stamp distribution in the inner city (not enough grocery stores or stamp-distribution outlets) had been turned down. There were insufficient funds, and that was that. Thirty-four hundred participants was the limit. On November 29, 1971, Senator Griffin met with Department lobbyists to discuss his position on the Butz nomination. On November 30, a deputy assistant flew to Detroit to inspect the ongoing program. On December 2, Butz was confirmed by seven votes, including Griffin's. On December 3, the Department discovered that money was available and authorized feeding an additional 12,000 mothers and children.

On December 12, a Department team, responding to a new demand from Detroit that the high-nutrition items removed from the package nearly 21 months before be restored, made another trip to Detroit. Nine days later, peanut butter and scrambled-egg mix went back on the list for the entire nation and the fruit-juice distribution rate was boosted. One vote at a crucial time, and "open, sesame." Bureaucratic miserliness yields swiftly to political expedience.

June 1971: The White House refused to release funds to permit 1,000,000 inner-city children to have food at summer recreation projects. This was the latest ironic twist in the budgetary lemon squeezer as applied to the special food service or Vanik program.

In light of the significant underspending that had taken place in the summer of 1970, leaving a surplus appropriation, and the realization that the program's outreach had been minimal in the past, Department regional officials went all-out to sell special food service to major cities. In Chicago, one federal official notified potential sponsors that "we want to reach more children" and asked whether they knew of "any nonprofit summer programs or day-care centers which will be in need of financial assistance with food costs? . . . If you know of any, please contact the USDA" (U.S. Congress, Senate. Part 6:1528). Detroit was urged to triple its capacity. Los Angeles was told that, if they got the children, USDA would get the money. San Antonio was promised $200,000 a month in food.

But the Washington bureaucrats were not as enthusiastic about promoting their product. First, the Department, reacting to a report of its Inspector General that some cities had claimed they were using volunteer services as their required local contribution (20 percent of program cost) when, in fact, no such services had been forthcoming, sought to ban the use of volunteer labor as part of the match. The cities won that round. Second, the Office of Management and Budget decided to hold the 1971 spending level to the 1970 figures to conserve funds.

The impact was dramatic. By the middle of June, eleven cities that had been stimulated by some USDA officials to get ready to feed half a million children were told by the program heads that the money was not available and that they would have to stick to the 1970 service figures. Deputy Assistant Secretary Olsson claimed that the budget was adequate because every state could operate without cutbacks and that "programs expanded beyond this level would only be counterproductive because of administrative problems" (New York *Times,* July 8, 1971).

Congress moved fast. It passed two bills extending the program's life and furnishing more funds. The Department held firm. Forty Senators, led by Republicans, wrote the President to complain; the mayors were furious. Finally, after a week of uncertainty, the OMB reversed itself and released an additional 15 million dollars. The states even managed to double this sum by wringing dry the rest of their child nutrition funds. But the summer of 1972 promises to be another hold-the-line, feed-no-more proposition, since the special food service budget is no larger than in 1971 (the Department sought 90 million dollars; OMB gave 49 million dollars).

July 1971: The White House substantially reduced food-stamp benefits for and, in some instances, denied eligibility to the upper-income poor. Although all welfare recipients were permitted to continue to receive stamps even if their income or assets exceeded uniform standards, as the final regulations took hold, the nonwelfare poor were not given the same treatment. As a result, 75,000 elderly poor persons living in twelve states were about to be cut off the program. In addition, the Department had promulgated new food-stamp purchase schedules drastically raising the cost of stamps to "the richest of the poor" without equally increasing the value of their allotments. The Department estimated that 1,750,000 persons would have their benefits reduced, but proffered no projection of how many in that group would voluntarily drop off the program rather than expend considerable effort and funds for an insubstantial return.

For example, welfare recipients and other persons in New York and elsewhere whose monthly income for a family of four was in the vicinity of $360 would have to pay $99 for $108 in stamps instead of $82 for $106 as before. This precipitous 62.5 percent drop in bonus value from $24 to $9 was designed, according to Assistant Secretary Lyng (U.S. Congress, Senate, Part 13: 972) "to feather out the benefits as income approaches the eligibility standards" in order to lessen alleged disincentives to earn additional income. The justification was that a person with a job earning $4,300 would decline a $4,500 job if the latter job would cost him $288 in food stamps annually, but not if the loss were limited to $108. How much less well he would eat if he stayed at $4,300 because no other job was available (the most likely circumstance) was not considered significant.

The response to the approaching excision of nearly two million participants reached a crescendo on the eve of the implementation of the new purchase schedules. What had been a muffled protest in April and July became an angry roar in December. Elderly participants in the White House Conference on Aging lobbied their congressmen. Senator Hubert Humphrey, Democrat of Minnesota, introduced a resolution to preserve the previous eligibility standards and purchase schedules for those who would otherwise be hurt by the new ones. In a dull moment on the Senate floor, with only three or four senators present, the resolution was tacked on as an amendment to the Children's Dental Health Act of 1971 and sent to the House. Twenty-eight senators petitioned Secretary Butz to fulfill his confirmation promise to support the food-stamp program by making the necessary regulatory changes without waiting for Congress to force his hand. Fourteen northeastern state spokesmen, including many Republican governors, appealed for a moratorium on the cuts. Senator George Aiken, Republican of Vermont, ranking minority member of the Senate Agriculture Committee and a supporter of food stamps in the 1950s, tried to persuade the White House to undo the damage. Finally, it was revealed that the Office of Management and Budget had impounded 202 million dollars in food-stamp monies that represented the increase in appropriations over the Department's budget request.

The scenario was complete. Orchestrated pressure was used to force the Department merely to fulfill the will of Congress. Secretary Butz accordingly retreated and ordered modifications in the regulations to ensure that no previously eligible participants would lose any benefits when the new purchase schedules went into effect. This meant formally loosening all controls over the withheld 200 million dollars.

A victory? Not really. All the effort went not to expand the program but merely to hold the line against the forces of budgetary constraint.

August 1971:   The next act in the school lunch comedy of errors took place in August 1971, a few days before school opened. The Department, trying to correct the funding imbalance induced by their famine, then feast, administration of reimbursement rates in 1970–71 (itself a product of the ever-present desire to underspend), proposed a new set of regulations limiting reimbursement for free and reduced-price lunches to 35 cents over-all, or much less than half the states received in April, May, and June. The rationale? According to a statement on August 4, 1971, by Assistant Secretary Lyng, "Fiscal discipline is always difficult, but it is absolutely essential . . . if we're to live within our budget."

The state school lunch directors reacted as if to a declaration of war. Nearly every state had planned for the fall in reliance on the spring reimbursement structure. Now the Department was scrapping that structure and replacing it with a new one that entailed cutbacks in the majority of states. Although the exact impact of the Department's action was never certain, 37 states claimed that their programs could not be expanded to reach any more needy pupils and some insisted that they would have to shut down many of their lunch rooms. The problem, of course, was that many states that had reached only a few among their poverty enrollment in 1970–71 had had much more to spend than 35 cents per lunch because their money was spread over a small number of lunches. With the same or only a slightly larger amount of money available in 1971–72 to divide among many more lunches, an income-expense gap was inevitable unless (unlikely, if not impossible) state funds filled the breach. If not, the children would suffer.

The national funding status was familiar—Congress had made the money available. The Office of Management and Budget wanted no part of it. At the end of June, Congress had enacted a special appropriation of 100 million dollars in customs receipt funds to carry out the provisions of the National School Lunch Act relating to the service of free and reduced-price meals. While this money was specifically intended to support summer feeding in recreation programs, much of it was still available for the regular school lunch program. But, as Assistant Secretary Lying semicandidly admitted in a Senate hearing in September, the Office of Management and Budget controlled the amount expended and wanted no more going out than the Administration had sought in January 1971, regardless of how conditions had since changed.

With a majority of states adversely affected, the outcome in the Senate was hardly in doubt. On October 1, the Senate passed a resolution calling for an average reimbursement rate of 45 cents per free and reduced-price lunch.

September 1971: No cutbacks. Merely a Departmental refusal to spend any funds to revamp the food donation or commodity distribution program.

October 1971: No sooner had the free lunch reimbursement rate been saved than the White House countered by seeking to curtail the number of children entitled to receive such a lunch. The White House proposed a regulatory change to deny any state the right to stipulate a higher eligibility standard for free and reduced-price lunch than the federally promulgated poverty level. The probable consequence: a loss of lunch to approximately 1.5 million children in thirty-one states and the District of Columbia where a higher standard had already been in existence.

Again there was a round of senatorial protest (59 senators wrote a letter of complaint to the President seeking his intervention), private criticism (Dr. Jean Mayer, the President's former nutrition advisor,

called the proposed cuts "mean-spirited") and Congressional action
(the House Education and Labor Committee voted 31 to 0 to override the cut-off of children). The President swiftly ordered the regulations rescinded. This time, the Congress put an end to further scenes
and hauled the curtain down with a resolution raising reimbursement rates to a minimum (not average) 46 cents per meal, wiping
out the incentive to serve reduced rather than free meals, and grand-
fathering into the law all state eligibility standards in existence before
October 1, 1971.

November 1971: The White House trial balloons tightening up reimbursement rates for breakfast and day-care meals; changes were
finally put into regulations in February and March of 1972.

December 1971: The White House continued to refuse to permit
commodity distribution alongside food-stamp dispensation in Seattle
or anywhere.

It took political pressure from overseas to settle the last budget-
engendered food-program dispute of 1971. Although Congress had
specifically—and at the administration and Department's insistence—
authorized a county simultaneously to distribute commodities and food
stamps (but not both to the same family in any given month) when
the state indicated its willingness to pay for all of the delivery costs
entailed by commodities, or in the face of an emergency, the Department emphatically refused to permit this to occur in any county under
any circumstances. The law it had asked for in 1969 and 1970 it was
anxious to bury unused in 1971.

Seattle sought to test the Department's obstinacy. It had over
110,000 persons unemployed, many with assets like homes that were
unsaleable and too valuable for them to meet the food-stamp purchase
schedule demands after meeting house, auto, and insurance payments.
A lawsuit to force the Department to implement the law led to a
finding by a federal district court that the Secretary had been arbitrary and capricious in refusing to do so in the face of the severe
economic hardship in Seattle.

The Department, however, was not ready to accept the court ruling
and implement dual programs. The Office of Management and Budget
was concerned that the principle might be extended nationwide, resulting in costly double programming. An appeal to a higher court
was seriously contemplated. Then the city of Kobe intervened, bringing about a policy change that the intervention of Washington's Republican governor and Republican state officials had been unable to

achieve even when making the request to White House domestic affairs chief John Ehrlichman, a native of Seattle.

Kobe employed the powerful weapon of humiliation. Kobe, Seattle's "sister city," shipped one half-ton of rice noodles and canned food to a church-sponsored group to distribute to the poor. The Department saw the handwriting on the wall and caved in.

So the budget operates to divert the thrust of programs to feed the hungry and to force Congress and the concerned public to spend more time fighting retrenchment in existing food assistance activities than in devising new and better mechanisms for overcoming malnutrition.

A potential solution. The catalogue of failures to deliver is dreary. All levels of government, but especially the federal government, stand condemned for their inability to end hunger in America.

What is to be done? Is the answer to perform plastic surgery to improve existing food programs, especially food stamps? Is the solution to guarantee ready access to free food stamps to the needy everywhere in the nation and free school lunches for every pupil from daycare to twelfth grade (or else lunch stamps for the needy) with surplus commodities purchasable at a discount? Are more and better food programs the best means to end hunger?

Or, as the preceding roll call of inadequacies implies, might more of the same be equivalent to throwing good money after bad?

The major reason that the jigsaw puzzle pieces of food programs the federal government has constantly been carving out since 1935 will never mesh to cover all of the hungry poor is that the government began by asking the wrong question: "How can we feed the poor?" The answer, inevitably, was this plethora of programs of bureaucrats and by bureaucrats, supposedly for the ultimate benefit of the poor:

"We" want to make sure that "they" eat correctly. So we send out 50 million dollars' worth of nutrition aides to instruct "them" in how to invest their 24 cents a meal.

"We" want to be certain that "they" do not waste their food resources on bingo or alcohol or narcotics or anything else nonnutritious. So "we" restrict the convertibility of food stamps. So "we" try, if "we" are Senator Paul Douglas, Democrat of Illinois in 1964, to exclude carbonated beverages from the food-stamp eligible-item list after supporting the stamp program because participants could go into the grocery stores and be indistinguishable from other patrons of the stores. So "we" refuse to permit "them" to get cash as change in food-stamp transactions where less than 50 cents is at stake.

"We" want to guarantee that impoverished mothers of infants under one give their children more milk and formula. So "we" give "them" food certificates for milk and formula which "they" use to buy the milk and formula "they" previously were buying, and the rest of the family spends the extended income on other needs.

"We" don't want "them" to have to make any hard choices among food, rent, medical care, clothing, or other needs. So "we" propose to tie up 30 to 50 percent of "their" purchasing power in the form of food stamps rather than give "them" cash they might reallocate elsewhere.

"We," the benighted 85 percent of this country who live above the poverty level, know best what is good for "them," the needy 15 percent. At least, "we" think "we" do.

The time has come to reorient our thinking about the problems of hunger in America. We should admit, as we knew all along, that hunger is only a symptom of poverty and that we must treat the disease, not merely alleviate the symptom.

The question ought to have been—from the beginning—not how can we feed them, but how can they feed themselves. We should always have focused not on creating an administrative jungle of mechanisms for delivering food to the poor, but on developing the simplest, most dignified method of enabling them to determine when and how to meet their own food needs. We should always have acted as our brother's helper, not his feeder or keeper.

An adequate income provided in a just, nondegrading manner has always been the solution. Cash. Not stamps. Cash. Not coupons. Cash. Not vouchers. Cash. Not certificates. Cash. Not credit slips. Cash.

"Our" social blindness has hurt "us" as well as "them." Because of "our" desire to feed "them" rather than give "them" freedom of choice, "they" have gone hungry and "we" have become entangled in the undergrowth of our administrative jungle, wasting manpower and funds incessantly. Because "we" insisted upon stamps, coupons, vouchers, certificates, and credit slips rather than cash, "we" have had to hire thousands of middle-class bureaucrats to perform services for "them," "we" have had to waste more millions upon the delivery mechanisms than "they" ever could have on bingo or booze. Since "we" wanted to make sure that "they" got stamps that could be applied to food needs, "we" made sure that 14 million-plus of the poor got no stamps at all, many because the stamps were too expensive or too difficult to use, some because their local governments refused to cooperate and the federal government acquiesced.

The costs of our institutionalized distrust of "them" have been great, primarily in terms of the loss of human potential, undermined by and forever lost of malnutrition, secondarily in terms of operating expenses wasted in support of the battalion of caretakers. It is not difficult to document these costs.

Cost barriers to participation. The stark facts of nonparticipation are self-evident. Under current income eligibility guidelines, approximately 29 million Americans qualify for food stamps (25.5 million poor and nearly 4 million just above the poverty line of $3,940, but under $4,320 in annual income for a family of four). Perhaps 23 million of these people live in areas that furnish food stamps. Only 11.1 million receive the stamps. What happens to the other 11.9 million? They are either program push-outs or program dropouts.

The former predominate. They are the ones who choose not to participate in a program that inexorably demands that they invest a specific chunk of their monthly income in food one or two times a month. For instance, a family of four earning $200 a month has to come up with $26.50 every two weeks or $53 on or about the first of each month. A family of six with $350 from work or welfare has to pay out $48.50 semimonthly, or $97 monthly.

The poor are unable effectively to control their meager cash flow to meet the program's inflexible demands. They may get paid on the first but be out of sufficient money to pay for the second installment of stamps on the fifteenth because of intervening needs. The family of four may not have $26.50 in hand by the fifteenth, the only day when stamps are issued. They may have the full sum available by the twentieth, but that is too late. The food-stamp program was not and cannot be tailored to match the to and fro of their income and expenditures. If they have no money or less than the tables call for at the set date, that is that. Stamps may be allegedly available, but they are practically foreclosed from using them. IOU's are not accepted in exchange for stamps.

The new regulations try to ease the iron rigidity of the purchase requirement by permitting any household to elect to purchase as little as one quarter of its allotment at issuance time. But the household cannot recoup that portion of its stamp allotment it is unable to pay for, which means that it will be only a one-fourth or one-half-program participant. Nor are there any indications yet of widespread reliance upon partial purchase as a means of escape from the harsh cost bind.

On the other hand, if the poor were to be given cash, they could buy food when they wanted to, so long as the cash held out. If they chose to allocate some of their limited funds to finance medical care instead of food in any given month, they would not be denied the rest of their food-related cash grant. That is not the case with stamps. For example, if a family of four earning $200 a month could only afford one fourth of its food-stamp allotment one month in cash ($13.25 for $27 worth of stamps instead of $53 for $108), the boost in its food purchasing power for that month would amount to only $13.75 ($27 minus $13.25). Were food stamps, as we recommend, to be eliminated and the monthly bonus translated into an extra cash grant of $55, the family could deploy that $55 as it chose. Indeed, it might apply $30 of this $55 to doctors' bills and still have $25 left over for food purchases, more than the $13.75 subsidy that would obtain under the food-stamp program under the facts described.

The mathematics underline the reality: cash is invariably preferable to stamps in terms of the way all of us, except perhaps the very rich, manage our funds. In Mississippi, the grocery stores that do the best food-stamp businesses are the ones that illegally lend the shoppers money to afford the stamps on the understanding that the stamps will be returned in trade. Private ordering readily evades program controls.

Nonparticipation is primarily, but not exclusively, attributable to the absolute dollar payments the purchase of stamps compels. Other factors work to deter the poor from buying in, among them the relationship between the percentage of income mandatorily invested in food and the percentage of income thereafter available for nonfood purposes, and the physical and psychological agonies and obstacles associated with the distinct processes of stamp certification, issuance, and use.

The Administration revised its welfare reform program in the spring of 1971 to meet sugggestions by the House Ways and Means Committee, especially from Representative Sam Gibbons, Democrat of Florida, that food stamps he converted to cash, thereby raising the cash floor of families of four without outside income from $1,600 to $2,400 in states like Mississippi, Arkansas, Alabama, Louisiana, and South Carolina. Prior to that, the welfare proposal of $1600 coupled with the food-stamp allotment attendant upon such income ($34 cash for $108 in stamps) would have forced stamp users into the following pattern:

		Month	Year
(1)	(a) Cash (welfare)	$133.33	$1600
	(b) Less cash spent for food stamps	−34.00	−408
	(c) Total cash available	99.33	1192
(2)	Value of Food Stamps	108	1296
(3)	Total Purchasing Power (1c + 2)	207.33	2488
(4)	% Total Purchasing Power Tied Up in Food	52%	

It was only the cashing-in of stamps that saved the $1,600 poor from having to devote 52 percent of their purchasing power to food or be penalized by receiving no food aid whatsoever. For families at the $3,000 income level, the percentage of purchasing power in food stamps would be 38 percent, absent any merger of stamps and welfare. As Representative Gibbons argued:

What family in America, poor or otherwise, wants to be compelled to receive over half its total purchasing power in the form of scrip which can only be used for one of its needs—food—and this on penalty of receiving no family food assistance at all unless it submits to this compulsory budgeting?

What family wants even more than one third of its purchasing power tied up in food, untouchable in emergency? The average American family spends only 16.5 percent of its disposable income on food. Granted, the average family's income is higher than that of the typical poor family, but must the poor be locked into a forcible formula which makes them spend three times the average for food alone? (U.S. Congress, House, 1970:80)

Recently, Senator McGovern and Dr. Mayer have combined forces to attack the Administration's welfare reform proposal because of its elimination of food stamps. To the extent that this is a condemnation of the possibility that, under the complex pattern for determining welfare grant levels, households in nineteen states and the District might not get the full value of the food stamp bonuses they now receive translated into cash, such an attack makes sense. To the extent that this is an attempt to obtain $2,400 as a cash base with food stamps on top, such an attack seems to be good strategy. To the extent that this is a determination that $3,000 in cash and the equivalent of $444 in food-stamp subsidy is better than $3,444 in cash, such an attack ignores the needs of the poor in favor of nutrition dictation.

Noncost obstacles to participation

The certification process is a barrier to participation for those not on public assistance. Welfare recipients are supposed to be automatically cleared for stamps at the same time they are determined eligible for welfare, but eligibility is only one step en route to full utilization of stamps. Issuance is another. The authority to purchase stamps has to be alchemized into the stamps themselves through the exchange of the buyer's cash for the government's cash. Although originally most of these transactions took place in county welfare offices, the trend has been to involve commercial banks as the dominant stamp-sellers (more than 7,000 now issue stamps). While the banks may be more conveniently located and more accessible to the poor than welfare offices, particularly in rural areas, this is not invariably the case. Urban ghetto areas may not contain any banks that deal in stamps and, if the welfare authorities have, as is often the case, entirely abdicated the issuing to the banks, long distances may have to be covered to secure the stamps.

The problem is that, even though the banks demand and receive an average of one dollar from the state or county welfare departments for performing the service, the banks are increasingly reluctant to issue stamps. They make no or very little profit by virtue of their involvement and are often afraid of losing some of their regular clientele, who do not want to rub shoulders with food-stamp purchasers. Thus, banks either forsake the food-stamp trade entirely, forcing the sales back onto ill-equipped welfare agencies, or else treat the food-stamp customers as second-class citizens, confined to special facilities (drive-in windows) or special days and hours. The consequence? Stamps become harder and harder to purchase. None but the most persistent stay the course. It is not startling that one of the most consistently expressed user demands, especially among the elderly, is that the federal government undertake to mail people their full coupon quota by direct certified mail. Issuance is one stage in the flow that most stamp users would like to skip.

Before the stamp purchase is consummated, the user has to obtain an authorization-to-purchase card specifically setting forth his purchase price and allotment value. When the program was small, the cards were distributed at the time of certification or kept on file at the welfare office that sold the stamps. Today, the cards are generally sent out through the mails, timed to arrive on the first of the month. Given the difficulties of depending on prompt mail service, it is not surprising that some families receive the card after the first, either too late to purchase the first installment for the month or one day after the head of the household spent part of the funds reserved for stamps.

The mailing system was commenced in the District of Columbia in February 1971 in order to give the administrators a few days' breathing space to check on duplicate applications against a master file. To get at a handful of cheaters, the entire program serving 110,000 people monthly was brought to a two-to-three day standstill at the start of every month, while the delayed authorization cards came through the mails. In response to a wide variety of interim emergencies produced by this new procedure, the District welfare department began to make emergency grants of an estimated $33,000 a month to families who couldn't survive the two-day lag without cash for food. In other words, a substantial cash input was needed to prime the pump of the stamp economy. Cash was substituted for stamps, but only on an interim basis.

The difficulties of getting certified and obtaining an authorization-to-purchase card and gathering the right amount of cash to exchange at the bank (or office) for stamps are compounded by the problems associated with using them in grocery stores. To begin with, some stores simply refuse to accept food stamps, no matter how instantly redeemable at the applicable bank and Federal Reserve they may be. Not only do recipients have to bypass nearby or preferred stores and travel to find an accepting store (nearly 150,000 retail grocers do accept stamps), but also they are singled out for inevitably discriminatory treatment in the stamp stores' check-out lines.

They are just like regular patrons except that regular patrons do not have to separate their purchases into two separate piles—one containing most foodstuffs, the other composed of sanitation supplies, like napkins or soap, and clearly labeled imported food items, including lean Argentinian hamburger. The former may be paid for with stamps; the latter may not. Indeed, there may even be a third pile for returnable bottles whose contents are stamp eligible but whose form is not, so long as a bottle deposit must be paid. Stamps were declared out-of-bounds for container deposits following a December 1971 Department of Agriculture ruling effective this March.

And what if stamp purchasers want to eat some fried chicken from Colonel Sanders's Kentucky Fried Chicken carry-out counters, or ice cream at Mr. Softee's mobile vending wagons? The Solomonlike Department has ruled in favor of the ice cream, but not the chicken, although a federal court has permitted the latter.

Suppose the food-stamp customer has to offer $2.50 worth of stamps in payment for $2.45 worth of approvable groceries. Does the clerk accept the stamps and give the user a nickel in return? Not if the store wants to keep its certified status. The store must, as of March 1, 1972, as was the case before 1971, give the customer a token or credit slip redeemable only in eligible food and only at that store (or its chain counterparts). The House Agricultural Appropriations Subcommittee apparently got upset in the summer of 1971 when it discovered that stamps were being exchanged for cash in change transactions and persuaded the Senate to join in urging that the "threatening" practice be stopped. The Department proposed a change in regulations in fear of abuses of the cash change "privilege" and of careless use of the change for nonfood needs. "They" shall be fed. "They" cannot be trusted.

The degradation of the poor

With distrust in the ability of the poor to take care of themselves as its hallmark, the stamp program carefully and prominently labels each and every recipient a potential wastrel. Shame and stigma automatically accompany every stamp-bought bag of groceries. There is no way to avoid being advertised to the store-going public as a "poor," no way to hide the fact that a stamp-user's freedom of choice differs from the same freedom exercised by the two hundred million other Americans who buy their food with cash.

The food-stamp poor do not suffer their indignities gladly. But, at times, they exhibit a peculiar inability to realize the precise remedy their complaints point to—the substitution of cash for stamps. At a nationwide meeting of seventeen local and national organizations committed to improving the food-stamp program in February 1972, the groups agreed first that food stamps be retained until every family of four was guaranteed $6,500 a year and then proceeded to criticize the program as intolerably degrading, to demand that the purchase of nonfood items be authorized, to call for permission to receive cash for change less than fifty cents, to recommend that restaurant meals be purchasable with stamps by the elderly and disabled. These reforms are achievable only when stamps are replaced by cash.

Many spokesmen and advocates for the poor have recognized these problems and support switching cash for stamps, and, by acting to violate the regulations governing their use, the users of stamps daily express their interest in abolishing stamps in favor of cash. Stamps are highly negotiable—many persons sell them at face value or at a discount to friends, strangers, or local grocery stores. Every week since the beginning of 1971 the Department has issued news releases announcing that, on the average, three to five stores have been suspended from participating in the program for as much as a year for permitting ad hoc cash-ins or allowing food stamps to be exchanged for cigarettes, toilet paper, soap, or other nonfood items carried in grocery outlets. The Department maintains a large squad of compliance officers who receive reports of suspicious activity and conduct visits to the stores oriented both toward education (to remind them of the rules of the program) and compliance (to investigate and warn). The Department has to be ceaselessly vigilant to halt the cashing-in of stamps, to stop the poor from enjoying the same freedom the rest of us enjoy.

The administrative burden

The food store compliance effort is by no means the only aspect of administering the food-stamp program that consumed departmental resources that might be better spent in the form of cash grants to individuals. There is no clear price tag on the policing effort, but the best estimates put it in excess of 5 million dollars annually.

What about other forms of program fraud, such as counterfeiting of stamps? The Department has persuaded the Bureau of Engraving and Printing to place the same detailed etching of Lincoln on the $5 food coupon that is on the $5 bill to deter counterfeiters. But theft still accounts for nearly half a million dollars in stamp losses a year, and negligent losses cost the Department $230,000 in Illinois alone in 1971.

Another of the Department's major program-related expenditures is for the printing of the coupons. To produce enough of this second form of money to yield a monthly average of 276 million dollars in coupons, the Treasury has to allocate four of its thirty printing presses for twenty-four hours a day at an annual cost to Agriculture of 15 million dollars.

The Department's food-stamp headaches are regulatory as well as fiscal. It has to wrestle with the fact that it has been responsible for creating four forms of scrip for food: the stamps, food-credit slips (as change for fifty-cent food stamps), food certificates (twenty-five-cent pieces of paper good only for milk, formula, or instant baby cereal) and that old standby, cash. The fifth form of scrip is an invention of the Office of Economic Opportunity's dying Emergency Food Program —food vouchers to enable recipients to buy food stamps or groceries directly.

The Department's administrative problems in controlling the proper flow of noncash are compounded by those of the state and local food-stamp officials. New Mexico is faced with an increase in statewide administrative costs of from 1.3 to 3.4 million dollars and the legislature won't appropriate the money to hire the people to implement the program. Louisiana claims it can't afford to pay for any fair-hearing officers for most of 1972. Every state has a tale of fiscal woes flowing from dispensing food stamps.

None of the states is anxious to engage in much outreach work proselytizing for participants, because states are federally reimbursed for only 62.5 percent of the cost of personnel involved in outreach and because outreach expands the rolls, which has the additional fiscal impact of requiring more stamp-certification workers (again 62.5 percent at federal expense) and more funds for stamp issuance for which the federal government pays nothing at all. It is this latter sum particularly, which averages between seventy-five cents and $1.00 per transaction with each household entitled to a minimum of two transactions a month or twenty-four a year, that bites deeply into local budgets. Issuance alone accounts for approximately 100 million dollars a year or slightly under 5 percent of bonus costs. When certification, outreach, and fair-hearing expenses are added on, it is understandable that a state might even conclude that it is better to expand and improve the commodity-distribution program, and not food stamps, since the commodity program is less costly to administer.

Who is for food stamps?

There are, of course, some substantial food-stamp constituencies, as there would be for any program that has 11.1 million participants a month. Perhaps the most vocal opposition to any cashing-in of stamps would come from the food industry, the representatives of the 150,000 retail grocers whose profits have been shown to rise by an average of 8 percent when the community gets food stamps. The grocers' obvious fear is that, if people were given cash to spend instead of food stamps, recipients might, out of choice or necessity, spend less of it on food. The result? Fewer profits. So, too, some state and local employers whose livelihoods depended on food-stamp certification or issuance might become jobless were stamp distribution to be terminated. In short, the economic interests of many in business and officialdom are linked to the stamp program.

The self-interest of these groups in retaining food stamps is understandable. The concern of the nutritionists is somewhat less comprehensible. If having stamps means (as current statistical patterns reveal) that one half of the eligible individuals will never receive their benefits, while some of the participating half will try either to cash in a portion of the stamps illegally or else use a portion of them for non-nutritious purchases, how does transforming stamps into equivalent cash and doubling the number of recipients create any greater danger that the poor will be malnourished? To assume that is to assume that at least two out of every three poor households will drastically misallocate their cash income and ignore their food requirements either because that income is too low to satisfy other basic needs or because adequate nutrition is not highly valued.

If the assumption is made that the poor will not opt to buy sufficient food, then the food-stamp program is no more tenable than its cash counterpart. The only social measure that could guarantee nutritional adequacy would be a nationwide requirement of submission to daily intravenous feedings or daily recommended dietary allowance injections, or daily nutrient pill consumption. This massive invasion of privacy may be the only realistic assurance social programming can ever give that malnutrition will be ended in America itself for all time.

Whither commodity distribution?

As food stamps go, so goes commodity distribution, indeed, sooner. The commodity program is irreparable. There is no way to deliver a storageable month's supply of desirable foods containing thirty days' worth of recommended dietary allowances to every poor family in America in the absence of administrative outlays that would essentially duplicate the existing system of food enterprise, including buying freezers for the poor. Anything short of that is only the present program warmed over. No one wants to retain commodities—the recipients, the President, the nutritionists, HEW—no one, that is, except the Department and some processors to whom the Department is politically responsive, since it is only the processors, not the growers or the ranchers, with whom the Department contracts and who profit in any way from the Department's food-purchasing activities.

Allowing the poor to select their own commodities when they want them, in the size packages they want them, and where they want them is the preferred substitute. Stamps can help perform that task. Cash does it better.

Whither child nutrition?

Cash is clearly the solution to the second most significant problem confronting the school lunch program—overt and covert discrimination against the recipients of free and reduced-price lunches. The cash grant would have to be adequate to permit every child to pay for his own meal just as middle-class and rich children do. The level of the cash grant could, of course, be somewhat lower to the extent that the federal government maintained the general school lunch assistance program and subsidized everybody's lunch across-the-board.

In addition to this general assistance, the federal government would have to continue to help schools without food service facilities or with facilities that are either deteriorated or insufficient to meet the demand. The help would come in the form of financial aid to purchase the necessary equipment, hopefully without any requirement for state or local matching. This federal program is essential to overcome the primary barrier to universal school lunch service for the poor.

Whither other nutrition programs?

Cash aid would do away with the need for all but four federal food assistance programs—the general school lunch subsidy and equipment aid referred to above and two programs designed to feed those who cannot be expected to feed themselves: the very young, whose mothers and fathers are at work or otherwise absent from the home, and the elderly.

Since the principle of furnishing cash, not food, is that the poor will do a better job feeding themselves than bureaucrats could, the principle has a natural limitation. It does not extend to those who must be fed by others if they are to survive nutritionally. Poor children in day-care centers must be furnished meals. Poor elderly persons who are physically unable to prepare meals for themselves and are housebound should have food brought to them at home in ready-to-eat form. Poor elderly persons, who could cook if they so chose but are psychologically deterred from doing so, or who are not housebound but lack effective cooking facilities in their rooms or apartments, should have meals prepared for their benefit in group settings in community centers and the like.

The solution here is a major expansion of the special food service program for day-care children (or, preferably, a nationwide child development program that would nourish as well as educate children under six) and a major expenditure of funds and energy to implement the newly-passed nutrition program for the elderly (the President is apparently seeking 100 million dollars for this purpose as of July 1).

To help them feed themselves

Cash will not completely solve the problems analyzed above unless (1) the cash provides an adequate income floor for everyone, permitting each member of the household to afford and receive (at home, at work, or in school) nutritious meals three times a day, regardless of whether the member is an infant, elderly, pregnant, nursing, or adolescent and (2) that income is furnished through a simple, comprehensible, exclusively federally-controlled administrative mechanism that assures that no individual is dependent for his entitlement upon the level of annual appropriations and (3) that administrative mechanism does not degrade the human dignity of the recipients of the income or destroy their family life.

That is a tall order for a social program to fill. But it is the only feasible way to end hunger and malnutrition in America for all time.

REFERENCES

Bettelheim, Bruno.
 1970 *Food to Nurture the Mind.* Children's Forum.
Kotz, Nicholas.
 1971 *Let Them Eat Promises.* New York: Anchor.

New York *Times.*
  1971   July 8.
U.S. Congress. House. Committee on Ways and Means.
  1970   *Family Assistance Act of 1970. Report of Committee on Ways and Means on H 16311.* H. R. Report #91–904. 91st Congress, 2nd session.
U.S. Congress. Senate. Select Committee on Nutrition and Human Needs.
  1971   *Nutrition and Human Needs, pt. 3: Food Stamp Regulations.* Hearings April 29, 30; May 14.
———.
  1971   *Nutrition and Human Needs, pt. 6: Summer Feeding Program and USDA Decision to Withhold Funds for sec. 32, June 25 and July 22, 1971.* 92nd Congress, 1st session.
Weekly Compilation of Presidential Documents.
  1969   Weekly Compilation of Presidential Documents, 5 (January–June). Washington: Office of Federal Register, National Archives and Records Service, General Services Administration.
White House Conference on Food, Nutrition and Health.
  1970   *Food, Nutrition, and Health. Final Report.* Washington: Government Printing Office.

Chapter 8   HUGH J. SCOTT

Large and Predominantly Black School Systems: Financing Public Education

PUBLIC education is currently facing a serious financial crisis—
especially in those urban areas where there is a heavy concentration of black students. The financial predicament of many school districts is so serious that some are being forced to reduce drastically
programs and services which are already considered inadequate or to
completely close the schools for extended periods of time. In February 1972, the Council of the Great Cities, an organization comprised
of members representing the public school systems of twenty-two of
the largest cities in this country, sent out an urgent appeal to its members to attend an emergency meeting in March for the purpose of
developing co-operative efforts to confront the problem of insufficient
funds. Of the twenty-two-member big-city school systems, nine had
pupil enrollments in the fall of 1970 which were more than 50 percent
black. At that time, the average black pupil enrollment for the twenty-
two systems was 41.7 percent. At a time when the schools are expected
to solve problems which have resisted solution in all other instructional
settings, the richest nation in the world seems to have run out of
money for education.

There is no school district in this nation serving a large black student population which is not confronted with the constraints imposed
by grossly inadequate funds for services and programs to meet effectively the educational needs of their students. In those school
districts where the scope and complexity of the problems are maximized by societal injustices and inequities, insufficient funds is the
standard reason given for denying requests for improved or expanded

127

services and programs and even for continuing many existing programs which can only be considered inadequate.

On September 14, 1971, the National Education Association did a survey of 103 school systems, including all of the largest systems enrolling 50,000 pupils or more. Telegrams were sent asking the superintendents if there were reductions in staff and school programs this year because of a financial crisis. Sixty-three school systems responded within four days with forty-one indicating some kind of rollback taking place. Thirteen school systems indicated a hold-the-line budget. Of those school systems polled, 23 were cutting back a total of 4,388 regular teaching positions.

It has often been humorously stated that money may not be the most important thing in the world, but that it is way ahead of what is in second place. Current circumstances in public education reveal the bitter truth in that expression. The saying "Put your money where your mouth is" certainly seems applicable to any assessment of the commitment of this society to public education. Our national priorities are easily measured by how we allocate our funds.

Public education, like all other services extended to large segments of the citizenry, is expensive, but it cannot be logically concluded that America does not have the resources to fund public education adequately. The undeniable needs of all students must be met if this democracy is to achieve credibility as a viable form of government. The resources needed to achieve this goal are available. Earl C. Kelley (1962:144) states the choice that confronts this nation:

> The people of the richest country in the world buy what they want. It is only a question as to what they value. I believe that we in education should not concede that the American people cannot afford a well-educated teacher and an attractive classroom for each twenty-five of our own young. We just have to care more about that than something else.

While expensive, education is the most important endeavor that a nation can undertake. It has been said that those who desire to be both free and ignorant desire what cannot be. The flight of both black and white Americans from public schools to nonpublic schools is alarming. The urban public schools of this nation are in a critical state, and the illness which has created the problems, both financial and educational, has crossed over the boundaries and infected the nonurban schools as well. The fight for the dollar has become the major concern of many boards of education and superintendents. The question is: How far are Americans willing to go to lend credence to their professed commitment to the value of education?

Some assumptions. Joseph Alsop has written that, if the worst racist in America set out to design a structure that would keep the black man enchained, he could do no better than to use the present system of public education (1967:22). The destructive effects of grossly inadequate funding for school systems with heavy concentrations of black students are evident throughout the country. These schools must be assessed either as operating in varying degrees of callous disregard for and detachment from the needs and problems of black Americans or as operating in a manner which demonstrates colossal ineptness in responding to those problems and needs. In this context, the following assumptions are offered as relevant to the exploration of the subject of financing public education for predominantly black school systems.

1. Historically and currently, race and socioeconomic status have been and are the chief determinants of success or failure in the public schools.
2. Far too many white Americans remain reluctant to support the provision of essential instructional services to black Americans on an equitable basis.
3. America has more than enough resources to finance adequately the kind of educational programs and services which can provide appropriate compensation for the host of disparities in the socioeconomic condition of most black Americans.
4. The continued resistance of many white Americans to racial integration in the schools has resulted in the flight of whites from those communities with a high percentage of black residents to surburban communities where blacks constitute an insignificant percentage of the population.
5. The ever-increasing proportion of black students in many school districts is a significant factor in the opposition of whites to adequate financing for public education in those schools.
6. The emerging commitment to increase public funding for non-public schools is directly related to the significant increase in the percentage of black students in many school districts.
7. Until such time as institutional racism is eradicated and its effects rectified, it will cost more to educate black students than white.
8. Unless something is done to reform fundamentally the nature and intent of public education in America, many communities will have public schools attended solely by blacks and poor whites.
9. The cost of public education increases in proportion to the

severity and scope of the impediments to the development of the
innate potentialities that are existent in the environmental setting.

Role of the school. The dire consequences of inadequate funding
for already inadequate educational programs and services for black
students are more evident when one fully considers the role of the
school and the importance of education in America. The public
school is the one institution in which society has pooled its funds in
an effort to provide benefits for all. In addition, the school is the
single institution which bears the heaviest responsibility for dispensing or promulgating those values which identify a group's consciousness of itself.[1] Education has always been an important means through
which the individual can improve his socioeconomic status. Schools
have become the major social institution, not only for preparing individuals, but also for their selection and placement in various positions in society. The level of entrance into the occupational world is
strongly predetermined by the level that is achieved in the educational
world.

Education is a form of social policy—a means by which the society
distributes power and privilege. Educational institutions reflect the
values of society by the way in which they are organized and operated
and by the way in which the various ethnic, religious, and racial groups
are treated. If black Americans are ever to bridge the gap between
aspiration and actuality, they must succeed in reconstructing the role
that the school performs in the lives of black Americans. The basic
tenets of this democracy give legitimacy to the efforts of black Americans to alter elements of the social structure in order to provide equality of opportunity for all. Any consequence of public education that
impedes or negates such efforts is illegitimate and dysfunctional.
White America has historically exercised an almost absolute control
over the nature and intent of public education for black Americans.
The deplorable fact is that this monopoly has resulted in black Americans being the most poorly educated, the most severely impaired, and
the most deliberately misinterpreted of all the major ethnic groups in
the public schools.

The most demanding and complex challenge that confronts public
education is the effective and equitable reconciliation of the differences in innate intellectual potentialities and the disparities in socio-

1. Statement extracted from the position paper prepared by the Black Caucus
at the Harvard University Conference on Educational Subsystems, January 25,
1968.

economic condition that exist among all groups. It is the clear responsibility of the society in general and the schools in particular to seek ways to compensate for differences in innate intellectual potentialities and to attempt to remove those socioeconomic barriers that deny opportunity to any group.

The question which we must continue to ask is: How do we gear our educational programs and instructional procedures and materials to student populations which share both similarities and differences in their life experiences and in their innate capacities to respond to those experiences? Also, the question which has to follow is: Are we willing as a nation to finance such an educational program? When there are unusually wide disparities among individuals, the teaching-learning process is heavily taxed and becomes extraordinarily complicated and expensive. As of yet, there is no school system which can legitimately claim to have resolved equitably the problems presented in the vast differences among individuals and groups.

The kinds of life experiences that can produce mutual understanding among and equitable relationships between the various ethnic, religious, racial, and socioeconomic groups represent the essential elements of a viable application of the concept of integration, both in society at large and in the schools. The fact that some Americans seem unwilling or reluctant to return to blacks those rights to which all are entitled presents a very formidable condition for society to deal with. In resolving this disparity in rights and opportunities, the schools must function to reform society.

Quality education. The cost of public education should bear a direct relationship to the resources required to provide for students what is defined as a quality education. It is my view that quality education should be defined on the basis of the democratic principles upon which this nation was founded, and it should have two critical and inseparable elements:

1. Education should successfully fulfill its responsibility to society and to its clientele by contributing significantly to the development of each individual's inherent potentialities.
2. Education should prepare its clientele to seek for themselves and for others opportunities to develop resources for improving the quality of communal living with respect to the legitimate needs, rights and responsibilities of individuals and groups.

Quality education, when applied specifically to black Americans, should be a designation used only to describe the efforts of those educational institutions which provide major assistance to blacks in fulfilling their legitimate needs and aspirations. Quality education must carry with it a commitment to demonstrate that "blackness" is not a regrettable human condition, but the proud heritage of one eleventh of this nation's population. It also requires that the schools fulfill their responsibility to rectify those conditions which have caused millions of black Americans to believe the specious evidence that they are inherently inferior.

It should be abundantly clear to any observer of this current crisis in public education that the black school administrator's role cannot be a passive one. The black school administrator, if he is to be effective, has no choice but to lend openly, actively, and professionally his expertise and status to the resolution of the problem of education for black Americans. In spite of the flow of criticism and abuse that can be expected from both whites and blacks, black school administrators cannot legitimately justify their abstention from direct commitment to their responsibility as educators and more especially as black Americans. It is imperative that black educators militantly participate in the establishment of an orderly process for bringing about those changes which will culminate in systems of education that do not permit the factors of race and socioeconomic condition to serve as the determinants of success in our schools and that provide quality education for all students.

Life in disadvantaged environments is not the most conducive setting to producing the kinds of qualities and learnings desired and projected by our schools. Once a child is convinced that school is irrelevant to his immediate needs and future goals, the task of education becomes almost impossible. School personnel must develop approaches to learning which are realistic and based on the life conditions faced by those students whose values and attitudes are formulated primarily from their perceptions of the conflicts, tensions, and frustrations of day-to-day life in the inner city. As James Olsen (1965:84) has stated, "Educators need to study class differences and then translate the insights they gain from that study into curricular and organizational modifications."

Equity versus equality. Nature has not plagued America's blacks by denying them the requisite innate intellectual potentialities. No ethnic or racial group has a monopoly on intelligence or other positive characteristics of human behavior. With this in mind, a normal child can be defined as an individual born with the appropriate distribution of those critical innate intellectual potentialities essential for effective participation in society. The possession of such innate intellectual potentialities in appropriate amounts is a fundamental prerequisite for adequate participation in society, but an additional essential factor to be considered is the amount of stimulation provided to promote the growth and development of those potentialities.

The development of an individual's innate intellectual potentialities is strongly influenced by the effect of the variables in his social, political, and economic environments. The presence of a host of depressant factors in an individual's environmental setting can impede development, and the existence of these factors necessitates compensatory action in order to prevent normal development from being stymied. While the vast majority of America's blacks are normal with regard to innate intelligence, they have been subjected to institutionalized impediments which have hindered their maturation process. Thus, the black child in such a restrictive environmental setting is not disadvantaged on the basis of his innate intelligence, but rather because his growth and development are taking place in a disadvantaged environment.

No child acquires his social drives and moral values—his basic culture—solely or primarily from his books or his teachers. The behavior of the child in school is the consequence not only of what happens in the school, but also what happens outside the school. Housing, family life, employment opportunities, community organization, mobility and many other aspects of life directly affect the learning process. The commitment to the premise that, if properly stimulated and taught, a group of normal children will learn does not answer the question: To what extent can the schools be reconstructed in order to compensate appropriately for the host of impediments which may be encountered in various environmental settings?

Teaching all of the children in society is a relatively new conceptual approach to public education in America. Successfully teaching large concentrations of youngsters who are in disadvantaged socioeconomic environments is a significant challenge. As inconsistent as it may seem, in the most advanced scientific and technological society in the history of mankind, as well as the most affluent, students are dropping out of school in the major urban areas at a rate ranging from 30 to 50 percent. The majority of the black students who do remain in school until graduation are not acquiring the basic skills needed to function effectively in this society. The large urban school systems with their increasingly black student populations are rapidly reaching the point where it can be said that the majority of their students are not acquiring the basic academic skills which they so critically need.

The range of abilities within any school system is tremendous, and the wider that range is, the greater the demand on the skills of school personnel and the higher the cost of education. The students who are the least expensive to educate and the least difficult to teach constitute the majority in most school systems, but this is not true of most urban school systems. While it is not possible for schools to guarantee that every child will learn to read adequately because of possible organic handicaps, schools can and should guarantee to every child a learning environment conducive to the full development of his potential learning capacity. Thus, the schools should direct their primary efforts toward creating an educational setting in which the right to read may be translated productively into the satisfying act of reading. This goal can only be achieved when reading instructional techniques are demonstrably viable, when educators are in effective command of these techniques, when the necessary materials and media are readily available, and when the critical support services to students are provided. These services by right ought not to be ignored, and of necessity ought to be developed and financed.

If the schools are ever to compensate for the delimiting factors of socioeconomic deprivation and rectify the massive condition of cumulative deficiencies in the basic skills in reading and mathematics, there must be more than an equal allocation of personnel and financial resources for urban schools. The commitment must be to go beyond equality to what can be called equity in the provision of resources in order to provide the necessary compensatory services for students hindered by social and educational inequalities. The priorities established in terms of programs, services, and funds should be aimed at alleviating situations where socioeconomic factors and academic deficiencies combine to present the most urgent challenges to public education. The quality, quantity, and intensity of resources supplied by a school system must be provided in direct proportion to the degree of severity of its students' needs, regardless of race.

The term *equalization of educational opportunity* has served well. But it must not be construed to mean sameness of program, or of number of dollars to be spent on every child's education, or of number of tax dollars to be paid by every taxpayer. It does mean that the opportunity must be tailored to each child's potentialities for self-realization, productiveness, service, and dependability as an American citizen. The primary function of the school is to provide instruction and experiences for learning. A public school support formula must be developed which provides equity among the school districts in providing their respective shares of the investment needed to achieve the assured educational program. Equity must apply to both the effort and the ability of the local districts in supporting their schools.

The establishment of a workable formula through which equity can be determined in the funding of critically needed programs and services presents a formidable challenge to public education. While there certainly must be some justifiable limit imposed on the cost of public education per individual, there also must be a rationale to direct the allocation of resources for public education which is consistent with the aspirations and hopes of the citizens of this democracy. The variables which have an impact on the teaching-learning process must be included in any formula or rationale used to determine the level of resources needed and the way they should be allocated. The following guidelines are offered in an effort to bring some degree of categorization to the determination of the relative cost factors as they apply to instructional programs and services:

Scope of the instructional task. How large is the specific population to be served? Will the target population require instructional resources in addition to what is now being provided in order to complete satisfactorily the expected performance tasks?

Complexity of the instructional task. What has been the past record of the target population's receptivity to instructional programs and services? What are the external and internal factors operating to impede the teaching-learning process?

Educational setting. Is the educational setting in which the instructional services are to be provided such that both external and internal reforms need to be initiated in order to increase the possibilities for achieving the assigned tasks?

Expected completion period. Can the instructional services be adequately mobilized and the projected outcomes achieved within the time frame established for realization of the educational objectives without additional resources?

Support services needed. Are the critical supportive services that are required to supplement the basic instructional effort available?

More and more black Americans are prepared to seek the "doctrine of debt" in education just as vociferously as it is being sought in other institutional settings. The "doctrine of debt" holds that society owes something to blacks for 250 years of slavery and 100 years of discrimination following slavery. The major objective of seeking preferential treatment for black students is not because black students are either the most or least qualified. It seems fair that a form of specialized treatment be accorded to blacks after centuries of having been the recipients of demeaning and obstructive treatment. Such a recompense seems necessary if past and present inequities and injustices are to be rectified rather than compounded and perpetuated. If equity in the allocation of funds for educational programs and services as compensation for socioeconomic disparities is judged as unacceptable, then public education can hardly be expected to serve successfully as the great equalizer which can alter elements of the social structure in order to provide equality of opportunity for all.

Conclusions. The inadequacies and inequities in the provision of public education for black Americans should be viewed in the context of the many other problems which engulf our cities. The problems confronting urban areas today make it difficult to look with any optimism to the future of the city. The serious problems that are presently going unresolved will not go away. Rather, it is likely that they will be compounded with each passing year. It is obvious that not enough is being done to solve urgent social and economic problems, so it is not difficult to expect that living in the cities will be even less desirable in the future than it is today. This dire projection will have even more drastic implications for the lives of most blacks.

Once we accept the conclusion that life in our cities has little relationship to humanistic values, we realize that this is intolerable. We cannot allow our cities to continue to deteriorate. Our cities are crucial to the vitality of this nation, and their decline has far-reaching economic and political implications. Yet we are faced with restricted resources to confront unmet domestic needs. A number of seemingly unanswerable questions are raised: How can we redirect our priorities in order that resources can be maximized in the resolution of humanistic problems? In looking at the complexities of urban problems and their inextricable interrelationship, how can we apply our resources and efforts in a way that will make urban areas at least habitable for the present and yet invest in improvements for the future?

Public school systems are responsive to the dominant social influences in the communities of which they are a part. Because education affords prestige and advantages in a competitive specialized society, it has great importance for members of minority groups. But blacks, as a group, have had far greater difficulty than most other groups in securing the necessary social influence on the nature and intent of educational opportunities provided to them.

Since public education reflects the dominant values and priorities of society, the conclusion can be reached that the serious failure of public education for black Americans, in particular, and for individuals from lower socioeconomic groups, in general, is in large measure a manifestation of the failure of our society. Inadequate educational opportunity creates and perpetuates inadequate living opportunity. Black Americans are an integral part of the total society, and this nation must provide effective education and quality living for all of its citizens.

The most important challenge which most black Americans face in their adult lives is that of finding successful employment. The level of education which is attained has a fundamental impact in terms of meaningful and satisfying work experiences and the level of income which can be commanded. The increasing cost of public education is staggering; however, when compared with the expanding economy, it can be seen in better perspective. The richest nation in the world can afford to provide public education for all its citizens in a manner that can compensate for socioeconomic disparities and serve to reform society as well.

Unless it is the intent of this society to promote quality education for black Americans, and unless it is willing to undergird this commitment with a redirection of resources to be applied in such a manner that will provide equity, then the historic efforts of black Americans to secure their full rights as citizens of this nation will represent slightly more than a tragic exercise in futility. The richest nation in the world has a choice to make. It will either finance public education for blacks in a manner consistent with legitimate needs or it will continue on its present course of action. For those who realize that this nation does have the resources and must only revise their allocation, the question becomes one of whether or not white Americans are willing to accept the premise that black Americans are not inherently inferior but have been the victims of institutionalized discriminatory practices so oppressive and obstructive that the public schools as presently constituted and financed are incapable of responding adequately to their legitimate needs.

This nation cannot long endure, one half poor and the other affluent. The unprecedented prosperity which has engulfed the affluent majority cannot prevent a large disadvantaged minority from rising to participate either violently and/or nonviolently in the rewards of prosperity. There is no doubt that America has the needed capacity to eradicate poverty and discrimination, but is there the necessary degree of commitment to pursue this end?

REFERENCES

Alsop, Joseph.
    1967   "No More Nonsense About Ghetto Education." *New Republic* 157, nos. 4–5, (July 22–29), Issues 2747–2748, 18–23.
Kelley, Earl C.
    1962   *In Defense of Youth.* Englewood Cliffs, N.J.: Prentice-Hall, Inc.
Olsen, James.
    1965   "The Challenge of the Poor to the Schools." *Phi Delta Kappan,* XLVII, no. 2 (October), 79–84.

Organization and Finances
of Public Schools: A Black Response
to a Black Assessment

A Comment on Hugh J. Scott's Paper

A T a time when President Nixon has called for a moratorium on
busing, has called for a down-and-out play by the Miami Dol-
phins, a professional football team, and has escalated the bombing
fever of the Vietnam War, Brother Hugh Scott, Superintendent of
Schools, Washington, D.C., our previous speaker, is being charged
with causing the President to call a moratorium on the consideration
of granting Home Rule to the District of Columbia. The President
chose to do this because Brother Scott decided that black children,
indeed all children, had a right/responsibility/obligation to learn
through the vehicle of the classroom how to hold the government accountable. The District of Columbia school children had been involved with welfare-rights mothers in a march on March 25, 1972
(Scott, 1972:1).

It may be that some of us would have been happier if the President
had stuck to his spectator role in the Super Bowl, called a moratorium
on the Vietnam War, marched with the children and the welfare
mothers on March 25, 1972, and left the bus-driving to us (Hunter,
1972). His actions have won the support of the conservatives, given
the white liberals another loophole, confirmed that his "benign neglect"
of blacks is more of the same-o, same-o, and upset a small number of
Negroes, particularly the Congressional Black Caucus (Scott, n.d.).

My first reaction to his busing position was that he was against the
further burning of buses until he escalated the Vietnam War. My

139

second response was that maybe he was beginning to hear blacks as being articulate spokesmen of their own causes until he pulled the rug from under Home Rule in the District of Columbia. My final reaction was that he was going to become the first President to attempt to finance quality education within those communities where the so-called minorities are, in fact, *the majority,* until I learned the 2.5-million-dollar proposed appropriation was not *new* money. Finally, there are a growing number of black people who are beginning to believe that Tricky Dick is not as tricky as the white liberals. He tells you when he does not want you to ride on his bus, even at the rear or on the way to school. The white liberals would have left you standing at the bus stop or filed a suit in your support after the bus had been burned or overturned.

The integration/segregation/quality integration/busing game of white America has about run its full course. White America, which has failed to educate whites effectively to respect blacks, is learning that it can no longer deceive blacks into believing that white-controlled education means quality education; that the problem is financial, not racial-cultural; that black is unhuman and ineducable, that whites have unlimited talents to educate. The myth of white male superiority is a legend, enforceable only with guns, genocide, and the like. My point: integration is losing its containment quality: scattering blacks will not have the effect in 1972 that it would have had in 1954. Witness events in professional sports, on college campuses, and in the collective actions being taken at the local, state, national, and international levels by blacks.

Black people are asking who owns the buses and how much whites are willing to pay to have their children sitting beside black students in classrooms. Historically, white youth have been educated to become masters over black people—and want to socialize with blacks at all costs. The black bourgeoisie "integrated" in order to prove that they were white, as good as or equal to whites, i.e., better than niggers. Poor blacks integrated to get a better education—not for social reasons. The former group considered themselves to be Dubois's "talented tenth": They were educated to cajole other blacks or to submit to white leadership. The latter group emulated the Booker T. Washington model: They acquired the skills to build their own nation. They knew better than white people that victims have to manage their own de-victimization. To turn one's destiny over to one's victimizer is to ensure no change in one's fortunes.

To complain that a lack of money is the problem is to mimic the bureaucrat who turns down requests because of a "lack of budget."

Teacher unions are doing well, doing no good. One of the best legitimate hustles one can find as a white person or a black person under white rule is that of a teacher.

There is a direct relationship between the amount of white-defined pathology and public appropriations. Can you imagine a grant being made to a community of normal, "nondisadvantaged," "nonculturally-deprived," "nonretarded" black children where there was no delinquency, drug addiction, prostitution, muggings, crimes, and the like? Foundations would probably finance studies to find out *why* there was such a lack of pathology. When pathology became operational, the government would begin to find it. It may be, then, that the demand by blacks for control over the programs that serve them may be a problem for a while. My point: The rate at which whites can locate paid employment as saviours of blacks is declining.

The Scott thesis: Summarized/reviewed.   Brother Scott viewed the financial crisis in public education as being of critical importance. It impinges on the destiny of black students. A Council of Great Cities in a study conducted in February 1972 found that of the twenty-two-member big-city school systems, nine had pupil enrollments which were more than 50 percent black. Blacks were the *majority* and not the minority in these nine systems. The average black pupil enrollment was 41.7 percent.[1]

Scott also reported on a study done by the National Education Association of 103 school systems, including all those with 50,000 or more students. The survey raised questions about financial cutbacks of the sixty-three respondents; fifty-one indicated some kind of rollback was taking place. Other findings were as follows:

(a). 13 school systems indicated a hold-the-line budget.

(b). 23 were cutting back a total of 4,388 regular teaching positions.

(c). 18 had reduced budgets for instructional materials as well (Scott, n.d.:2).

Scott listed nine assumptions as an explanation of the problem of white financing of black education (n.d.:4–6). All could be put into a single three-word category: *white institutional racism* (white narcissism plus white power plus white antiblackness).

Scott introduced a discussion of equity versus equality. He was

---

1. The incident involving the suicide of a black principal in Flint, Michigan, may prove instructive. See: Jerry M. Flint, "Behind a Black School Aide's Suicide: A Conflict in Basic Values," in the New York *Times*, March 19, 1972, p. 58.

essentially raising the question of whether white victimizers would promulgate educational justice by ensuring, not an equal distribution (based on per capita appropriations), but equitable distribution (based on essential/actual needs).

As have all black men who have succeeded in white America on the terms/credentials/criteria of the oppressor, Scott appeared to vacillate between the recognition of the fact of white institutional racism and a deeply held need to have the American Dream realized. Such a position tended to have him rely on white response rather than on the need for black self-determination, collective action, and co-operative economic development (Wilcox, 1972).

Scott pointed out after his speech that the blacks were the majority in Washington, D.C. They compose 71 percent of the population. The pupil enrollment is 143,000; the majority (91 percent) are black. As to the source of income of school support, 83 percent comes from the District of Columbia; 17 percent comes from the federal government.

When Scott decided that it was fine to have school children participate at the marketplace on the recent day-care/welfare-rights issue, an effort was made to chastise him and the Board of Education members. This was done by a Congressional committee. It was reported that Marion Berry, President, Board of Education, told the committee to take back its money. He implied that the District of Columbia board would play "nigger no more."

The question for Washington, D.C., becomes, not how they can get the federal government to raise the 17 percent, but how a collective black nation-building effort among blacks and others can generate the 17 percent from assessing Congress for the use of Washington, D.C., etc. My point: The majority of the students of the District of Columbia school system cannot depend on white racist benevolence. They can only rely on black self-government (National Black Political Convention, Inc., 1972:23).

REFERENCES

Hunter, Marjorie.
   1972   "Confusion Stirred by Nixon Stand." New York *Times*. March 19, 1972.
National Black Political Convention, Inc.
   1972   "Self-Determination for the District of Columbia." The National Black
          Political Agenda. Washington, D.C. May 19, 1972.
Scott, Hugh J.
   1972   "Quality Education and the Public Schools." In *Comment: The Execu-*

tive Office of the Superintendent. Washington, D.C.: The Public School System. March 27, 1972.

———.

Undated *Large and Predominantly Black School Systems: Implication for the Financing of Public Education.* Washington, D.C.: Public Schools of the District of Columbia.

Wilcox, Preston.

1972 *The Policy Implications of Community Control of Blackamerican Schools.* New York: AFRAM Associates, Inc. March 23, 1972. 20 pp.

Health Services in the Concentration Camp: Prospects for the Inner City in the 1970s

Health and the social order in the inner city

THERE is a widely held, though often unstated, belief that poor health services are the major cause of the appalling gap between the health of the poor, in the ghetto and in the inner city, and the health of the rest of the nation. It is false—despite the fact that poor health services do kill people, directly and indirectly, do cause months and years of needless pain, disability, and loss of human potential, and do assault the integrity and dignity of millions of people. There is an equally widely held belief that improvement in health services is the primary requisite for major and long-lasting improvements in the health of the poor and the urban minorities. It is also false— despite the fact that such improvements are desperately needed, must be fought for and won, and would, if effected, have some measurable effect on health.

The truth is that, for any population, and particularly for the poor, the black, the Puerto Rican, the chicano, the Indian, and the inner-city resident, the basic determinants of health lie in the social order. They lie in the social environment, the biological environment, the physical environment. They lie in issues like income and housing and food, the degree of exposure to environmental hazards, the quality of daily life, the social arrangements which form the ways in which members of a population can interact with each other and with members of other groups. They lie in risk factors which in part in-

145

volve personal behavior and choices but which also involve environmental and social patterns. They lie in the degree of power and control a population has over its own destiny, and in the degree to which
it has at least a possibility of meeting its own needs and fulfilling its
own aspirations.

The statement that health is primarily related to the social order is,
in this era of the magnificent achievements of scientific medicine,
usually given more lip service than serious attention, particularly by
physicians, who have always overestimated the usefulness of their
interventions. It might challenge too many of our professional premises
to recognize that there were enormous improvements in health, declines in mortality, and growth of populations in England, Scandinavia,
and parts of Western Europe (the area for which some records are
available) between 1700 and 1840, an increase which began a hundred years before sanitary reform and 150 years before medicine had
anything even remotely effective to offer against any disease. Most of
the reduced mortality was probably due to decreases in the toll of
infectious diseases, and this in turn probably reflected a doubling of
the food supply and improved nutrition (McKeown, 1971:29–49;
Hutchinson, 1966:303–311; Ernle, 1919; McKeown and Record, 1962:
94–122). Kass has cited evidence that the infant mortality rate among
the royal families of central Europe in the middle of the nineteenth
century was approximately 12 per 1,000 livebirths—a rate better than
the best in the world today—and that was before the germ theory of
disease, before antibiotics, before obstetricians, and without benefit of
pediatricians.[1] In this century, McDermott (1969:1–27) and others
have traced the associations between a rising standard of living and
the decline of tuberculosis, childhood diarrhea, and other major causes
of morbidity and mortality before specific medical therapies were
available. The improvements that came with stable food supplies were
followed by the sanitary reform movement of the mid-nineteenth
century—in considerable measure a social reform movement that arose
in response to the first great urban crisis, the disastrous living conditions of the urban workers in the first decades of the industrial
revolution. Significantly, this movement was led by physicians who
understood that poverty cripples and kills, that hunger and slum
housing and a polluted environment can damage and destroy human
life, that child labor and the exploitation of women and the elderly
stunt human potential (Simon, 1887:143–163). Only much later, in the

---

1. Personal communication from Edward H. Kass.

second quarter of the twentieth century, did scientific medicine begin to make a difference.

I intend these remarks as more than the usual superficial bow to history, to the problems that belong to some quaint and ignorant past and are irrelevant to contemporary society. In the eighth decade of the twentieth century, in the wealthiest society in the recorded history of mankind, how many black babies burned to death in slum housing last year? In rural Mississippi, a few hundred miles from this meeting, how many black children today are working in the cotton fields, together with their mothers and their elderly grandparents? How many drink water from drainage ditches and cry for food at night? How many white Appalachians literally have the earth ripped from their valleys and replaced by a bleak wasteland of slate and acid-poisoned water? How many elderly Americans of all races, living in social isolation, struggling to survive on fixed social security pensions, are measurably malnourished? How many coal miners die each year of Black Lung disease or related pneumoconioses? How many industrial workers labor in environments that are at once toxic and dehumanizing? How many adolescents of all social classes are addicted to drugs, in a contemporary epidemic which can only be explained as a function of the social environment? How many chicano, black, and Puerto Rican Americans consume their lives in that sad stream of humanity called migrant farm workers?

As professionals, to talk of health services and ignore these conditions is to diminish not only our relevance but our own humanity. Yet many health planners immerse themselves in the technical problems of medical service delivery as if they were the primary problems, relegate these other difficulties to the areas of "good citizenship" or "social concern," and define them as outside our proper medical or technical or professional business. In this they are unconsciously at one with much of organized medicine and its allies, defending themselves and their version of a medical-care system against the implicit accusation of our high infant mortality rate by saying the rate is due to "socioeconomic conditions"—as if "socioeconomic conditions" that maim and kill people are not a proper professional concern of physicians, or a factor which calls for a reorganization of health care!

There is thus no decent way, in my view, to begin a discussion of health services delivery for the poor and urban minorities without reference to these larger issues. In the narrow context of this conference, it means that every *other* paper—the presentations on housing and economic development and political power—is of possibly greater potential significance for health than is this one.

This does not mean that we should excuse the problems of health care delivery and ignore them, nor does it mean that the technical achievements and benefits of modern medicine are unimportant or irrelevant. We affirm that every human being has a basic right to health services, freely accessible and of high quality, in a single standard of care, provided with his informed participation (not "for" him by others), with dignity and decency and without regard to race or sex or age or income. To say this is merely to affirm that every human has the right to life, liberty, and opportunity, including freedom from needless and preventable pain, disability, the stunting of his or her full potential by disease and deprivation, or early and unnecessary death. Health services are—or should be—designed to serve the people, but they are only one of many crucial ways of providing service and of affecting health.

Even if we focus narrowly on the question of health services delivery, moreover, we must recognize that we are dealing not with one but with two American crises. There is a *health* crisis, which chiefly afflicts the poor and the nonwhite, though it is manifest among other groups in selected ways: coronary artery disease, lung cancer, or chronic pulmonary and renal disease. And there is a *health-care* crisis, which now affects almost everyone. It hits the poor hardest, of course, because they are the sickest, they are at greatest risk, they live in the most dangerous environments; but in fact we did not begin to pay serious attention to it as a nation until it began to affect the white middle class. The two crises are related, but separate. And *both* have their roots in the social order: the health crisis, because of the determining role of the social order in health; the health-care crisis because our arrangements for basic human services both reflect and express our social structure and policies.

It is the failure to recognize the dual nature of the crisis and its relationship to the structure of our society that makes many of the papers analyzing our inner-city health-care systems, and proposing changes, so inappropriate. There is, by now, a fairly standard format for such papers. First, one reviews at length the present health status and the terrifying health problems in the ghetto, and summarizes in detail the links and associations between poverty, minority status, illness, and death. Next, one discusses the importance of health-care services and the desperate need to increase them if health in the ghetto is to improve. Finally, one proposes an optimal system, a massive campaign for change, and lists all the essentials that must characterize the new system—a single standard of care, free access, health care as a right, citizen and consumer control, increased personnel and facilities, and so on.

This standard presentation is faulty in at least three ways. It perpetuates the fallacy I have already mentioned—that the health-care system is primarily responsible for the bad health of the poor, and that improvements in it are the primary road to long-lasting improvements in their health. Also, it promotes unrealistic expectation by suggesting that all we have to do is think up appropriate changes in the health-care delivery system, without reference to where the larger social order is now and where it is headed; yet it is this social order that will determine the major health needs and problems that any changes must address. Finally, it may seem to suggest that any major change in health care—let alone radical change—can and will be accomplished regardless of the existing political, economic, social, and racial climate.

I suggest that we start at the other end. If we are to plan health services delivery for the poor and urban minorities in the 1970s, then first we must try to estimate what life will be like for the poor and urban minorities in the United States in the 1970s. The estimate I find most likely was expressed in a parable called "Before the Law" written fifty-eight years ago by the Czech novelist Franz Kafka (1971). Kafka vividly describes the frustration and demise of a common man when confronted with an official holding arbitrary powers. The man has spent every day of his adult life pleading in vain for admission at what he thinks is the doorway to justice. As he lies dying—still on the sidewalk outside the door—the gatekeeper casually tells him the doorway leads nowhere, that it was an illusion constructed only to fool him, and that now it will be shut forever. Urban minorities and the poor would recognize every element in Kafka's parable—the sense that daily life is a waking, lifelong nightmare; the implication of a sinister conspiracy against their interests; the feeling of confrontation with a power so arrogant that it is used casually, almost indifferently, for oppression; the seeming futility of every available response; the statement that hope is a delusion and a waste. Kafka's parable is an almost perfect description of what it is to live as a black, a Puerto Rican, or a chicano in Los Angeles or New York or Chicago today. The meaning should not be restricted to something as narrow as the search for health care (though the black and the impoverished, to be sure, have been dying on the doorsteps of indifferent institutions for decades) but rather should be understood in a larger and even more chilling way. *For the dominant white majority*

*in the United States is even now, I believe, joining in the process of
shutting the door on urban minorities and the poor, cutting them off
from any prospect of full and equal participation in national life, in
the status of full citizenship, as human beings.*

The formula that is being used to induce this change is straight-
forward. Use the real fear of crime as a reason for limiting or
effectively destroying the Bill of Rights, insisting that this is a necessity to control crime and assuring everyone that the limitations, of
course, apply only to "criminals." Then equate political dissent,
criticism, radicalism, and even such liberal values as freedom of the
press with "crime," while simultaneously making sure to provoke active
dissent, demonstrations, and violence, either by blocking any hope of
redress of grievances by legal means or by the employment of agent
provocateurs and the use of police forces themselves to initiate and
conduct riots (thus police and other right-wing murders like those at
Kent State or Jackson State are not "crimes" and go unpunished).
Present the efforts of the black to win self-determination and an open
society as a *criminal* threat to the white majority, particularly to the
working-class and lower-middle-class white. By these means, one can
simultaneously: (1) enlist the support of the white majority for
oppression and the destruction of basic liberties; (2) divert its attention from the *real* sources in the social order of its own exploitation
and oppression and limit the possibilities of social and political
change; and (3) prevent the diversion of money from the private
sector, defense industries, and the military establishment to the tasks
involved in easing the unbearable conditions of life in the inner city,
the rural slums, or the Indian reservation. Compared to the cost of
reconstructing the country's major cities, building thousands of schools
and creating millions of jobs, the cost of doubling the capacity of the
nation's jails would be invisible.

In a society nominally committed to a democratic ideology, of
course, this process requires the adoption of euphemisms, code words,
and disguises. "Crime" has become such a code word, a euphemism,
justification for the oppression of the poor, the black, and other
minorities. In the same way, at the initiative of the government,
"busing" has been discovered as the euphemism behind which, at
last, the white majority can comfortably choose overt racism and
racial segregation: in short, apartheid. It is not just the schools that
will not be opened up; it is the housing, the suburbs, the jobs, the
political freedoms, and the civil rights.

I suggest that precisely this strategy is now being used to play
upon the fears of crime held by most Americans, and the racist

feelings held by many Americans, to enlist their support for repressive measures rather than for a reallocation of national priorities and national resources to address our social problems and inequities, and in the process to enlist their support for the destruction of any effective liberal political opposition. That this is the case, and the extent to which it has already succeeded, is documented in chilling and exquisite detail by Richard Harris of the national reporting staff of the *New Yorker* in a long and carefully researched article entitled "The New Justice." Among Harris's general points—aside from the documentation of their implementation in legislative act and administrative decree—are the following:

Those who are most deeply committed to the status quo are incapable of blaming society itself for its ills, because a conclusion of that sort would amount to an admission that society should be changed. Such people can ignore what is wrong and hope it will somehow be righted or simply go away; or, if the threat is large and lasting, they can select a few scapegoats and link them together with a conspiracy theory. That is the most common way out, and it was the way chosen by the far right in exploiting the crime issue.

. . . Conservatives are more realistic because they have such a low opinion of humanity, and are willing to put it to use. One way they have put it to use politically is by nurturing the white man's fear of the black man—a very deep, perhaps ineradicable fear by now—as the seed of their grass roots support . . . Richard Nixon harvested the crop in 1968 by repeatedly promising in the North that he would crack down on those who committed crime or fomented disorder and by repeatedly implying in the South that he would slow down the pace of desegregation. North and South, the message was the same: black men would be controlled . . .

If demands for social reform were to be silenced through exploitation of whites' fear and resentment of blacks, the agitation for civil rights for Negroes had to be discredited. One way to accomplish that was to equate it with crime. By now, the equation has been drawn and accepted by many people.

The danger today is not only that the Constitution will continue to be violated by the government, as it has been repeatedly in the past couple of years, but that the present administration will rewrite the essential protections contained in that document, *with the consent of the governed and the agreement of the Congress and the Supreme Court*, in the name of private and public security [italics added].[2]

2. From "The New Justice," by Richard Harris, *The New Yorker*, XLVIII (March 25, 1972), 44–105. Copyright © 1972, The New Yorker Magazine, Inc. By permission of the publisher.

In 1968, the National Advisory Commission on Civil Disorders (the Kerner Commission) concluded that the nation was "moving toward two societies, one black, one white—separate and unequal." The Commission found that "White racism is essentially responsible for the explosive mixture which has been accumulating in our cities since the end of World War II," and that crime, drug addiction, dependency on welfare, and bitterness and resentment against society in general and white society in particular are the result (1968: 1, 203–204).

Today we can conclude that the Commission's prediction is being fulfilled, that the process is being *led* by powerful forces in government, and that it may have, at least temporarily, the support of most white Americans. If this is true, the consequences to the health of the urban minorities and the poor in the 1970s will be the least of many disasters; but they will be disastrous, nonetheless.

The argument may be made at this point that I am being too "political," and that I am discussing politics, social, and racial concerns to the exclusion of health. I can only repeat that it is these "political," "social," and "racial" forces that will determine the conditions of life for the urban minorities and the poor in the 1970s and that the conditions of life will both determine their health and define the problems we will have to confront when we plan policy for health services delivery.

If this picture is correct, then one can make the following predictions about life for the urban minorities and the poor in the remainder of this decade:

1. The white suburban noose around the black, Puerto Rican, and chicano inner city will not only remain, but will be drawn tighter, with even less possibility of outward movement to improved housing or better communities for the expanding nonwhite populations.

2. Within the urban core, there will be a continuing decrease in the absolute amount of available housing, continued deterioration and abandonment of present housing, continuing use of urban renewal as black removal from commercially desirable areas, and continuing failure of federal programs, as exemplified by current policies which—with whatever good intentions—have simply enriched white banks, insurance companies, and real estate speculators, defrauded the poor, and made the Department of Housing and Urban Development one of the major owners of slum and abandoned housing. These trends, occurring simultaneously with continued nonwhite population growth, will result in sharply increased crowding and an even higher percentage of the ghetto population living in substandard, physically and

biologically dangerous housing. The increased population densities will result in secondary failures of supporting environmental services, particularly garbage collection, and will increase rat and insect infestation rates. These forces will exert enormous upward pressure on the infant mortality rate. Further, there is evidence from both animal and human studies to suggest that such sudden increases in population density operate to increase morbidity and mortality from all major disease categories, to decrease social cohesion, and to increase aberrant behavior and mental illness.

3. Inner-city schools will deteriorate still further in consequence of increased population density, a deteriorating physical environment, and increased social disorder. In consequence, the educational deficit of inner-city children will grow.

4. Unemployment—already in excess of 25 percent for young black males in the cities—will increase, during years in which a demographically young black urban population will have increased numbers reaching employment age. Increased capital-intensive spending in the private sector will intensify this trend, as will the flight of industry to the segregated white suburbs. The suburbs will have the jobs, the land, the industries, the tax base to support schools and other services, the wealth, and the whites; the central cities will be black, brown, and broke. Newark now has 16 percent unemployment, the highest percentage of substandard housing of any major northern city—and the highest infant mortality rate.

5. Welfare programs will be continued, since conservatives find even welfare preferable to the costs and social implications of providing nonwhite populations with any opportunity for economic self-sufficiency, but they will continue as at present to be: (a) inadequate to support healthy life, (b) increasingly used as regulators and controllers of the poor, and (c) operated in ways destructive of family and community life.

6. Control of almost all the basic institutions in the ghetto, including the human service institutions, will remain outside the ghetto in most significant respects, even if community control is apparently won over some local schools, hospitals and health centers, since the primary instrument of control—the budget—will remain in "downtown" political and governmental agencies not as susceptible to pressure from the poor and nonwhite.

7. Large-scale violence, demonstrations, and riots in response to these conditions are less likely than during the decade of the '60s, primarily because of the widespread recognition that they would be met by brutal and indiscriminate police and National Guard violence

and repression, with the general support of the dominant culture. Instead, "urban guerrilla" tactics—selective, smaller-scale and symbolic attacks on police and other institutional symbols—are likely to increase, and their occurrence will be used as further justification for repressive measures against "crime" rather than understood as a form of general social protest (which was, at least, understood of the 1960 riots).

8. Since all of these are conditions that breed crime, crime in the ghetto and inner city will increase. As at present, its chief victims will be other blacks.

9. Since these are the conditions that define anomie (social disorganization and normlessness), the drug addiction industry—already one of the largest industries in the United States—will continue to grow, and addiction rates will continue both to rise and to shift toward younger ages of onset.

10. The major social justification for these conditions will be what William Ryan has named and documented (1971) as "blaming the victim." One corollary of this tactic in the health field is already under way—the recent revival of "health education" efforts which implicitly or directly state that the health problems of the poor and the nonwhite are caused primarily by their own alleged apathy, ignorance, and lack of concern, and that if only they can be taught to "live right," save their (hypothetical) money, eat better, make earlier use of the (mythically) available health-care system, and clean up, they would be healthier and happier.

In summary, the predictions of the Kerner Commission have steadily been coming true. The difference is that, in 1968, this seemed to be a source of considerable concern and distress to the federal government and to the white majority; today, it seems to be a goal of federal policy and the overt and hostile hope of many whites.

Four years ago, in arguing that the Columbia Point Neighborhood Health Center (and the neighborhood health center movement in general) *had* to concern itself with these social and environmental issues as well as with the narrower questions of medical care delivery, I wrote (1971:241–250) that

Health action alone is not enough. In the urban crisis, and for the Negro population that is at the center of the urban crisis, it is absolutely clear that the biological, social, economic and political environment of the ghetto is incompatible with healthy life, and no amount of health service as such will alter it . . . To equip a concentration camp with a medical center is not only futile . . . it is an expression of the deepest moral cynicism.

The reference to concentration camps, then, was largely metaphorical. But if the description of our current social and political trends is valid, then the term becomes much more literal. A population living under conditions of physical misery and borderline survival, restricted to defined geographic and social areas with little prospect of mobility, blocked by majority prejudice and majority-sanctioned police power from equal participation in the social order, poorly served by the major institutions of American life and without significant control over its own institutions, with specifically limited personal freedoms and civil rights, with most of its efforts to change its situation (that is, to "escape") labeled "criminal" and used as a justification for still harsher imprisonment—and with all of this sanctioned by allegations of collective worthlessness and innate inferiority—such a population may fairly be described as living in a concentration camp. If the social arrangements are pervasive enough, there do not have to be barbed-wire barriers as a physical fact. Even the symbolic barriers may become internalized by the subject populations, which may indeed be the goal of present policies, just as it was the goal of the slavery and postreconstruction periods in the South.

If this is true, then we can redefine the question asked at this conference and addressed by this paper as follows: "What should be our public policy regarding health-services delivery to the network of concentration camps in which urban minorities and the poor will be living in the 1970s?" And it is against the background of that question that we can survey the present health state of these populations, predict the likely trends and problems in health (the western world, after all, is rich in ghetto and concentration-camp precedents and experience), and plan appropriate strategies.

Before turning to that task, I wish to make one point as emphatically as possible. Nothing in this analysis, nor in those that follow, is intended to suggest that we simply accept this oppression, passively resign ourselves to it, regard it as inevitable and unchangeable, or fail to fight against it—any more than, say, the recognition of the real nature of the National Socialist Party in Germany in the early 1930s constituted a valid reason for all Germans to abandon their resistance to it—nor should it be so interpreted. I am simply arguing, instead, that we use political and social reality as starting points, both for the planning of short-term health strategies and for the planning of ways in which health services can be made part of a larger program of resistance to oppression and movement for change. It is, to my mind, the standard and more academic analysis of health care—the one that merely addresses the technical issues—that inadvertently promotes acceptance of oppression by ignoring the social and political basis of health. It is not the imagery of a political analysis—words like "oppression," "concentration camps" and so on—that is extreme or rhetorical. What is really extreme is the quiet absence of any reference to the social order in most "technical" analyses.

Present health status and health-care problems of urban minorities and the poor. A recent request to the National Library of Medicine for a bibliography on health and poverty yielded a computer-printed list of references that was several inches thick—and covered only the relatively recent literature. There is no need here to review in detail the exhaustive research on this subject. It was summarized a few years ago in three sentences: "The poor are likelier to be sick. The sick are likelier to be poor. Without intervention, the poor grow sicker and the sick grow poorer" (Geiger, 1966b). To this might now be added: "The black, the Puerto Rican, the chicano, the American Indian, and the Chinese American are poorer and sicker than everyone else."

Pettigrew (1964:72–99), Falk (1966:171–177) and numerous others have documented the staggering health deficits that characterize the black population in the United States. Yerby (1966:5) has written eloquently of the process by which the poor are forced to "barter their dignity for their health care," and, with Bergner (1968:541) has described the barriers to health-care utilization that face low-income people. James (1965:1757) examined the shocking excess mortality in black Bedford-Stuyvesant (as compared with middle-class-white Flushing) in New York City. He estimated by extrapolation that the annual *excess* mortality among the poor in New York is 13,000 deaths, and concluded that it is appropriate to state that these deaths "are caused by poverty." The American Public Health Association (1970), the Citizens Board of Inquiry (1971), and the Urban Coalition (1970) have separately reported the details of a fact we have known for decades—that the poor are sick more often, get less health care, and die sooner (in all age groups and from almost all causes) than the more affluent, and that the situation is worst for the nonwhite poor. Weinerman (1968:381), Weiss and Greenlich (1970:456), Nolan (1967:34), and many others have shown the effects of poverty on reduced utilization of medical- and dental-care services. And this is just a small sampling of the relatively recent literature. Essentially, the same findings have been reported for more than fifty years.[3]

3. Perhaps the most adequate brief review was provided a few years ago by an HEW Program Analysis Group on the Delivery of Health Services to the

Poor (1967:3–4). The situation has not changed essentially since then. They reported:

Among persons with family incomes of less than $2,000, about 29 percent have chronic conditions with limitation of activity, as contrasted with less than 7.5 percent among persons with family incomes of $7,000 or more. This is partly a reflection of a greater proportion of aged among the poor. However, even in the age 17–44 group, the poor are affected at twice the rate of the nonpoor, and in the age 45–64 group, the rate is five-and-one-half times greater.

Persons with family income of less than $2,000 have more than double the days of restricted activity per year than persons with an income of $7,000 or more. For males in the working-age group 45–64, the lower-income group has three-and-one-half times as many disability days—49.5 in the under-$2,000-income group, compared to 14.3 in the over-$7,000-income group.

In one year, a larger portion of persons who live in low-income families have multiple hospital episodes than those in higher income groups. The length of hospital stay is longer for the poor (10.2 days for the income group under $2,000, compared to 7.2 days for the income group over $7,000, a relationship which holds for all but the 15–24 age group), and they are more often hospitalized for nonsurgical conditions. This exists in spite of the fact that the poor are much less likely to have hospital insurance to cover the bill.

If nonwhite status is used as a proxy for the poor, the clear health differential, by race, in this country can be interpreted as reflecting the unfavorable health status of the poor. While life expectancy for the newborn has increased significantly since the turn of the century for both white and nonwhite groups, a wide differential still exists (63.6 years for nonwhite versus 70.19 years for the white population).

Maternal mortality rates among nonwhite mothers are approximately four times those among white mothers (in 1965, 90.2 and 22.4 maternal deaths per 100,000 live births, respectively). In infant mortality, a similar trend exists (21.5 deaths per 1,000 live births among white infants, compared to 40.3 among nonwhite infants).

High differentials in nonwhite versus white mortality are found for tuberculosis, influenza, and pneumonia, vascular lesions affecting the central nervous system, and death due to homicide. For each of these, the ratios are greater than 2.1. There is also a higher nonwhite mortality from cancer of the cervix, a neoplasm almost entirely curable with early diagnosis and treatment.

Children under age 15 average two physician visits per year in families with incomes under $2,000, compared to 4.4 in families with incomes over $7,000.

In families with incomes under $4,000, 22 percent have never seen a dentist, as compared to 7.2 percent in families with incomes over $10,000.

22.5 percent of nonwhite children aged one to four have had *no* DPT immunization, compared to 8.6 percent of white children.

The following are a few salient reasons for the poor health status of the low-income population:

1. The current "system" in which the poor receive health services perpetu-

The picture is more vivid—it better connotes the realization that real communities, real people, real illness and death are involved—when it is described on a local level. DeVise and his colleagues, in "Slum Medicine: Apartheid in Chicago Health System" (1969), pointed out that the infant mortality rate in a black-Puerto Rican-poverty area of Chicago was 45.5 per 1,000 live births, more than twice the white nonpoverty rate of 22.2; the postneonatal death rate (deaths per 1,000 survivors to 28 days) was 15.6, more than three times the white rate of 4.9. They found that a map of the high-prevalence and high-incidence areas of tuberculosis was identical with a map of high-poverty areas.

In Washington, the Report of the Mayor's Task Force on Public Health Goals (1970) pointed out the constant association in that city between lower income and higher death rate—and added that the greatest irony is that the relationship of death rates to income is most marked for preventable or treatable causes of death. Thus, the poor in Washington are twice as likely as the rich to die of pneumonia, four times as likely to die of cirrhosis, and *forty* times as likely to die of tuberculosis.

In New York, a series of recent surveys (Stern, 1971:21) note the persistence of preventable diseases among the poor, particularly among children; evidence of malnutrition among the elderly on welfare, of rickets and grossly retarded physical development in low-income children, and suggestions of a vast amount of undiagnosed and unsuspected serious or potentially serious illnesses among the poor. Typically, the infant mortality rate in black Harlem was 200 percent higher than that in white, middle-class Riverdale. An inspection of 2,600 slum apartments showed more than 1,600 with dangerous lead levels—a rate of 62 percent. A study of 15,000 slum children yielded 1,900 cases of lead poisoning, an over-all rate of more than 1 in 8; among black children, the rate among those tested was 1 in 3 (Health Services Administration, 1972).

More than half the black people in the United States are under the age of 25. A sampling of recent data indicates how damaging our

---

ates fragmented emergency-oriented medical care which is often relatively inaccessible in terms of time and location.

2. Despite recent legislation, inability to pay for services remains an important barrier to the poor's quest for health care.

3. Medical facilities and health manpower are particularly scarce in areas with a high concentration of poor.

4. Environmental and nutritional deficiencies (not covered by this analysis) lead to lowered host resistance and greater exposure to health hazards.

social order is to the black community's most important resource, its children. Recent data from the National Center for Health Statistics show that children in the lowest family income group had the highest rate of time lost from school—43 percent higher than the rate for the richest children. Another study from the same source (HEW Publication No. [HSM] 72–1011, 1971) examined the reading and arithmetic skills of a national sample of children aged six to eleven. At six, white-black differences were negligible in both categories; at age eleven, black children suffered a 2.1 grade level deficit in reading and a 1.3 grade level deficit in arithmetic. Even more strongly correlated with the deficits than race was family income.

The damage to children, in fact, begins before they are born. Premature delivery and low birth weight are prime determinants of risk of infant death or impaired health. In this country, the data for decades have shown a higher prematurity rate among poor and black infants. What is perhaps not as well known is that the problem is worsening. From 1950 to 1967, the percentage of premature births among nonwhites *increased* significantly, from 10.2 to 13.6. The increase is *not* due to changes in the age of the mother at birth (HEW Publication No. [HSM] 72–1030, 1972). Of the "nonwhite" group which suffers this higher rate, 90 percent are blacks. Only recently has epidemiologic evidence begun to accumulate which might lead to effective intervention in this problem.

As we have already indicated, the primary causes of these burdens of ill health, increased disability, and excess death must lie in the physical, biological, and social environments. But this does not gainsay the fact that health care *resources* are most lacking for the poor and the urban minorities—the groups in greatest need. Inner-city poor and nonwhite communities desperately lack physicians, dentists and every other category of health personnel; they lack facilities; they lack transportation to get to sources of medical care; they lack access to hospital beds. Over and over again, low-income and nonwhite citizens suffer fragmentation of their health services—well-child care in one place, care for sick infants in another, care of adults at yet another source, in-hospital care unconnected with any of these. For the poor and the nonwhite, the search for medical care is usually a degrading journey through a hostile system, a maze of specialty clinics, an obstacle course of late-night emergency rooms. Most of all, urban minorities and the poor lack the ability to pay—and in this nation, by and large, good medical care is still a commodity, with mark-ups for profit built in, most available to those with money and available at highest quantity and quality to those with the most money—like automobiles, or stocks and bonds. Medicare and Medicaid have improved the picture slightly for the low-income consumer, and enormously for the provider, but *they have accomplished no essential change in the system*. Glazer (1971) and others have recently cited an increased volume of physician visits by the poor, and arrived at the incredible conclusion that income is no longer a significant barrier to access to good health care! What they fail to understand is that increased utilization of an almost hopelessly ineffective system—the inner-city health-care system of aging physicians struggling through high-volume practices without benefit of hospital staff appointments; fragmented and distant outpatient departments; and chaotic emergency rooms trying simultaneously to serve as sources of primary care—is unlikely to accomplish any significant improvement in the health of the poor.

No review of the health and health-care problems of the inner city could be complete, finally, without mention of the drug addiction epidemic which threatens to destroy what is left of the urban minority community and to overwhelm its already overburdened health-care resources. No one really knows the full dimensions of the problem, particularly in school-age populations. One source has recently estimated (Freedman, 1972:1) that in *New York City alone* there are now 400,000 addicts, of whom about 100,000 are under age 20, with an *annual* increment of 30,000 new cases (and treatment programs reaching a grand total of 20,000 cases). If one takes the extremely conservative figure of fifty dollars a day as the average addict's need, then drug addiction in New York alone costs 7.3 *billion* dollars a year. If one assumes, equally conservatively, that New York has only one tenth of the national addict population, then heroin addiction alone (for these figures exclude the estimates for barbiturate, amphetamine, and other addictions) represents an annual national expenditure of 73 billion dollars. It is time we called this by its proper name—the Drug Addiction Industry—and recognized that it is one of the largest industries in the nation, a bright new addition to our Gross National Product. Every ghetto child over the age of five knows that the industry functions exploitatively for the enrichment of police forces (both local and federal), corporate crime syndicates, and local political and judicial machinery controlled by the latter; this is, perhaps, one reason why both local and federal criminal-justice approaches have been so ineffective (there is no shortage of heroin, and its street price does not change in response to widely publicized "crackdowns" and seizures). But medical responses have fared little better; one reason may be the paucity of hard epidemiologic data on prevalence (the New York City estimate quoted above may be an understatement

—or a fourfold overstatement), on age of onset, on the ratio of known cases to total users, on geographic distribution.

Strategies for health-care policy

In the face of all this, what are we to do? Certainly not give up in despair. We recognize that the health crisis and the health-care crisis are part of a larger and worsening social, economic, and political crisis for urban minorities and the poor; but that recognition does not imply acceptance. We cannot merely await the arrival of full "concentration-camp" status, as it has been defined in this paper, and cynically plan health services for it without concerning ourselves with the struggle for larger social change, for a decent and just society. Yet neither can we focus solely on the long-term social, racial, and political campaigns which must be joined, and meanwhile ignore the current human needs, the sickness and death and lack of resources which are a consequence of poverty and racism. We must, if we can, devise a strategy which will at least begin to meet these immediate health and health-care crises—and which will also be a part of, or at least consistent with, a larger social and (if you will) political effort at change in the three environments. And we will have to do this, furthermore, in the full awareness that key measures that are now being proposed—particularly national health insurance —have not been prompted primarily by concern for the needs of urban minorities and the poor, and certainly not by any desire for very fundamental social change. Rather, they are responses to the fact that the white middle class and lower middle class are finding the search for health care (as with other aspects of life) increasingly difficult. (In an analogous way, Medicare finally acquired the political support necessary for legislative approval, not because of concern for the poor, but because the middle class could no longer afford the health-care costs of its elderly parents. Heroin addiction blighted the ghetto for twenty years without arousing the dominant culture's concern—but became a national "crisis" almost overnight when it spread to the middle-class suburbs.) A part of any strategy for urban minorities and the poor, therefore, must be to capitalize on solutions designed primarily for others, and try to use them—for both short-term and long-term purposes—as bases for the development of more significant changes.

Chief among these solutions is national health insurance. Without it, I believe, little real change can be accomplished. With it, we can make a beginning—always keeping in mind, however, that health care alone is *not* the primary pathway to ending the health disasters among the poor.

A great deal depends, of course, on the kind of national health insurance that is approved. The report of the HEW Program Analysis Group cited earlier, was specific in arguing that any plan concentrated primarily on funding mechanisms—pumping money into the existing health care system, without requiring major changes in it— would be almost useless:

> It is strongly felt that support for only the *financing* of health services will guarantee neither improved health status nor equality in the receipt of health services by the poor. Indeed, a substantial increase in demand for services through financing programs without a concomitant increase and redistribution of currently scarce health resources can be expected to lead to inflation of health-care costs and continued inaccessibility to services for many of the poor. Support must be given to improving the organization and delivery of health services for the general population and, particularly at this time, for the poor (1967:2).

In partial recognition of this fact, even the minimal plan of the present administration proposes to foster some reorganization of the system and to emphasize the development of what will be, in effect, prepaid group practices. Such measures might at least make medical care more efficient and less costly than the present combination of fragmentation and fee-for-service. But nothing in such a plan is in itself likely to increase the health-care resources available to the inner city, particularly to increase the supply of physicians and dentists, nor in other ways to equalize the distribution of manpower or facilities between the poor and the affluent. National health insurance would put a floor under the poor and the more affluent alike with regard to health care; it will not narrow the gap between them any more than social security pensions have narrowed the gap between the elderly poor and the elderly middle class. To the extent that influence will still be able to purchase medical care above and beyond the floor of national health insurance, then—as usual—everyone will be equal, but some people will be more equal than others.

It is important, therefore, to work for a form of national health insurance that will provide financing *and* a significant reorganization of the medical-care system (particularly eliminating fee-for-service mechanisms) *and* additional funding and special incentives for health-care programs in minority and poverty areas, with corollary funding for the construction of a whole network of new physical facilities in such inner-city population concentrations.

On the other hand, the health maintenance organization does offer some significant opportunities. Its precursor was the neighborhood health center advanced to, and adopted by, the Office of Economic Opportunity in 1965. That concept, although never fully implemented in any single case, called for the following major changes in the health-care system:

1. A shift in focus and concentration from hospital-based, complex secondary and tertiary care to primary care;

2. A shift in the hub of the health-care universe from the hospital—often outside the community to be served, frequently unresponsive to it, and almost always beyond its effective control—to the neighborhood facility, one that would be *in* the community, *directly* responsive to its particular needs, and *under* its control. This shift is not merely geographic; it involves more than what is usually expressed by "decentralization."

3. A shift in the relationship between neighborhood facility and central hospital—so that it is the latter that is, at last, understood as the "satellite"—less frequently used by most patients, used for limited and special purposes by others—and the neighborhood as the "center," not only of care, but of policymaking;

4. Removal of all the systematic barriers to access to care: transportation, cost, convenience, hours of operation, fragmentation, bureaucratic self-preservation;

5. Community (not just consumer) control, at least of the local and central source of care as a start, rather than provider control;

6. Prepayment on a capitation basis (which is, of course, precisely what OEO funding represented for the population served by the health center);

7. Finally, and most important, the redefinition of medical care as health care, the recognition of the origin of many "medical" problems in the social order, and the inclusion in health-center services of programs designed to deal with the environment, with job training, with housing, with legal service needs, with economic development as related to health—thus providing both an effective base for, and an expression of, full-scale community organization. In effect, the hope was to run the equation backwards: if the social order determines health levels, then why not use health centers to help improve the social order (Geiger and Gibson, 1965; Geiger, 1966b; Geiger, 1971)?

Against the subsequent realities, these 1965 hopes perhaps now seem Utopian; nonetheless, they give some indication of what must be sought for in medical care organization under national health insurance. The possibility of accomplishment will be brighter to the extent that HMO funding and operation depend on the decision of the individual consumer to choose to deliver his nationally-funded health care prepayment or capitation to a particular provider, or of organized groups of consumers in a community to do so. This puts some economic muscle behind the principle of community control, in a way not possible with OEO health centers funded by annual grants from a federal agency and thus really controlled by that agency rather than by consumers. "Choice" is meaningless, however, unless there are resources to choose between.

Urban minorities and the poor must therefore concentrate their efforts on attempting to get HMOs (by this I mean prepaid group practices in health centers in their own neighborhoods) that are locally based and subject to local control; that focus on primary care, while maintaining links to hospitals; that define "health care" in the broadest possible terms, including transportation, training, outreach, and environmental services as an absolute minimum; and that provide the opportunity—for example, through the formation of a wide variety of community corporations—to keep the federal health-care dollar *in* the low-income community and turn it over through *local* medical equipment supply firms, pharmaceutical wholesaling firms, etc. It may be argued that nothing about the provision of health care should be corporate; but until that occurs—if it ever does—the urban minority and poverty communities are entitled to their piece of the action.

(Unfortunately, much of the current thinking about HMOs seems to be aimed not at improving and enlarging health care but rather at cutting costs, to the tune of frightening-sounding predictions as to the total bill. Seventy billion dollars a year is, apparently, a huge amount for health, but a trifle for drug addiction. In any case, it is as nothing compared to the present social costs of neglecting health. The issue here is, of course, one of national priorities. In the same week that a two-billion-dollar-a-year day-care program was vetoed by the President, plans were announced for a fourteen-billion-dollar space shuttle.)

I still believe strongly in the merits of the community-based neighborhood health center; the experience and documented impact during the past five years of nearly 100 such centers, serving more than one million of the poor, justifies that belief. But I must also recognize that—even if progress is made beyond our most optimistic hopes—it is unlikely that such centers, funded through a functioning national health insurance system, can be developed in sufficient numbers to meet most of the needs of the inner city *in this decade*. Particularly in the crucial area of primary care, the hospital emergency room and the hospital outpatient department are now the most important single resource for urban minorities and the poor, and they will continue to be so between now and 1980, regardless of the planned structure of the health-care system thereafter. If we really wish to change the fragmented, episodic, ineffective, and often degrading health-care experience of these groups in this decade, therefore, we will have to do something to help the hospital (particularly the municipal hospital) emergency room and OPD *now,* without abandoning the longer-term strategy of decentralized health-center networks. The poor—and the inner-city hospital—cannot wait, particularly in the face of the acute dangers to health represented by what I have called "concentration camp" status.

Such an interim agenda for immediate action might include the following major features:

1. The categorical funding (by the federal government and *by the suburbs*) of expanded inner-city hospital emergency rooms, to double or triple their staffing and patient capacities. Even more important, the thrust of such funding should be to reorient and reorganize the emergency rooms toward their largest actual function, nonemergent care, without abandoning true trauma and emergency services. Aside from federal monies, the necessary tax revenues can no longer be generated by the cities alone. In this area of municipal services, at least, the tax base must be broadened (on a county or regional basis) to include the wealthier suburbs. Such funding should be devoted not only to expanded physical facilities and staffing for inner-city emergency rooms but also toward the reorganization and rationalization of outpatient departments into multispecialty, primary-care-centered group practices, instead of the present self-serving arrangement of fragmented specialty clinics.

2. A significant proportion of inner-city primary care is now provided by a generally aged, hugely overworked corps of solo practitioners operating, without benefit of hospital staff appointments or paraprofessional assistance, on a fee-for-service basis. The system is costly, ineffective, and of dangerously variable quality. Special incentives *now* might induce such practitioners to move into salaried, prepaid group practices, linked to existing hospitals, and operating primarily on Medicaid and Medicare reimbursements even prior to national health insurance. Such incentives might include *federal* construction of group-practice facilities in ghetto areas, with title vested in community corporations, for lease at nominal rates to such groups; funding for the provision of paraprofessional workers to such groups from hos-

pital payrolls; and links of various sorts to existing municipal hospitals (the technology of multiple-channel cable television, which will be available in the cities in any case, may be particularly suited to this move). Later, under national health insurance, such groups will become neighborhood health centers or HMOs. More important, they may provide an incentive now for the recruitment of newly graduated physicians to the inner city The Martin Luther King Hospital–Charles Drew Postgraduate Center in Watts represents a step in this direction.

3. An *immediate* step can be taken toward the ending of the present double system ("public" and "private-voluntary" hospitals) and its double standard of care by a federal requirement that "private-voluntary" hospitals, as a condition of approval for Medicare or other federal funding of any kind, must provide a defined (and significant) minimum percentage of their ambulatory and in-patient services to indigent patients, rather than "dumping" such patients into the municipal hospital system. The Department of Health, Education and Welfare has recently proposed regulations to this effect, analogous to the Title VI civil rights regulations that were briefly enforced upon private hospitals. They would not bring the end of the dual system, which is the only way to achieve a single standard of care, but they would represent an immediate improvement in the resources available to the inner-city population. As with every other item in this agenda, effective enforcement and action would occur only if reasonable mechanisms for accountability were simultaneously developed.

4. The provision of funding, through local consumer corporations, of some of the current neighborhood free clinics, preferably in network arrangements with hospitals but without destruction of the autonomy of the neighborhood facilities.

5. The development, particularly at municipal hospitals, of modest community-medicine research and planning units for three purposes:

a. The provision of technical assistance to the various neighborhood and community groups comprising the consumer constituencies of the hospital.

b. The development, from patient and community data, of the epidemiologic information on patterns of demography, illness, and utilization, which are the only real basis for the development and evolution of services into a practice of community medicine (as opposed to the mere practice of medicine in a community) that is responsive to the problems of the group or population served.

c. The performance of evaluative, epidemiologic, and cost-benefit studies to determine the real long-term yields of highly specialized services (e.g., coronary care units) on which millions of dollars in equipment and staffing are now invested.

6. Next, efforts at greatly increasing personnel training must continue—but with far greater emphasis on the production of family health workers, physicians' assistants, and nurse-practitioners than on the production of physicians. The former roles, on the evidence from other nations, are more productive and less expensive; furthermore, they are more immediately accessible as career choices to the population most in need, while physician recruitment during the remainder of this decade will remain overwhelmingly a white-upper-middle-class phenomenon. A significant manpower shortage in health and other human services matches significant unemployment among urban minorities and the poor, and they should be put together. No one should urge these populations to settle for a system under which they have all the physicians' assistants and the suburbs have all the physicians; but—despite the understandable suspicions—an effort should be made to change the view that physicians' assistants, nurse-practitioners, and other new professionals represent second-class care rather than the rational system long since adopted by many other nations (with improvement rather than loss of quality). To insist on physicians for tasks that can be done not only more efficiently but with higher quality by others is counter-productive.

7. In view of the data cited earlier, and despite the general truth of the observation that categorical programs are a poor substitute for primary care available to all, I believe the inner city during the 1970s will urgently require special programs for the children who comprise such a very large fraction of the poverty and minority populations, and whose health deficits now begin so early. Every school of significant size should either have its own health facility—and a case can be made, on the basis of the data on learning differentials, that this is essential to effective education—or be linked to an existing full-scale health center. And it is in the primary schools, in particular, that the educational preparation and exposure to a variety of health careers must begin if recruitment into the health professions at

every level is ever to be truly available to significant numbers of the poor and nonwhite.

Finally, it is in the schools—given our present lack of epidemiological knowledge about the origins and distribution of drug addiction and our present inability to offer adequate medical therapy—that we have our best present opportunity to combat the drug-addiction industry.

The key to all these programs is *local accountability* of health services—a process for which the doorway is at least potentially opened by any version of national health insurance funding that would allow groups of consumers—communities, in other words—to organize, effectively pool their funding, and demand at least a share in the control of the programs designed to serve them.

This is, to be sure, hardly what the larger society is likely to have in mind. I am suggesting, however, that the needs for health care—and the prospect of national health insurance—be used as the basis for a massive effort at local community organization (even on a block-by-block basis, if possible) in the inner city, despite the fact that it is other issues—housing, jobs, food, police brutality—that traditionally have served as the best basis for such organization. The reasons for such a community organization concentration on health services are threefold. First, the prospect of an expanded network of local health centers or HMOs means there will be an expanded number of local community organizations which can be used as a focus for organizing people to push for further social change. Secondly, health is a particularly good umbrella for efforts at social change, because it still has the highest sanction in the dominant society and is therefore more difficult to resist. In simpler words, there are undoubtedly large numbers of people in the dominant society who don't give a damn about dead black babies, but even they cannot yet afford to say so publicly—or to fight efforts at change with the same fury they muster over housing or jobs.

But it is the third reason that is most important. Health and health services may be the issue on which at least a beginning can be made in the establishment of a social and political liaison that must be forged if the political power is to be found, not only to support these health services reforms, but also to reverse the accelerating rush toward polarization and apartheid. The liaison is that between the nonwhite poor and the white working poor and lower middle class. These latter groups suffer many of the same hazardous environments; they suffer at least some of the same kinds of economic exploitation, and they have many of the same true enemies—yet it is of course precisely these groups that are the target of massive efforts to convince them that their real enemies are crime, equal rights, blacks and other minority groups, welfare recipients, liberals and radicals, and to lead them down a pseudopopulist path toward the acceptance of further repression. Perhaps a beginning can be made on the relatively neutral issue of health care. To those who are skeptical, I would point to the recent successful effort to organize black and poor white workers together in the pulpwood industry in Mississippi—and if it can be done in Mississippi, it can be done anywhere.

Some of the barriers to this liaison are the fault of liberals and radicals themselves, who have for far too long ignored the needs of the white working poor—or made effective organization and liaison impossible by conspicuously rejecting the values most dearly held by them. Some of the difficulty undoubtedly relates to the fears engendered by the legitimate and long-overdue emergence during the 1960s, of the concepts of black (or Puerto Rican, or chicano, or Indian) power, autonomy, and independent development. No middle-class white can tell either population how this difficulty is to be overcome, but it seems to me that a way must be found both to preserve the movement for minority-group autonomy *and* to emphasize the community of interest between them and working-class whites; and perhaps the campaign for change in the health-care system is the place to begin.

Finally, I would suggest that any effort to improve the lot of the urban minority and poverty populations—in health care, housing, jobs, or other areas—is doomed to failure unless simultaneous efforts are made to improve the social order for the rural poor. The largest single movement of people in the history of this nation—the migration of blacks from the rural south to the northern and western cities—helped to make the urban ghettos what they are today; it occurred first because rural people wanted better jobs and housing and educational opportunities, and later because there was no alternative for pure survival (Newman, 1962). If rural poverty deepens, if mechanization makes even more workers surplus and drives them from the land, if the small towns and small cities continue to be devoid of job opportunities, while the inner cities decay and the suburbs remain all-white islands, then the movement to the cities will accelerate again. No one seeks coercively to block migration, as southern landowners and their state governments conspired coercively to induce it, but tens of thousands of people are entitled to a viable alternative, to the possibility of a decent life where they are, and the future of those now in the cities also now depends, in part, on the provision of that alternative. Some of the roots of what we call the urban crisis are in fact, in the black-Mississippi phrase, "out in the rural."

This is a relatively modest program for the improvement of health-care resources in the inner city—immediately and in the developmental stages of a single-standard national health-care system organized through national health insurance. But even this limited proposal would represent the diversion of funds and resources from services to the middle class and the suburbs—something that seems unlikely.

A few other aspects of this proposal should be mentioned briefly.

First, it does not directly address the issues of black (or Puerto Rican or chicano) separatism versus a continued push for integration by ghetto communities—a question that currently concerns and divides many of them. The health-care system provides a good illustration of some of the practical problems: complete black autonomy in the development of black community institutions is unlikely when (a) the funding and some scarce professional manpower must, of necessity, currently come from outside the impoverished community, and (b) there is no national commitment to a general principle of control by consumers, quite aside from questions of race or income. The present proposal does emphasize local control and local autonomy and in particular suggests that federal fiscal enfranchisement of the consumer for his health care does offer the possibility of such consumers organizing themselves as community groups.

Second, these proposals do not address the issue of radical political change (neither, on the other hand, would they await that day to have effect). As such, they are likely to be attacked in some quarters as liberal diversions from the true tasks of changing the whole system. Such criticisms, however, are rarely accompanied by effective proposals to do anything that could meet the desperate needs of those who suffer *now*; this is what I have called the dilemma of human versus political priorities. The masses in ghetto and inner-city communities have in fact been much more interested in what can be done to meet their needs *now* than in political abstractions favored by those who usually hurt less. As the people closest to the issue of pure survival, moreover, they have been quickest to recognize that meeting some real needs is the quickest way to organize a community base for further action, and that—far from being pacificatory— such steps create rising expectations and rising demands. The task is to devise first steps that can be accomplished now, that will not be mere missionary or charitable palliation, and that will help to move in the direction of further change. That may happen if, in that process, emphasis is placed on the development of true community participation through freely chosen representatives of the mass of consumers, rather than through self-identified and self-selected "community representatives" from among the elite.

Finally, I would point out again that these proposals would have at best a modest impact on the health of urban minorities and the poor in this decade; they are designed simply to minimize the losses that will result from our present social, political and economic policies. Even the full-scale evolution of a national health-care system will do little to reduce the health gaps between the nonwhite, the poor, and the rest of affluent America. Only major changes in income distribution and the distribution of power and resources—in short, basic changes in the social order—can do that.

REFERENCES

American Public Health Association.
  1970 "Health Crisis in America." New York.
Bergner, Lawrence, and Alonzo S. Yerby.
  1968 "Low Income and Barriers to Use of Health Services." *New England Journal of Medicine* 278:541–546.
Citizens Board of Inquiry into Health Services for Americans.
  1971 "Heal Thyself." Washington, D.C.
DeVise, Pierre, et al.
  1969 "Slum Medicine: Apartheid in Chicago Health System." Community and Family Studies Center. Chicago: University of Chicago.
Ernle, R. E. P.
  1919 *English Farming, Past and Present*. London: Longmans Green.
Falk, Leslie.
  1966 "The Negro American's Health and the Medical Committee for Human Rights." Medical Care 4, No. 3 (July–September), 171–177.
Freedman, Alfred.
  1972 Hospital Tribune 6, No. 4 (February 21).
Geiger, H. Jack.
  1966a *Progress Report to the Office of Economic Opportunity*. Boston: Tufts University School of Medicine, Department of Preventive Medicine.
_____.
  1966b "The Poor and the Professional: Who Takes the Handle Off the Broad Street Pump?" San Francisco: 94th Annual Meeting of the American Public Health Association, November 1.
_____.
  1968 "Health and Social Change: The Urban Crisis," The Lowell Lecture, February 13, 1968. Reprinted in *Metropolis in Crisis: Social and Political Perspectives* (2nd edition), edited by J. K. Hadden and F. E. Peacock. Springfield: pp. 241–250.

————.
1971   "Progress Report: Building a Program, Creating a Community Institu-
       tion." Mound Bayou, Mississippi: North Bolivar County Health Council,
       Inc. January. Mimeographed.
Geiger, H. Jack, and Count D. Gibson.
1965   *Proposal to the Office of Economic Opportunity.* Tufts University
       School of Medicine, Department of Preventive Medicine, Boston.
       March 1965. Mimeographed.
Glazer, Nathan.
1971   "Paradoxes of Health Care." *The Public Interest,* No. 22 (Winter
       1971): 62–77.
Harris, Richard.
1972   "The New Justice." *The New Yorker,* March 25.
Health Services Administration.
1972   *Newsletter.* City of New York: Health Services Administration, Feb-
       ruary.
Hutchinson, J.
1966   "Land and Human Populations." *Listener,* September 1.
James, George.
1965   "Poverty as an Obstacle to Health Progress in Our Cities." *American
       Journal of Public Health* 55.
Kafka, Franz.
1971   "Before the Law." In *Franz Kafka: The Complete Stories,* edited by
       Nathan N. Glazer. New York: Shocken Books.
McDermott, Walsh.
1969   "Demography, Culture and Economics and the Evolutionary Stages of
       Medicine." In *Human Ecology and Public Health* (4th edition). New
       York: Macmillan.
McKeown, Thomas.
1971   "A Historical Appraisal of the Medical Task." In *Medical History and
       Medical Care.* London: Oxford University Press.
McKeown, T., and R. G. Record.
1962   "Reasons for the Decline of Mortality in England and Wales During
       the 19th Century." *Population Studies* 16 (November).
National Advisory Commission on Civil Disorders.
1968   *Report.* Washington, D.C.: U.S. Government Printing Office.
Newman, Dorothy K.
1962   "The Negro's Journey to the City." *Monthly Labor Review* 88, No. 5
       (May).
Nolan, R.
1967   "Social Class Differences in Utilization in a Pediatric Clinic." *American
       Journal of Public Health* 57.
Pettigrew, Thomas.
1964   *A Profile of the Negro American.* New York: Van Nostrand.

————.
1970   *Report of the Mayor's Task Force on Public Health Goals.* Washing-
       ton, D.C.
Ryan, William.
1971   *Blaming the Victim.* New York: Pantheon Books, Random House.

Simon, John, editor.

1887   *Public Health Reports.* London: J. & A. Churchill. Published by the Sanitary Institute of Great Britain. Vol. I, 1887.

Stern, Michael.

1971   In New York *Times,* May 31, 1971.

U.S. Department of Health, Education, and Welfare.

1967   "Delivery of Health Services for the Poor." Office of the Assistant Secretary (Planning and Evaluation). Washington: U.S. Government Printing Office, December.

———.

1971   "School Achievement of Children by Demographic and Socioeconomic Factors." *Vital and Health Statistics,* Series 11, No. 109, HEW Publication No. (HSM) 72–1011, November.

———.

1972   "Trends in 'Prematurity', United States: 1950–67." *Vital and Health Statistics,* Series 3, No. 15, HEW Publication No. (HSM) 72–1030, January.

Urban Coalition.

1970   "Rx for Action." Washington.

Weinerman, R., *et al.*

1968   "Social Class and Medical Care: Emergency Room Services." *Medical Care* 6.

Weiss, E., and M. Greenlich.

1970   "Effect of Social Class on Utilization." *Medical Care* 8.

Yerby, A.

1966   "The Disadvantaged and Medical Care." *American Journal of Public Health* 56.

Housing Problems of Minorities: Policy Considerations

A national perspective

BY the year 2000, less than thirty years from now, America will be a nation of some 300 million persons. If our present response to the nation's housing and urban growth problems continues, we can expect a serious decline in the quality of life for all Americans.

Americans have become an urban people, and have exhibited an increasing preference for living within metropolitan areas. Since 1900, our population has increased by more than 100 percent, while the number of persons living in metropolitan areas has increased by more than 350 percent. In contrast to earlier times, most of our recent metropolitan growth has occurred, not in the central cities, but in the suburban rings. Between 1960 and 1970, population in the central cities grew about 1.3 percent. The population in suburban rings, however, increased by more than 33 percent. Indeed, by 1970, the central cities had replaced nonmetropolitan areas as the slowest-growing parts of the country. The fact that 70 percent of the country's population lives on about 1 percent of our total land area testifies to the fact that our patterns of growth have not been rational. The primary tools used to control the use of land are zoning and subdivision regulations. These tools, however adequate when first initiated, have long since outlived their usefulness and now stand as the primary barriers to orderly urban growth and the provision of decent housing for all Americans. Local governments have shown themselves incapable of coping with present realities.

The private sector has also failed us. Even when given legislative inducements and tax shelter, private builders have tended to maximize their subsystem at the expense of the total system of housing delivery. Present legislative tools are designed more for the needs of special interests than for those of the consuming public in the federally supported housing-delivery system. Banks, builders, speculators, and investors in the 50-percent-tax bracket seem to be the chief beneficiaries under present legislation. Housing costs are not really lessened for the ultimate consumers. What actually occurs is that families are allowed enough in subsidy to pay the increased costs of housing—a benefit that runs primarily to those who either have access to, or control, the flow of investment capital. The housing-delivery system is not really an industry at all, but rather many subindustries, combined in a grossly inefficient manner.

Of all the elements which influence construction cost, location, and orderly urban growth, the one element which stands out as the key is *land*. It is for that reason that one of my chief recommendations focuses on land.

At present, we are continuing on a path that will ultimately lead to complete stratification of our society along racial and economic lines. The visible manifestation of this stratification is, and will increasingly be, segregated residential patterns, but the malaise does not end there. The impact of continuing in our present rut goes far beyond the smaller question of racial segregation of communities and extends into vital indices of the quality of life. Where and how one lives affects where his children go to school and what kind of education they receive in preparation of life. These questions affect our perception of other racial, ethnic, and income groups. The quality of public services one receives is in large measure a function of where one lives. Access to such fundamental amenities as shopping and recreational facilities is affected by where one lives. It is increasingly clear that the relationship between home location and job location can cause hardship and loss of economic opportunity. In all the above areas, and many more, the quality of life of Americans is profoundly affected by their housing conditions. Minorities and poor persons continue to suffer disproportionately in this situation. What is generally not comprehended is that the rest of the nation also loses by our present system of allocating housing resources. The artificially imposed restraints of race and income have trapped minorities and low-income groups in the inner city and have occasioned the overconcentration of problems in the inner city which, in their cumulative impact, threaten the orderly governance of most of our major cities. No one really gains under the present system, and we all stand to lose much more by it. Under present conditions, most Americans find it difficult, if not impossible, to obtain decent housing at prices they can afford. In this context, individual families seek to gain relative advantage without much concern for improving the over-all housing picture. Vested interest groups vie in the political arena for laws and regulations which favor their clienteles. Minorities and low-income persons have exercised less power in the political process and, hence, walk away from the political table with less than most other groups.

Status of housing in the United States, 1972

Few would quarrel with the statement that this country is presently in the midst of a serious housing crisis. Current rhetoric, however, would have us believe that the magnitude of the crisis has diminished during the past decade due to greater efforts on the part of local governments and the implementation of various statutory provisions incorporated in the Housing Acts of 1949, 1965, 1968, and 1970. It is true that the number and percentage of substandard units has been reduced from close to 15 million units in 1950 to approximately 7 million units at this time, but it is seldom pointed out that this aggregate decline can be attributed, for the most part, to the up-grading of nondilapidated units via the installation of adequate plumbing facilities. Indeed, the fact that 75 percent of the replaced or repaired substandard units were located in areas outside of SMSAs (Standard Metropolitan Statistical Areas) suggests that little has been done to attack the problem of inner city blight and decay (Report of the President's Committee on Urban Housing, 1967:26–28).

We must also question the applicability of housing quality criteria utilized by the federal government to the conditions present in central cities. More specifically, census enumerators place units without private toilets, bathtubs or showers, or piped hot water in the substandard category, but rarely is there an investigation made of the operational characteristics of the total plumbing system. (This applies equally to heating and electrical systems.)

Large-scale, multifamily structures do not easily lend themselves to census-defined quality categorization. It is not inconceivable that a substantial number of multifamily units are functionally substandard but have never been enumerated or categorized as such. In summary, despite percentages and numerical declines, a thorough analysis would clearly indicate that no significant progress has been made in approaching the goal of a decent home for every American household.

In answer to persisting conditions of housing dilapidation and decay, the federal government has embarked upon a program to add approximately 26 million new or rehabilitated housing units to the total supply by 1978. To achieve the goals outlined in this program, the annual rate of housing production would have to double that achieved since the Housing Act of 1949 and be 42 percent higher than that accomplished in any single year prior to 1969. It would also be necessary to increase the annual output of subsidized housing for low- and middle-income families. The present rate of production nationally is approximately 2.0 million units total, subsidized and unsubsidized, measured against an annualized goal of 2.6 million for the decade. These goals are admirable, but the programmed production, as large as it might be, is not geared to the reality of the situation that confronts us. To illustrate, all administration figures are based on the conditions enumerated in the 1960 census. It has been stated (U.S. Bureau of the Census, 1967:I, 5) that "The 1960 census evaluation program indicated that dilapidated housing in the United States, as determined by the 1960 census, *is understated by at least one third*." Thus, a more realistic estimate of dilapidated housing conditions in the year of enumeration would be close to 2.5 million units, rather than the original figure of 1.87 million. Furthermore, in considering the nation's needs over the decade 1968–1978, the estimators failed to include in their forecasts a figure to compensate for the significant number of deteriorating units with all plumbing facilities that existed at that time. If such units were included in the original calculations, the nation would be faced with the task of either replacing or rehabilitating 15 million or more deteriorating and dilapidated units. If we add to this figure the estimated number of new household formations for the decade, the total need approaches 29 million units—fully 3 million units above the current goal. The unacceptability of the current estimate is heightened by the fact that the base figure of 29 million does not include an allowance for demolitions, conversions, and mergers or an increase in vacancies. Therefore, to achieve the goal of a decent home, the original estimate should be revised upward by almost 10 million units. It should also be stated that incorporated in the administration's production goals are four million mobile homes. We must view the recent insertion of such units with a great deal of skepticism.

How do the above goals relate to the needs of blacks and other members of the minority community? First, there is some evidence that members of a minority group require one third more in annual income than whites to achieve a standard rental housing unit (Haugen and Heins, 1969:660–672; Rapkin, 1966:333–345). Yet, each year, some minority-group members fall deeper into poverty. It is true that substantial income gains have been made in the past few years, but these gains have been far from evenly distributed. In the poorest ghetto communities, we have a crisis situation. Thus, in areas such as Watts and Hough, poverty has actually increased and family income has not risen at all (U.S. Dept. of Commerce, 1965). Even for those capable of escaping from the state-of-emergency areas, the situation is far from acceptable. In 1970, a black college graduate still had a median income below that of a white high school graduate, and while the white unemployment rate stood at 4.5 percent, nonwhite unemployment was 8.2 percent, almost double. In the 19-to-25 age group, nonwhite unemployment remains a staggering 24 percent.[1]

The Kaiser Commission has estimated that, by 1978, one in four nonwhite families will need housing assistance, and yet the goals legislated by Congress call for the production of only six million new or rehabilitated subsidized housing units within the ten-year period 1968–1978. Such a figure is not only 1.8 million units less than the amount calculated by the Kaiser Commission, but also totally inadequate when we consider that approximately 60 percent of all American households are unable to afford the price of a new unsubsidized housing unit (Welfeld, 1970:37–38).

The number of blacks living within the suburban rings of all metropolitan areas of the country remained at a relatively static 4 percent from 1960 to 1970, but during the same period the percentage of blacks inhabiting the central cities of our metropolitan areas increased from 16 percent to 20 percent. Ten percent or more of the black households in central cities in 1968 occupied housing units that were either dilapidated or lacked basic plumbing facilities. This was nearly three times the rate for white central-city inhabitants. Furthermore, as the distance from the central city increases, the percentage of substandard housing units occupied by blacks also increases. In 1968, sixteen percent of the housing units occupied by blacks in the suburban rings were substandard. The percentage rose to 56 in areas outside of SMSAs. The homeownership-to-rental ratio continues to show a disparity between whites and nonwhites. During the period 1960–1970, the relation improved slightly.

TABLE 1

	White Owner-Occupied	Rental	Nonwhite Owner-Occupied	Rental
1960	64%	36%	38%	62%
1970	65%	35%	42%	58%

1. Statement by Conrad Taeuber, Associate Director, Bureau of the Census, before the House Committee on Banking and Currency, June 3, 1969.

In summary, the disparity index for nonwhite households is uniformly high in all geographic subdivisions of the United States.[2] In New York City, nonwhite households typically pay more than their white counterparts for far inferior accommodations. In areas such as Cleveland, Chicago, Baltimore, Washington, D.C., and Los Angeles, they are compressed in those sections of the city with the oldest and worst housing stock. And in smaller cities such as Memphis, Raleigh, and Shreveport, the historic pattern of residential segregation has been increased so that, in these and other areas, more than 75 percent of the black population lives in census tracts that are populated almost exclusively by blacks.

Housing and urban development programs

Taken as a whole, housing legislation over the last thirty-five years stands as one of our national failures. It has been a failure because it has not substantially effected a solution to the nation's housing problems, problems which have worsened in many respects. No one who is familiar with this nation's vast material, technological, and human resources can deny that we have always had the potential for solving our housing crisis. Some observers cite the magnitude and complexity of our housing problems involving billions of dollars, years of concentrated effort and the co-operation of all levels of government and private enterprise. Anyone familiar, however, with the Marshall Plan, which gave billions to Europeans to rebuild Europe's cities, certainly is entitled to be less than impressed with such an argument. Anyone vaguely familiar with the space effort, or any of a dozen or more such national efforts, which required the co-ordination of private and public efforts, knows that this nation can solve problems even of the magnitude of our housing problem. The failure, then, stems from something other than physical resources.

Legislative attempts have failed for several reasons. Chief among them are failures of commitments on the parts of both the private sector and government. The private sector functions on the basis of anticipated profits. In many instances, the private-profit motive has been mitigated by an enlightened self-interest which caused builders and financial concerns to view the larger needs of the nation. Unfortunately, those elements within the housing system which have had the sensitivity and insight to comprehend that their own best in-

2. The disparity index is explained in the Report of the President's Committee on Urban Housing, Volume I, Housing Needs, p. 55.

terests are best served by meeting the housing needs of all American families have not predominated. In the aggregate, the construction industry (a loose alliance of land developers and building contractors), organized labor, and financial institutions have not acted, either as individual components of the "housing system" or in concert with other elements, to offer all or even most Americans a meaningful and equal chance to acquire decent housing. Each part of the total housing system has acted as a subsystem that has sought to maximize its success at the expense and to the exclusion of other subsystems and, most importantly, to the detriment of the nation's over-all housing-delivery system.

It should be clear, however, that many elements of our society other than builders, organized labor, and financial institutions have contributed to the present morass in housing. This is especially true if one understands that the crisis goes far beyond an artificially contrived short supply of housing. It became apparent more than half a century ago that the private sector, left to its own devices, would not solve the nation's housing problems. Government entered the picture; first, local governments, chiefly through restrictive zoning, artificially excluded "undesirable" elements of society to "protect" their white oases from poor and black families.

The aftereffects of the national depression prompted government at the federal and state level to play greater roles in housing. Federal legislation, for example, provided mortgage money for middle-income families with a very low downpayment. The return of thousands of GIs after World War II was a further stimulus to federal involvement. In most instances, the federal legislation has either failed to work, has worked in unexpected ways, or has worked with very modest success. In the case of FHA mortgages, for example, 30 million American families were assisted in purchasing homes. It is clear now that these families, predominantly white and middle class, were assisted in fleeing the inner city, with its black and poor, to the white suburbs, from which they excluded the black and the poor. This same observation applies with equal force to every major federal program in housing.

All of this was accomplished with federal subsidy and assistance. In the case of urban renewal, funds actually went unclaimed for years because white builders, faced with the option of building on inner-city land purchased at reduced prices and generating only modest profits, chose to build in the suburbs. In many cases, cities diverted much of their urban renewal effort to so-called central business districts, to revitalize decaying commercial cores with federal funds.

As a result of the urban renewal experience taken as a whole, hundreds of thousands of black and poor families were pushed out, never to return. On balance, urban renewal has not helped the minorities and poor of our inner cities.

As a solution to the nation's housing problems, the low-income housing program commonly known as "public housing," whereby the federal government has provided financing to local government agencies to construct and manage low-cost rental housing, has had mixed success and failure. Although it has been the only solution available for approximately 3.5 million eligible families and individuals, only a million such units have been built since the beginning of the program in 1937. Further, public housing tends increasingly to be concentrated in relatively few localities because local housing agencies must be authorized to build by local governments. Local governmental approval has politicized the process adversely. It is readily apparent on even casual examination that there are location patterns for the building of public housing. These patterns affect the quality of life for those who must live in "projects" because the poor lack the resources to obtain either private housing or even the subsidized housing built for those with slightly higher incomes.

The usual configuration for public housing is that the developments are either all white or all black. In most cities with sizable minority populations, public housing sites are invariably the worst sites possible. This is true primarily because the political process of site selection permits local residents to object and to block the building of public housing in their communities. Most white communities are hostile to public housing, and politicians at the local level are acutely aware of this. They usually wind up taking the course of least resistance and choose sites in the center city, frequently on clear urban-renewal land.

Such a site often foredooms the development by placing it in an unworkable community configuration. In all too many instances, health, day care, recreational, and shopping facilities are inadequate or completely lacking. Frequently, the development causes further racial impaction and concentrates families with severe problems. Lack of pride in defaced buildings and lack of enlightened management often lead to vandalism by persons, usually teenagers, living in the building.

Problems of the surrounding community also enter into the calculation of the effect of site location. Much public housing is built in the heart of existing black ghettos. We have already indicated the almost universal hostility of white communities to public housing. Conversely, black communities, with little or no say in the political process, get public housing in their neighborhoods whether they want it or not. The net effect has often been a compounding of the problems of the ghetto rather than a solution to the housing problem of a given community. Vandalism from outside the development frequently gives the developments a "war-torn" look. Add to this the aesthetic bleakness of most public housing and the problems of security, and one can begin to understand how we got the concentration camps known as Pruitt Igoe in St. Louis or Robert Walker Houses in Chicago.

The net effect of the public housing programs, when seen in the above light, has been further to trap poor and minority families into a life style more appropriate to a prison than to a home. These bleak, dreary structures stigmatize the families living in them, because white society generally regards them as residential cesspools seething with everything loathsome and distasteful. Perhaps the most damning comment on the failure of public housing is that even poor black families regard public housing as a place of last resort. The program has come full cycle, and we now find public housing being bulldozed down in a number of cities. On balance, public housing has created more problems than it has solved. Its only justification is that it provided shelter.

After public housing and urban renewal, Congress, in its wisdom, passed legislation beginning in 1964 that introduced the concept of "interest subsidy." Under these programs, the federal government subsidized the cost of housing by paying some of the interest on the mortgage. In the 221(d) (3) BMIR (below-market-interest-rate) program, government paid the interest on mortgages for moderate-income housing down to 3 percent. Later programs such as 235 and 236 provided subsidies on interest which brought the final mortgage down to as little as 1 percent. These programs have created as many problems as they solved. Approximately 241,000 units of 235 (single-family) units have been built (or rehabilitated) since the inception of this program, and 176,000 of 236 (multiple units) have been built. Unfortunately, most of the families served by these programs were middle-income, and the majority of these families were white. Abuses in the program began on Day One. They reached the level of a public scandal and caused the loss, through foreclosure, of hundreds of thousands of dollars from the FHA Special Risk Insurance Fund and have defeated tens of thousands of families in their quest for better housing. Many of these abuses could have been mitigated or even eliminated by counseling and by enlightened administration of these programs. The real problem, however, is much more fundamental. The real problem is that the legislation is structurally unworkable if our goal is to provide sound housing for persons of low and moderate income. It was inevitable that private interests, such as builders and brokers, would take advantage of the programs, to the detriment of individual families.

It should be clear, at this late date, that the federal government has been long on rhetoric and short on actual commitment. This can be seen in inadequate authorizations and even more so in the gap between authorizations and appropriations. The problem further degenerated with the creation of a fourth branch of government (not provided for by the Constitution) known appropriately as the TOMB (The Office of Management and Budget), a place where things are buried. This adjunct of the executive branch was created by an executive order to perform the administrative function necessary for orderly budget planning and control of disbursements, presumably to insure that money disbursed would not exceed money available to the federal treasury. However, these functions have expanded under the present administration to the point where TOMB has, in effect, the power to thwart completely the explicit intent of Congress. In March of 1971, it was estimated that TOMB had impounded 700 million dollars of funds authorized and appropriated by Congress for community development programs. This action amounts to an unconstitutional usurpation of power in clear contradiction of the "separation-of-powers" doctrine.

Congress must take the blame for its failure to preserve its prerogatives, but the people of this nation suffer the burden of this breakdown of our federal system. This phenomenon is explained in large part as symptomatic of a deeper malaise. Our nation has never reached consensus on whether government really belongs in housing and, if so, to what extent, in what manner, and for what purpose. Programs in the 1930s, for example, were designed more to provide jobs than to build housing. The federal government has historically acted in response to existing conditions and with rare exceptions has never passed bold, innovative housing legislation which dealt either with the fundamentals of housing economics, production, or marketing, or with a long-range solution of our housing problems. Only after years of neglect by the building industry of the moderate-cost housing needs of the nation did the federal government react with subsidy programs designed to supplement the difference between what a family could afford and what decent housing cost. If we assume that which we have a right to assume—that American families were the intended beneficiaries of these supplement programs—it is ironic that just about everyone but the individual family benefits from the supplements. Existing federal subsidies tend artificially to perpetuate housing which most Americans cannot afford.

Actually, 60 percent of American families cannot afford to purchase the unsubsidized single-family homes being built at present. Federal figures indicate that median family income for whites is $10,236, but that the average cost of a three-bedroom single-family home exceeds $28,000. This predicament is even worse for black families, who have a median family income of only $6,279, a mere 61 percent of what white families earn. This means that more than 88 percent of non-white families are unable to purchase new unsubsidized housing being built now. It should also be clear that millions of white families earn considerably less than the national median family income and that 3.7 million whites live in poverty.

It is evident now that existing federal legislation will not be funded at the appropriately high levels necessary to affect our national housing crisis significantly. Furthermore, even if authorizations and appropriations were geometrically increased, there is little reason to believe that our short-range goals of adequate supply would be reached, and no reason whatever to believe that our long-range goals would be achieved. It is not a record that our nation or Congress can boast about. It is, in fact, a bleak and pitiful performance that stands in stark contrast to our traditional ability to deal imaginatively with difficult national problems.

The dynamics of minority housing conditions

In any one year, new construction amounts to approximately 2 percent or less of existing supply. This new supply, according to accepted economic theory, is supposed to generate a chain of moves in a housing market that results in lower-income households upgrading their conditions by replacing wealthier families who occupy the new units. This, in a simplified version, is a model of the "filtering process." Now, since black families, in general, have lower incomes than white households, they are almost totally dependent upon the existing stock to supply them with decent accommodations at a price they can afford. The proper operation of the filtering process can improve their conditions, but for this to occur, not only must there be an acceptable level of new construction; there also must be a high level of maintenance in the existing inventory. If maintenance practices are less than acceptable, most of the benefits (in the form of upgrading) that would normally accrue to lower income households never materialize. In most central cities, the housing stock has not been well maintained.

In absolute terms, there was virtually no change in the total volume
of new privately financed construction within metropolitan areas from
the 1950s to the 1960s. In each decade, approximately 11 million units
were built within SMSAs. In fact, privately financed new starts in the
period 1960–1970 were higher in relation to net growth in metropolitan
area households than they had been in the 1950–1960 period. This
was due to the fact that, from 1960 to 1970, central cities experienced
an absolute decline in the number of white households that was not
compensated for by a concomitant growth in black households. Re-
membering that new construction persisted at a high level during the
decade of the '60s, we should have seen extensive filtering, upgrading,
and increasing vacancy rates.

However, the data suggest otherwise. Table 2 indicates that the

TABLE 2

TREND IN RENTAL VACANCY RATES FOR RENTAL UNITS
WITHIN METROPOLITAN AREAS, 1956 TO 1970

Inside SMSAs

	Total	In Central Cities	Outside Central Cities
1950	2.8%	NA*%	NA%
1956	4.5	NA	NA
1957	4.0	NA	NA
1958	4.7	NA	NA
1959	5.0	NA	NA
1960	6.5	NA	NA
1961	7.0	NA	NA
1962	6.9	NA	NA
1963	7.3	NA	NA
1964	7.5	NA	NA
1965	7.4	7.4	7.4
1966	6.5	6.5	6.4
1967	5.5	5.7	5.2
1968	4.8	5.1	4.2
1969	4.0	4.7	3.8
1970	4.6	4.9	4.1

SOURCE: 1950 date from U.S. Bureau of the Census. *U.S. Census of Housing:
1950. Vol. 1, General Characteristics,* Chapter 1, U.S. Summary. U.S. Government Printing Office, Washington, D.C., 1963; 1956–1970 data from U.S. Bureau
of the Census, *Current Housing Reports,* Series H-111, No. 63, Part 2, "Vacancy
Rates and Characteristics of Housing in the United States: Annual Statistics
1970," U.S. Government Printing Office, Washington, D.C., 1971.
* Not Available.

vacancy rate for rental units within metropolitan areas has been declining since 1965. Within all central cities, the rate was 7.4 percent in 1965 and 4.9 percent in 1970.

For certain central cities, the decline in vacancy rates was even more precipitous. In Los Angeles, the decline from 1960 to 1970 was 4.5 percent. In Detroit, during the same period, it was 7.7 percent, and in Philadelphia, 4.4 percent. In New York City, during the 1960s,

TABLE 3

HOUSING ABANDONMENT LEVELS NATIONALLY IN 1971

City & Location	Total Number	Dwelling Units No. Abandoned	Percent Abandoned
Northeast			
Paterson, N.J.	49,335	18,119	36.6
Utica, N.Y.	32,770	9,820	28.0
Allegheny County, Pa.	533,196	13,380*	2.5
Baltimore, Md.	305,464	10,000	3.2
Erie, Pa.	42,677	4,743	11.0
Monessen, Pa.	5,320	165	3.1
Philadelphia, Pa.	673,390	23,833*	3.5
Southeast			
Jacksonville, Fla.	174,189	15,000	8.6
Owensboro, Ky.	16,927	666	3.9
Winston-Salem, N.C.	44,899	1,850	4.1
Midwest			
Cincinnati, Ohio	172,000	4,500	2.6
Toledo, Ohio	121,000	9,100	7.5
Joplin, Mo.	15,934	360	2.2
St. Louis, Mo.	238,441	9,000	3.7
Southwest			
Oklahoma City, Okla.	138,378	6,000	4.3
Tucson Ariz.	89,256	9,400	10.5
West Coast			
Oakland, Calif.	147,000	5,738	3.9
San Jose, Calif.	150,211	17,069	11.3
Portland, Ore.	152,043	4,550*	2.9

SOURCE: Philip Friedly, "Experimental Approaches to the Amelioration of Housing Abandonment and Neighborhood Decline," *Proceedings of the American Real Estate and Urban Economics Association*, VI, 1971 edited by Norbert J. Stefaniak and Byrl N. Boyce, p. 151.

* This figure represents number of buildings and is a better approximation of number of dwelling units the lower is the housing density, i.e., the closer it conforms to single-family dwellings.

where more dwelling units were added to the existing housing supply than in any other ten-year period since the early years of the twentieth century, the rental vacancy rate dropped by .7 percent to a meaningless 1.5 percent.

With fewer households to house and more units to do the job, one would expect a very flexible and loose market. The key to this paradox lies in the startling level of abandonment that has become visible in many of our older central cities. In New York City, for example, enough housing was abandoned during the 1960s to accommodate every household in the state of Wyoming. In addition, I should note that abandonment is not a problem that is exclusive to cities such as New York. As Table 3 suggests, smaller cities spread throughout the country are struggling with the same problem.

The continued appearance of abandonment on the urban landscape suggests that the real estate and financial institutions which traditionally collaborate in owning, managing, and financing housing stock in the central city—particularly those which are concerned with rental housing in the black submarket—are not operating in a manner which preserves sound housing. The question is whether or not their problems are structural in nature. If, as seems to be the case, they are structural, then our future housing policies must reflect that understanding. Present programs of rehabilitation, code enforcement, and urban renewal have had an insignificant impact on these problems. It should be clear that the problem of losing sound housing in the inner city is fundamental and hence requires a more fundamental solution. What most real estate economists fail or refuse to understand is that racism is a structural part of housing economics. No student of the subject will deny that there is an economic and even a class aspect as to who gets what and why in the housing market, but failure to recognize the racial psychology of those who operate, control, own, finance, and manage center-city property is a myopia with dangerous consequences.

Recommendations

In order to solve our housing problems, we must recognize as national goals the need for sound housing, in adequate supply, at a price which families can afford, and available equally to all persons regardless of race or income. This should occur in the context of orderly urban growth and as part of a national plan. We need an entirely new legislative approach. Such an approach must be geared to the reality that orderly urban growth and sufficient amounts of decent housing cannot occur under our present system. We need a national land use and urban growth policy, with an effectively organized and funded agency empowered to plan and implement it.

We must also abandon our indirect, complex, and largely ineffective approach in favor of one which places the problem in its true, national perspective. We must recognize the futility of dealing with individual units of government which lack the resources, the willingness, or even the comprehension of the problem of urban growth. There are thousands of overlapping, competitive, narrowly provincial, and even hostile jurisdictions which are unwilling to deal with such problems as decent housing for poor and low-income families. These smaller jurisdictions are the least logical place for decisions of such national import. We need to view land as a national resource and devise an effective system for allocating that national resource. I am not suggesting that all land be removed from the private market. On the contrary, I am suggesting that a small percent of total land capable of being developed be set aside for the planned use of land for urban growth and that such land be acquired in advance of need. Such a land-banking phenomenon could have the greatest impact in less developed areas standing in the line of potential urban growth.

By rationally planning the improvement and development which must inevitably occur, we could maximize the opportunities to create sound and balanced communities and to adjust the competing needs for residential, commercial, and industrial uses. History tells us that the use of land as an instrument of national policy is not new. The federal government is already one of the largest landholders in the nation. Land has been set aside for defense, parks, and other federal needs. Land has been regulated, sold, and even given away by the federal government for homesteaders and railroads, for example. And the power to acquire land through eminent domain for public uses is well established.

Under present speculative policies, the price of land increases at an average of 15 percent a year, a cost ultimately borne by the consumers of housing. In large part, that speculative cost is occasioned by value added by public improvements. An agency should be created at the federal level with broad powers. It should have, as its mandate, both a planning function and an implementing function to act where state or other governmental units are unwilling or unable to respond to such a plan. It should have the power to sell bonds and to build directly, using conventional or public funds. It should have the power of eminent domain and the power to override local zoning. It should have adequate funding for operations and should be regionalized. It should seek to co-operate with existing units of government but be mandated to act where such units fail to perform. In effect, such an agency would act as a houser of last resort.

There is no shortage of models. We need only look to the European experience of planned communities for good and bad models. The experience of New York State through its Urban Development Corporation provides a good example of what can happen when an agency has the power to act unilaterally. What I am calling for is much larger in scope and would require more of a planning function than the NYSUDC. The National Urban Growth Agency I have proposed should have the power to build new towns, as well. The present new town legislation is guilty of the same criticism I have leveled generally; that is, it is indirect and seeks to induce co-operation with the private sector and must wait upon others to initiate development. The agency I have proposed would also be charged with insuring equal availability to families irrespective of race or income, thus insuring minorities an equal stake in and access to new construction sponsored by such an agency. A special emphasis should be placed upon the use of minority contractors in all such development. This approach deals primarily with the supply part of the housing problem and would provide greater options to minority families and relieve the increasing density in urban ghettos by providing viable options to minorities.

On the demand side of the equation, we should abandon the hopelessly complex and grossly ineffective system of interest subsidy in favor of a Family Housing Allowance. It is immediately obvious that interest subsidy follows the unit and not the family, while a Family Housing Allowance (again a more direct approach) follows the family. By placing money in the hands of families, we increase the effective demand of families to a point (predetermined) where they can afford to purchase standard units wherever (assuming they are available) the family pleases. Such an approach has a double benefit. It eliminates a negative and accentuates a positive. It eliminates the automatic stigma placed upon housing which is built under federal subsidy programs and recognizable as government housing. The extreme of the hurtfulness of this stigma is the hostility felt toward public housing tenants. The same stigma, perhaps more subtle but equally pernicious, obtains in all federally supported developments.

The Family Housing Allowance approach accentuates the positive by providing an effective means of free choice in housing location. It is such an elemental consideration that it is frequently overlooked, but families ought to have the right to live wherever they want, even if they require some form of subsidy to obtain sound housing. This ability to choose takes on an even greater importance for minority families locked into concentrated ghettos, in part because of their inability to pay for sound housing. Such a system is somewhat analogous to an income-maintenance program or a guaranteed income. It is not unreasonable that they be linked together, even though the present prospects for a guaranteed income at a reasonably high level are very poor. An increased demand factor in our present context of short supply could admittedly have the negative effect of raising the cost of standard units. The question of the effect of increased demand on production of new units as well as its effect on the cost of units should be the subject of a large-scale experiment. Such an experiment should deal with market controls, as well as market response.

The suggestion of a Family Housing Allowance, however, is offered here in conjunction with an approach which would increase the supply. Both parts of the equation, supply and demand, must be acted upon simultaneously for maximum benefit from either. Either one of the approaches alone would have some measurable benefit, but together the benefits of the supply stimulus of the National Urban Growth Agency and the demand stimulus of the Family Housing Allowance would be greater than the sum of their parts.

REFERENCES

Haugen, R., and J. Heins.
  1969 "A Market Separation Theory of Rent Differentials in Metropolitan Areas." *Quarterly Journal of Economics* 83, No. 4 (November).
  1966 "Price Discrimination against Negroes in the Rental Housing Market." In *Essays in Urban Land Economics,* edited by J. Gillies. Los Angeles: University of California, Real Estate Research Program.
Report of the President's Committee on Urban Housing.
  1967 *Technical Studies. Vol. I. Housing Needs. Federal Housing Programs.* Washington: Government Printing Office.
U.S. Bureau of the Census.
  1967 *Measuring the Quality of Housing, An Appraisal of Census Statistics and Methods.* Working Paper #25. Washington: Government Printing Office.
U.S. Department of Commerce, Bureau of the Census.
  1965 "Characteristics of Selected Neighborhoods in Cleveland, Ohio." Current Population Reports, Series P-23, No. 21 (April).
Welfeld, Irving H.
  1970 "Toward a New Federal Housing Policy." *Public Interest,* No. 19 (Spring).

PART III

Policy Strategies
and Alternatives

Comprehensive Planning
and Population Control

I AM deeply appreciative of the opportunity you have offered me to participate with you in this very important conference. I want to talk with you today about national urban growth policy with particular reference to the need in the nation at this time for a more comprehensive and balanced approach to the development of metropolitan areas. I am particularly concerned that, until recently, the urban policy of this nation has failed to take significant account of the resources contained in metropolitan area suburbs which could be employed effectively for the purposes of contributing to the solution of national and regional problems of poverty and discrimination.

In discussing these matters, I should put in perspective my view of the situation in which attempts to eradicate poverty and discrimination are made. We live in a nation that appears deeply committed to maintaining wide-scale disparities in opportunities between economic classes and between racial groups. In terms of income and other indicators of social and economic position, the blacks and other minority groups today are not much further along than where the Constitution placed the slave for purposes of determining the number of voters in a district at the time of the adoption of the Constitution. That is, the black man is equivalent to about two thirds of the white man.

During the past few decades there has been only insignificant redistribution of the income of the nation from the wealthy to the poor. Latest income data suggest that the lowest 40 percent of income earners in the nation still earn a few percentage points more income annually than do the wealthiest 5 percent. The lowest 40 percent earn about 18 percent, the upper 5 percent about 15 percent. It is still the case that the richest 20 percent of income earners earns roughly eight times the income of the bottom 20 percent. Although Washington bureaucrats are happy to demonstrate that poverty has been drastically reduced in the nation in the past decade, in making such a claim they rely on an absolute standard of poverty, a poverty line established by the Social Security Administration. However, when poverty is understood as a relative rather than as an absolute concept, it can be seen that the gap between those who have and those who have not remains about as great as it has been during the postwar period.

In the field of housing it is clear that the nation's housing goal is to maintain a large supply of indecent housing in unsuitable living environments in locations not of choice for millions of American families. The national housing program allocates significantly more resources to those who have wealth than to those who have not. Secretary Romney has been one of those who has highlighted the fact that the Internal Revenue system operates to afford a far greater subsidization of housing to those who can take advantage of the special deductions given for mortgage interest payments and local real estate taxes than is provided in subsidy through other programs to low- and moderate-income families.

I do think it is best for real estate analysis of the situation and for competent planning to occur that the policy of the nation in relation to housing and to opportunity in general be understood in these terms. This is more than a rhetorical ploy, although the rhetoric of accomplishment or nonaccomplishment is significant. It is an attempt to confront the reality of indifference in public policy to the needs and aspirations of those classes of the population that are so seriously deprived of a chance to compete adequately in this society for the great resources that do exist within America.

A sound and sensitive national urban development policy calls for a very significant alteration of the present system of distribution of wealth and opportunity within the United States. It must be understood that the basic issue confronting urban populations is not an urban problem; it is primarily a national problem. It is a national problem of social and economic justice. It is the injustice inherent in the maldistribution of income, wealth, education, health, housing, leisure time, and other essentials that creates the serious deficiencies in life opportunities that afflict such a large number of residents of urban areas. Further, it is the lack of opportunity for so many that fosters so much of the tension and conflict in our society at this time.

Of course, it is true that there are problems that are uniquely urban in America—congestion of population and traffic is a uniquely urban phenomenon. Certain aspects of pollution are unique to urban areas. But problems of crime, welfare, housing deterioration, unemployment, alienation are not, in the first instance, urban problems; they do occur in urban areas and it may be that urban culture tends to promote certain of them, but, essentially, they are problems that could be solved, and must be solved, through a different set of national policy commitments.

Thus, it is essential to the solution of the urban problems of this nation that there be a significant redistribution of public resources away from the wealthy to those who have relatively little, those who are of lower income, or moderate income, or working-class status. To many who are of middle-income status, it is unfair and irrational for middle-class and working-class people to bear the major burden of supporting federal, state, and local programs. A more rational solution would be one which looked to a much greater burden being placed upon corporate wealth and the wealth of the very rich. The national tax structure has not been a subject area that urbanists have examined very carefully. I propose that more can be done to alter conditions of life in communities by adjusting the tax system than it can be through the host of federal and state urban-oriented programs presently in operation.

I think it must also be understood, as we look for solutions to urban problems, that no significant gains can be made in alleviating the conditions of lack of opportunity in our society until there is a vast reordering of national priorities. This reordering must involve a termination of destructive foreign endeavors and the establishment of domestic programs aimed at enhancing opportunity. In the words of an old campaign slogan, we must stop bombing and start building.

From another perspective, public planners and urban policy makers must recognize that they are of necessity concerned with the theories of distribution. They are concerned with the intensely political issue of who gets what.

The major issue I wish to speak about today involves the redistribution of responsibilities within metropolitan areas for solutions to problems of poverty and discrimination. To do this, I would like to discuss the work of the organization with which I am associated, the Suburban Action Institute. I do this because Suburban Action's work is aimed directly at the task of utilizing suburban resources for social actions in ways that they are not being utilized today.

Suburban Action is a nonprofit, tax-exempt organization whose work is aimed in general at opening the suburbs for the benefit of low and moderate income and nonwhite families. It was created to redress the imbalance in national urban growth policy which has failed to examine or employ suburban resources adequately for these social purposes. What are these resources? They are vacant land suitable for residential development, a growing number of new jobs, and very significant fiscal resources. Let me discuss each of these.

The suburbs of America's metropolitan areas contain the vast majority of vacant residential land suitable for development. Our central cities are greatly restricted in the amount of such land that they have available upon which decent, new communities could be constructed. Land costs in the central cities due to their shortage of vacant land are relatively high. The suburbs, on the other hand, are loaded with vacant land. One has only to travel twenty or thirty miles out from the center of a metropolitan area to come upon literally thousands of acres of unused land suitable for residential development. What makes this vacant land particularly attractive for development at this time is the fact that the overwhelming number of new jobs in metropolitan areas are located in the suburbs.

Approximately 80 percent of the new jobs created annually in metropolitan areas over the past two decades have been located within the suburban areas. Almost 100 percent of the increase in blue-collar jobs has been within the suburbs and it is also true that almost 100 percent of the increase in jobs for males has taken place within the suburbs.

It is now well known that more Americans live within the suburbs than in central cities or nonmetropolitan areas. Sometime in the late 1960s, the suburbs became the predominant place of residence. Less known, but equally important, is the fact that sometime in the 1970s the suburbs will become the predominant place of employment within metropolitan areas. Our studies indicate that the suburbs today contain approximately 45 percent of the jobs within metropolitan areas.

Just because the vacant land for new development exists primarily in the suburbs and just because the new jobs of America have been moving to the suburbs in increasing numbers, it does not necessarily follow that urban development policy should look toward the suburbs for providing housing opportunities for racial or economic minorities. Certainly the case should be examined that policy should operate toward bringing back jobs to the cities and that the vacant land that already exists in the cities should be better utilized to provide the basis for adequate housing. It is not the intent of the Suburban Action Institute to restrict development in the cities. It is our belief, however, that utilization of the job and land resources of the suburbs can relieve the cities of the tremendous burden they now have and make more possible a satisfactory solution.

It is important to understand that there are both moral and pragmatic arguments for what we are proposing. We find it improper and unjust for public policy to restrict the opportunities of minority, economic, or racial groups to inner-city areas. We think that it is the role of public policy to afford maximum choice of location for residents. We believe that a residence is more than just a shelter, that it is a location, that it represents a location within a region, a location in which an individual can seek out employment, education, and other opportunities. We can find no justification for a policy that would restrict the choice of location because of income or because of race. Moreover, we think that any policy that does so limit choice violates equal-protection provisions of the Constitution.

Suburban Action was started at a time when the federal government was actively engaged in policies of rebuilding ghettos through the Model Cities Program. It was our feeling that, insofar as ghettos represented an area in which people were constrained to live because of their race or economic class, federal policy aimed at making such restricted areas more livable was an unacceptable federal policy.

A ghetto is a condition, not a place. If the condition of restraint or limitation is removed, then the place may become an acceptable location. By offering opportunity to ghetto residents to reside elsewhere, the condition that creates the ghetto is removed. However, if present ghetto residents, offered the choice to move or to remain, chose to remain, then we would not think that the area in which they chose to remain would be a ghetto; it would be, perhaps, an ethnic neighborhood. But the distinction between a ghetto and an ethnic neighborhood is of great importance.

It is important to observe that there have been many spokesmen in the ghetto communities who have argued against suburban programs on the grounds that they would tend to disperse the ghetto population and would tend to disperse political power that blacks are gaining in central cities. It is also clear that a large number of spokesmen for the black community support the Suburban Action position. For example, Percy Sutton, who is the borough president of Manhattan, has served as the chairman of the Advisory Board to Suburban Action and, of course, Roy Wilkins has been a major proponent of action in behalf of the NAACP to break down exclusionary suburban practices. And just this week at a conference at Harvard, sponsored by the Black Congressional Caucus, a predominantly black group attending a housing panel voted unanimously to adopt a strong resolution calling for the elimination of restrictive barriers to suburban development for low- and moderate-income families and for nonwhite families.

As I indicated earlier, one of the basic reasons for our proposing the opening of the suburbs for development of housing and other opportunities for economic and social minorities is the tremendous growth of employment in the suburbs. The year we established Suburban Action, we highlighted the fact that, during that year, IBM had made the first page of the New York *Times* with the announcement that it had created some 300 jobs in the ghetto of Bedford Stuyvesant. But that same year, without any notice at all by any paper, IBM had created approximately 3,000 jobs in Westchester County. Where was opportunity? Clearly, it was appropriate for IBM to be constructing new job opportunities in Bedford Stuyvesant, but clearly there was great opportunity being fostered in the suburbs, and there was no reason, that we could see, why minority families should not be privileged to take advantage of those new opportunities. In fact, it was of the utmost importance that those jobs, plus the thousands of other jobs being created in the suburbs, be made available to families locked into center cities.

At one time, we conceived of the suburbs as being bedroom communities, but that just isn't the case today. Today, in many suburbs, there are as many people commuting to the suburbs as commuting out of them. We recently published *The Suburban Lock-Out Effect,* which documented this fact for Westchester County, New York. Westchester has always been the prototype bedroom community. But with the tremendous growth of new jobs and because the restrictive zoning practices have excluded working-class people from living within the county, it is now the case that almost as many people commute in to jobs in Westchester as commute out to New York City and other places for jobs. Frequently, the upper-class commuter objects to our actions on the grounds that he has chosen to live in the suburbs, and he takes a long commute; why, then, shouldn't the working-class man also have to commute the same distance? What is the answer to this? We would respond that the upper-class white has been able to reject living in Harlem and all the intermediate communities between the inner city and his location in the suburbs. He had a choice to live in those communities; he rejected them. For the working-class man, white or black, his choices are not so great. He has a very limited area in which he can choose to live. Further, for the working-class man the cost of commuting great distances is relatively much higher, that is, proportionate to his income, than it is for the upper-class executive.

One of the worst situations in the United States exists in Mahwah,

New Jersey, where the Ford Assembly plant employs some 6,000 workers, half of whom are white, half of whom are nonwhite. Because of zoning practices of Mahwah and surrounding northern Bergen communities, the working men at the Ford Assembly plant cannot afford to live near where they work. In fact, the majority of them are traveling vast distances, 30 miles or more, a day, from Newark or from New York City, to their jobs in suburban Mahwah. Suburban Mahwah as a community receives great tax advantages from the Ford Assembly plant and carries none of the burdens of having to educate the children of the workers who work there, nor to provide other services to their families. New York, Newark, and the older industrial suburbs that house the workers at Mahwah must pay these public costs to service the family while receiving none of the benefits from the industrial activity.

It is important at this point to highlight the fact that many suburban communities have grown relatively wealthy in terms of their fiscal position because they have been able to attract industries and upper-income families. They have successfully employed regulatory measures to zone out families who would be tax burdens to the community. At the same time, it is the case that the federal government provides fantastically large subsidies, in the way of tax savings to homeowners, to the residents of these wealthy suburban communities. Thus, we would claim that one of the major resources that at least some of the suburbs have is fiscal ability far beyond that possessed by the older industrial suburbs and by the central cities of the metropolitan regions. The withholding of these resources from economic and social minorities is as discriminatory as is the withholding of the resources of vacant residential land and new jobs.

In sum, the suburbs of America are the new America. They are where the majority of new residential and employment growth will take place. They are the place where major new investment will occur. They are the place where minorities are excluded. And because of the exclusionary practices of the suburbs, the nation has developed a pattern of spatial segregation of both races and income groups that is far greater than anything we have ever before seen. What is to be done about this?

The Suburban Action Institute is primarily an action-oriented agency. Our work is directed towards eliminating the barriers to the growth of opportunities for minorities in the suburbs. We are engaged in many different approaches to this goal, but I would like to emphasize the three major areas of our work.

Perhaps the most important part of our work is the elimination of

restrictive barriers to developing low- and moderate-income housing.
Our efforts here are involved primarily in litigation against exclusionary zoning. Exclusionary zoning is that set of zoning practices
which results in closing suburban housing and land markets to low-
and moderate-income families and to nonwhite families. Exclusionary
regulations are those which prevent relatively low-cost forms of residential development and which tend to increase the value of land so as
to force more expensive dwelling units to be constructed.

The practices which are exclusionary include the following:

Large-lot zoning. The requirement that a single-family home be
constructed on an exceptionally large parcel of land, such as an acre
or two acres or four acres or five acres or ten acres, results in greatly
inflated land prices. Zoning as a police-power measure must relate to
public health, safety, and welfare. The requirement that a home be
on such a large lot is unrelated to health, safety, and welfare. In fact,
the only time when such large-lot development might be required
would be in a situation where public water and sewer facilities were
unavailable and where a private developer could not construct an
adequate sewage-treatment plant. In that circumstance, an acre requirement might be considered.

*The prohibition against the development of any form of multi-
family housing, or the restriction of multifamily development to a
very small percentage of the vacant land of a community.* It is
typical in many suburban communities for one or two percent of the
vacant land to be zoned for multifamily use; but because of this great
restriction, the value of the land upon which multifamily housing can
be constructed in the face of great demand for such housing increases
significantly, and the resultant development on the land is typically for
relatively affluent families.

Prohibitions against large numbers of bedrooms. Quite frequently,
suburban zoners, in order to exclude children (children are some of
the most hated of all people in the suburbs, because they must be
educated, and education requires teachers and buildings and, thus,
taxes), restrict the permitted multifamily unit to one-bedroom units
and occasionally a small percentage of two-bedroom units. As a consequence, the occupants of multifamily units are generally not families
with large numbers of school-age children.

The requirement of an excessively large interior-floor area in each dwelling unit. In order to increase the economic status of development, the cost of development and the resulting taxes paid to suburban communities quite frequently require the homes to be of exceptionally large interior size. It is not infrequent that a suburban community requires a home to be of 1500 or 1800 square feet, whereas a home of 900 or 1,000 square feet would be entirely reasonable for purposes of health and safety.

We think that these regulations and a number of other zoning practices are discriminatory against the interests of families with low and moderate incomes. I might also point out that frequently the exclusionary action of a suburban community tends to zone out families of middle income. Thus, where the cost of new housing under the zoning regulations is $40,000 or more, the effect is essentially to zone out all families with incomes below $18,000 or $20,000. That estimate is based on the rule of thumb that a family should pay no more than twice its income for a new home.

In order to strike down exclusionary zoning practices Suburban Action has become involved in a number of tests against the exclusionary practices of suburban communities. Thus far, we have had just one case go to trial. In that case, in Madison Township, New Jersey, Judge David Furman invalidated the entire zoning ordinance of Madison Township.

I should tell you a bit about Madison Township. It is not a wealthy community. It is a community whose median income is about the average for the state of New Jersey. It is a community that grew rapidly from 7,000 in 1950 to 22,000 in 1960 to 48,000 in 1970. After such rapid growth, the townspeople said, "Enough; we've grown so large we've had to build too many schools. We've named one after every astronaut." Perhaps after running out of astronauts for whom to name new schools, the townsfolk decided to stop all growth and to prevent their taxes from going up higher. So, in 1970, they adopted a zoning ordinance which placed most of the vacant residential land in one- and two-acre zones, although one- and two-acre development had never taken place since 1930 in that township. Most of the development in the 1950s and 1960s had been on small lots of about a fourth or a third of an acre. The township adopted a number of practices similar to the type of exclusionary regulations that I mentioned before.

It is important to note that in this case not only was the Township of Madison sued for its discriminatory practices, but the suit also was against the State of New Jersey for permitting a state enabling act to remain on the books despite the fact that the enabling act had permitted Madison and other suburban communities to practice *de jure* residential segregation. Judge Furman did not throw out the state statute, but he did save it by giving it a very important new meaning. He stated in his decision that a locality must rezone in such a way as to take account of the needs of the surrounding region.

The words of the decision are so important that I should like to read to you just a small part of the conclusion:

In Madison Township's approach to the objective of balance, its attempted cure is a worse malady than whatever imbalance existed. About 8,000 acres of land, apparently primed for low- or moderate-income housing development, have been taken out of the reach of 90 percent of the population, prohibitive in land and construction costs. The acreage available for multifamily apartment units is minuscule. Families with more than one child are barred from multifamily apartments because of the one- and two-bedroom restrictions, restrictions without any guise of a health or safety purpose.

The exclusionary approach in the ordinance under attack coincides in time with the desperate housing needs in the country and region and expanding programs, federal and state, for subsidized housing for low-income families.

Regional needs are a proper consideration in local zoning. . . .

In pursuing the valid zoning purpose of a balanced community, a municipality must not ignore housing needs; that is, its fair proportion of the obligation to meet the housing needs of its own population and of the region. Housing needs are encompassed within the general welfare. The general welfare does not stop at each municipal boundary. Large areas of vacant and developable land should not be zoned, as Madison Township has, into such minimum lot sizes and with such other restrictions that regional as well as local housing needs are shunted aside.[1]

That is a magnificent opinion. The case is on appeal to the higher court and we are confident that Judge Furman will be upheld.

A second major area of Suburban Action's work involves action against corporations moving facilities to exclusionary suburbs. A corporation that does not provide housing in its new location for its workers is discriminating against those who cannot follow their jobs or who can only maintain their jobs with great transportation costs. Corporations which have opened new headquarters or facilities in exclusionary suburbs are involved in employment discrimination in violation of Title VII of the Civil Rights Act of 1964.

Suburban Action has requested the federal Equal Employment Op-

---

1. Oakwood at Madison, Inc., v. the Township of Madison and the State of New Jersey, Dkt. No. L–7507–70 P.W. (1971), 11, 12.

portunity Commission to initiate action against a number of corporations, which plan to move their headquarters to exclusionary communities. The staff of the EEOC has given support to our position. Their support appeared in a memorandum which was leaked to the Washington *Post* last summer. However, up to this time, the commissioners of that federal agency have not yet responded to our call for action. We do not know what decision they will make.

RCA had planned to move its headquarters from New York and Camden, New Jersey, to New Canaan, Connecticut. New Canaan, one of the wealthiest communities in the country, is very clearly an exclusionary community. Its vacant residential land is zoned primarily for two- and four-acre development. Suburban Action is involved in litigation against New Canaan's zoning ordinance. But it also requested the EEOC to prevent RCA from moving to New Canaan unless it provided adequate housing in that community for its minority workers. As a result of our activities, RCA has not gone forward with its proposed move to New Canaan. It has withdrawn its application.

Since we began our actions against exclusionary practices, we have been concerned that, if we should win in the court, we may not win any significant victories for minority families. Court determinations that exclusionary practices are unconstitutional would not necessarily produce a condition in which the private market constructed housing for low- and moderate-income families or nonwhite families.

To assure the construction of such housing in the suburbs, Suburban Action has encouraged nonprofit groups to acquire large numbers of tracts of vacant, residential land in exclusionary communities. It is our hope that well-developed site plans will be drawn up for these tracts, and development of between five to ten dwelling units per acre be proposed. I am working to establish a nonprofit corporation which will pursue this means of developing housing.

If the town rejects an application for development of these new, mixed-income communities, then it will be necessary to appeal the rejection of the application. We are confident that the courts will uphold the right to construct housing for classes of the population that are presently excluded from these communities. These nonprofit corporations will demonstrate that the planned unit developments will represent the very best of modern residential development practice. We are extremely conscious of the need for environmentally sound solutions to land development.

There is, of course, much more that I could say about the work of Suburban Action, but I've tried to highlight the most important parts of our activity. There has been a significant awakening in America, a recognition of the role the suburbs could play in contributing to solving problems afflicting metropolitan areas. We are confident that, in just a few years, the exclusionary barriers that prevent development of housing for minority families in the suburbs will be overturned by courts throughout the nation.

In conclusion, I think it would be appropriate to call upon urban affairs centers, such as the ones at Fisk and Vanderbilt, to begin undertaking the necessary studies to examine the means for fostering social interaction in the suburbs. It may be hoped that, in the not too distant future, it will be possible for large-scale, mixed-income development to take place in the nation's suburbs. Such development will strongly modify the nature of the social mix of the suburbs. We would kid ourselves if we think that this will be an easy task. Many problems face us in creating an open society in the United States. It isn't necessary for me to tell a conference here at Fisk that that is the case. But I do think that it is important that we begin now to develop the research required to increase our knowledge about how we may deal with the social, political, and economic consequences that could flow from a victory in this area. Such a victory, when it comes, will have implications for the nation that may equal those that flowed from the Brown decision in 1954.

REFERENCE

Oakwood at Madison, Inc. v. *The Township of Madison and The State of New Jersey,* Dkt. No. L–7502–70 P.W., Superior Ct., N.J. (1971), 11, 12.

Exclusionary Suburban Zoning: One More Black Rebuff to the Latest Liberal Crusade

THE checkered history of white liberal attempts to redress the wrongs that have been done to blacks has lately manifested itself in skirmishes by lawyers and other professionals, mostly white, to break down by court action the restrictive suburban regulations, most frequently zoning and subdivision ordinances and building codes, that force up housing costs and thereby effectively exclude moderate- and low-income families. As with earlier episodes in this history, endorsement of this latest white liberal movement by the black community is somewhat less than unanimous. Before I examine the reasons for this most recent division between white liberal and black nationalist, let me summarize the circumstances.

The imaginative legal techniques employed by many suburbs to insure high-cost, low-density development have been exhaustively, if not always rationally, catalogued. Large-lot zoning and total exclusion of apartments, excessively strict subdivision standards, and building-code provisions that have no basis in health and safety are just the head of the list. These substantive ukases are buttressed by highly discretionary administrative provisions that permit local governments to pick and choose among development proposals with one eye on the economic (and racial) class of the persons who might occupy those developments.

The effect of such restrictive devices is both obvious and documented. A study prepared by the Suburban Action Institute (Kristensen, Levy, and Savir, 1971) looked at the problem in New York's Westchester County. In 1952, the zoned capacity of the county was more than three million persons. By 1969, it was down 40 percent to just over one-and-three-quarter million—thanks chiefly to large-lot zoning. In 1950, the average size of newly created building lots was 0.3 acres; by 1968 it was 1.5 acres. This, of course, has produced an artificial shortage of land on which to build—both directly as a result of the larger lots and indirectly as large landowners hold land out of development in the hope of future zoning changes.

Building on large lots is beyond the means of low- and middle-income families and, indeed, beyond the capabilities of well-meaning sponsors of housing for those families. Not only is the land cost prohibitive, but development costs are pushed out of range by sub-division regulations that price streets and utilities on a front-foot basis. Add to this, of course, whatever the building code has imposed under the banner of health and safety.

Even smaller suburban lots are priced out of the low- and middle-income market by the artificial land shortage which places a premium on those few areas with small lots. When this artificially constricted supply is met by the increased demand of the white middle-class fleeing the central city, housing prices climb. In the ensuing competition for a relatively inelastic housing supply, the higher incomes of the white middle-class commuters enable them to outbid families seeking low-cost housing close to suburban job markets. Nor can the low-income families hope to rent rather than buy. The few apartments that many suburbs permit are frequently of the luxury high-rise, high-price type.

In short, the poor—and even those with moderate incomes—who are not already housed in pockets of suburban slums are generally foreclosed from leaving the central city. As a matter of principle, that is bad enough, but the practical problem comes when the same suburbs which exclude the urban worker woo the employment centers out of the city. The push of high rents and taxes in the city, and the pull of suburban acreage and officially sponsored inducements, coupled with the good road system between suburb and city, have increasingly attracted corporate headquarters, research laboratories, offices, and plants out of the city and into the suburbs. Nor should the amateur sociologist overlook the desire of corporate executives to have their places of business a few minutes by car from their suburban homes.

The result is that thousands of low- and moderate-income workers cannot find work in the cities nor housing in the suburbs. The public transportation system, designed to bring white white-collar workers from the suburbs to jobs concentrated in the central city, is incapable of bringing large numbers of central city residents out to scattered suburban job sites. Thus is created the pattern of "reverse commuting" that chokes both sides of the median strip of our expressways with city-to-suburb black workers and suburb-to-city whites. The sardonic result is exacerbation of unemployment in the central city, despite labor shortages in many suburbs.

These, then, are the suburban devices of discrimination—and the consequences. Recently, courts have begun to listen to the protests that these local laws infringe on constitutional rights, and the white liberal has begun to take pride in his contribution to the cause. But, just as he dares hope for success, he is met head-on by the indifference or outrage of black leaders. His problem, he learns, is that he is an integrationist—which, of course, is what he thought he was supposed to be. The charge is that his aim is either to dabble with meaningless problems in the suburbs while ignoring the agonizing problems in the black ghetto or to scatter the black population into the suburbs— "disperse" is the fighting word—just as it is gaining real power in the city.

I have been in this struggle for some years and thought I was on the side of the angels. Naturally, I am taken aback at this reaction, as any red-blooded liberal should be.

No man can tell another what is right for him, and it would take notable gall for a white man, no matter how well-intentioned, to presume to tell black people what is right for them. I suspect, however, that there are few of us who cannot benefit in some way from a bit of discussion before making a major commitment. And it seems to me that the black citizens of this nation face one more tough decision: Are they going to oppose, encourage, or be indifferent to efforts to construct substantially more housing in the suburbs that will afford some blacks in the central city an opportunity to move out?

Whatever I have to say on the subject has the inherent flaw of being the opinion of an outsider, although—if the most recent commentators on the fate of the WASP are to be taken seriously—that of a vanishing minority. Perhaps occasionally—when the stakes are high and the competing convictions are sincere and strongly held—a brief view from the outside can help bring the issue back into focus.

The threshold difficulty in attempting to address the growing black hostility toward efforts to open up housing in the suburbs is to pin down the bases for it. A special *Black Journal* telecast on National Educational Television early in February 1972 brought together nearly a dozen black leaders. Listening to them made it evident that a number of forces underlie the move toward separatism.

First, there was a rejection of integration as an impossible goal.

Integration won't work, so the argument runs, because the white man doesn't want it to work. This attitude reflects the black's understandable refusal to believe in the sincerity of the white community. It is a conviction justified by events such as those in Richmond, Virginia, where, just as black power in the city was about to take over, the city annexed white Chesterfield County, thus diluting the black vote. That particular maneuver has run into difficulty in the courts, but Atlanta blacks have witnessed the same struggle in the Georgia legislature. Some blacks see the entire movement toward metropolitan planning and metropolitan government as nothing more than an effort to "draw the circle wider" and to dilute black power in the central cities.

The black belief in white insincerity is not lessened by the apparent truth that the monetary advantages of so-called liberalism have not escaped the rich white. Circulars offering investment opportunities in low- and moderate-income housing are now common. The financing packages, by taking full advantage of tax laws, emphasize getting the investors' total investment back out of the project as rapidly as possible. When the tax gimmicks run out, the investor has very little interest in the project and very little incentive to try to keep it going.

Blacks may legitimately ask if such investment schemes are fostering the increasing rate of owner-abandonment of low- and moderate-income housing. Then again, that problem may be due to white get-rich-quick interests which throw up shoddy housing on poor sites —sometimes with the co-operation of local federal authorities.

Suspicion of white motives is increased when blacks observe that it is frequently the other guy's suburb that the white establishment liberal is proposing to integrate. There is no "suitable site" in the wealthy, built-up suburb of the white liberal, or land values are "prohibitively high" there. Too often suburban integration for the upper-class white Establishment leader means moving blacks into the lower-class white suburb.

Thus, one source of black opposition to suburban low-income housing is the belief that the result would be, at best, new ghettos in formerly lower-class white suburbs. This is a real risk for two reasons. First, present zoning law tends to accelerate the concentration of low-cost housing in the community that takes any. It is easier legally to exclude all subsidized housing than to hold it to a managed program—just as it is safer to keep out the first gas station at the intersection than to try to keep out the second or the third. Second, land values in some suburbs are so astronomical that promoters of subsidized housing are priced out. And these same wealthy suburbs frequently can plead that they have not been out proselytizing industry and have therefore a lesser sense of guilt.

A second major cause of black opposition or indifference to efforts to open up the suburbs appears to grow out of this same distrust of white objectives but goes beyond the belief that the white man is simply insincere to the belief that he is determined to destroy the black race. Some black leaders express this in terms of genocide, a physical extinction of a race which the white man no longer finds economically necessary and regards as a social annoyance, in addition to that. Black cultural nationalists see white efforts at integration as, at the very least, a conscious attempt at cultural genocide. Black spokesmen such as Roy Innis use *integration* and *assimilation* as equivalent words. Certainly, there may be cause for such attitudes when influential whites such as Nathan Glazer and Daniel P. Moynihan make statements such as "The Negro is only an American and nothing else. He has no values or culture to protect" (1963:53). Apparently, some white people have decided that, if they must live with the black man, they had better start making him white. About the time white men started thinking that way, Negroes started calling themselves black. Perhaps some white men are willing to ignore the fact that black Americans are black; certainly many blacks are not.

The black's belief that the white man's integration will be less than just, coupled with the fear that it will dissipate the power of the black race to help itself, combine to produce the conviction that the integrated black man will be integrated but unequal and powerless to do anything about it. At that point, the issue begins to look like one of survival. Black spokesmen who see it as such feel justified in advocating solutions that may infringe on the freedom of other blacks to choose integration.

The black's refusal to be assimilated on white man's terms suggests more than a negative fear of cultural extinction. It reflects a positive attitude of black pride. Since the mid-sixties there has been a growing black belief that to succeed the black man does not need white men, and there is, as well, a heightened awareness that black culture, with its origin in history more ancient than the establishment of white America, includes more than black spirituals. It is a pride that has at last grown weary of begging for admission into American society. Blacks have at once grown too proud to beg and too confident to feel the need.

The outside observer cannot ignore the existence of contrary attitudes which also motivate black separationist thought. In addition to strong feelings of black pride, some black leaders evidence a definite distrust of their own race. Speaking on the *Special Black Journal* telecast, Roy Innis spoke of the black masses being led by an elite few black leaders down the path of racial genocide. Elijah Muhammad exhorted the black race to stop asking the white man to do things for it and to start doing something for itself. Other black leaders feel that the successful black man will leave his race behind if given a chance. They fear integration will result in a constant skimming of the best black talent, a not unheard-of ethnic occurrence, by the way.

At the extreme, this black distrust of the black race takes the position that black men just cannot handle the white world. Western society is a game played by rules that white men wrote and have lived with for thousands of years, and some blacks feel that their race could never overcome that disadvantage, and so they propose starting a new game.

Another force behind the black separatist movement is the self-interest of some black leaders, a motivation that whites should be able to understand. Some black politicians and some leaders of black institutions argue that blacks should stay in the ghetto because only in that way can the black political power and black institutions controlled by these men be preserved.

Another factor is the belief of some black leaders that all the talk about the integration of the suburbs is simply a gambit to mask continuing neglect of the inner-city ghetto. Blacks distrust advocates of "dispersal"—such as Moynihan—who sometimes talk as though dispersal is just the easiest way to get around the white man's problem. "To the extent that a society has problems due to concentrations of race," says Moynihan, "that society would minimize those problems by spreading them out" (1970:2253). If integration is just a way to avoid dealing with the problems, it becomes as they say, part of the problem; it does not help black people; it just sweeps them under the metropolitan rug. When, on top of this, such a dispersal program becomes an excuse for abandoning programs aimed at ghetto improvement, black opposition to dispersal is easy to understand.

Furthermore, blacks are not convinced that suburban integration in the '70s will be anything more than the sterile public housing programs of earlier decades, one more gesture to treat the physical effects of racism while ignoring the causes. Such programs will not work any more in the suburbs than they did in the cities.

Finally, the evidence is inconclusive that integration *per se*, on any terms, has benefited black people. Probably the only place where there is any tally is in education. Black children may show some improvement after transfer to a white school, but the cause there is no doubt a better school—not an integrated school. Thus, black separatists reject arguments suggesting that the black race will somehow be improved by integration as factually unsound and just plain insulting.

Probably the only point at which these various factors converge with each other and, indeed, with black integrationist thought, is the belief, common to them all, that the critical goal must be power for the black race: power that will enable it either to establish and run its own society or power that will insure the black race that integration into the American society will come on terms which are fair and just to black people. Both the segregationist and the integrationist more and more reflect Benjamin Franklin's attitude that, in a revolution, the revolutionaries must hang together or hang separately. Realizing the limits of the power available to blacks, black leaders feel an urgent need to concentrate that power somehow to achieve whatever goals black men ultimately settle upon.

These, then, are the forces which seem to underlie black separatist views. The solution proposed by black separatists is to forget the suburbs and black integration into them and to concentrate upon building a power base in the central cities. The solution proposed by some goes so far as positively to oppose efforts to open up the suburbs to blacks who would like to move there if they could find the right price.

This is a solution which concerns me both in terms of what I believe is morally right and in terms of what I believe is practically advantageous for the black citizen.

My moral concern operates on two planes. First, I believe simply that people must eventually learn to endure each other. They don't have to play bridge together; to trade lawn mowers or spouses; or to support the same candidates for the school board. Just accept the fact that, with luck, you may like your neighbor; worse luck, you may not. I believe that no nation can survive for long in an acceptable manner with an uneasy peace between two separate factions, each refusing to admit any common interest with the other. Furthermore, the intolerability of such a situation inevitably will lead to a desire on the part of each faction to eliminate the cause of the problem. We have cold wars only so long as each faction doubts its ability to annihilate the other without severe losses to itself. Again, it seems painfully obvious that when the factions are a 90-percent majority and a 10-percent minority, separated geographically, possibilities of genocide become very real.

My second moral objection to the separatist position is perhaps more narrow, but just as basic. It comes down to the absence of a right of any person to impose his wishes on any other person. Many black separatists feel that if their view of right is to prevail, it requires more than their personal opposition to integration, it requires that other blacks be denied the free choice to integrate if they wish. When I am told that I should not break down the legal barriers erected by suburban municipalities, my concern is not for the black segregationist who doesn't care about the barrier but for the black who would, but for the barrier, choose to live where he now cannot.

The separatist's answer to my morals is that this is war, and my morals really don't matter. And I don't expect to sell the idea of opening up the suburbs on the basis of morals, mine or anyone else's. To the contrary, I suggest there are compelling pragmatic reasons in the self-interest of the black race which require that those legal barriers be torn down.

If it is to be war, at least let us not ignore the strategy.

First, look at the great cities, for it is these urban centers which black separatists have most recently staked out as the focus of emerging black power.

The black man is to inherit the city. There seems little doubt that if the black man wants it, he can have it. Even on straight-line projections of current trends, blacks will soon be a majority in a host of central cities. Given the white man's proclivity for running when some ill-defined "tipping point" is reached, the estimates could prove quite conservative.

A bleak prospect faces the black inheritors of the central city that no racial romancing can cover up. The white will control the state and federal legislatures under the one-person, one-vote doctrine. The white who now owns most of the urban land will be increasingly inclined to sell or abandon it—certainly he is not likely to maintain it. Tax revenues can be expected to plunge even faster as white flight accelerates. Concurrently, demands for increased municipal services must be expected from the long-deprived black population.

Currently, central cities compensate for dwindling local property and sales tax revenues through state and federal aid. Blacks who profess nothing but distrust for white society cannot expect this arrangement to continue when city limits become the dividing line between black society and white society. The benefits now grudgingly bestowed upon urban centers by legislatures can be expected to disappear under such circumstances. Professor Paul Friesema summed it up when he said:

If black political leaders expect any help at all in providing services to their constituents, they may have to go, hat in hand, to the Man at the state house and in Washington. Black municipal leaders are likely to have very little political maneuverability. Verbal attacks on the white man, or any other acts smacking of militancy, may have to be severely curtailed, for it simply will not do to offend white legislative bodies that are already indifferent, at best, to needs of the Negro city. Black city leaders may come to dangle on white man's strings while receiving little more than crumbs (1969:77).

If blacks need proof that control of the cities will not mean control of their own destinies, they need look no further than to what is happening right now. As black power in the cities has grown, the power of cities to deal with their own problems has decreased. As Charles Allen put it:

[R]egional Planning Agencies, Metropolitan Governments and Councils of Government . . . control such vital areas as mass transit, highways, open space, water and sewers, pollution, federal planning programs, and comprehensive health programs. Even though the central cities are becoming blacker, and new and more dedicated black politicians and civil servants are taking the initiative, whites are still able to take from the cities municipal facilities and services that serve the white purposes and not the black purposes. The resources of the cities are not being addressed to the problems of the city (1971:42).

As city boundaries become racial boundaries, one of two results seems inevitable. Either white-dominated state and federal legislatures will ignore black urban centers or they will once again absorb the black population by the creation of regional all-purpose governments controlled by suburban white forces.

In this country, power means economic power—the rest flows from it. In my view, if black America accepts or, indeed, encourages, the flight of white America, with its jobs and money, to the suburbs, the victory in the city is a hollow one. Whites could more easily ignore black problems and blacks would have fewer resources to help themselves. On top of this, dealing with the problems of poverty, poor housing, education, drug addiction, delinquency, gangs, jobs, health, and public facilities will become all the more difficult as those problems become increasingly concentrated in our deteriorating central cities.

This, then, is what I see as the unhappy result of the solution to racism posed by black separatists. It is not enough to say that your solution has problems. What is needed is a solution with fewer problems, and one that meets black objection to the current style of integration.

My solution begins with the basic premise that black people cannot trust white people. I should hope that is not true across the board, but it is, nevertheless, too late in the day to ask blacks to rely on the good faith of white America. If, as I suspect, the basic source of black opposition to suburban integration is distrust of the white race, then I fail to see the wisdom of a solution that gives to whites the rich suburbs, while isolating and concentrating blacks in a few emasculated central cities where they become easy prey. It sounds like Bill Cosby's routine about what if the American Revolution were a game. The rules are that all of the colonists wear nifty buckskin and moccasins and hide in the rocks while all of the British wear bright red coats and march very slowly in long straight lines—beating a drum as they go. Never before have revolutionaries agreed to wear the red coats.

If white self-interest is the problem, then the solution, it seems to me, is to figure out a way to take advantage of that white self-interest which for so long has been turned against the black race. In my opinion, the goal of the black race in this country should be to so insinuate itself into American society that every time the white race seeks to bestow a benefit upon itself, it must, at the same time, bestow a benefit upon the black race. It should be the goal of the black race to be so absorbed into American society that it becomes impossible for the white race to run from its problem.

White American society is hung up on race. It simply has been unable to cope with the irrational fears that plague it. Some of white America stands in front of school doors. Some of it lies in front of school buses. Some of it violently assaults little children. Some of it simply flees the problem, running even further into wooded suburbia and extending even further the high-speed transportation networks that keep it within reasonable commuting distance to the city where it must work but cannot bring itself to live.

Still others are hung up on carefully avoiding any appearance of racial prejudice. In so-called liberal sectors of white society, it has become a genuine *faux pas* to have racial prejudices. The more blatant forms of racism are never seen in these circles. It has become socially important to have a few black friends. But the problem is still there. The polite white liberals who refuse to talk about race still run from it. It may be the schools, it may be crime in the streets, it may be deteriorating public facilities, it may be a back yard for the kids to play in, or it may be a fear of losing his hard-earned downpayment in a changing neighborhood, but something invariably drives the white liberal out of the city and into the suburbs. So long as there is some place for the white man to run, he will try to run from his racial problem.

To me, then, one answer to both the white man's problem and the black man's problem is to deal with housing on a metropolitan basis rather than as a matter to be determined by each suburb or by each ward of a city. This means enough blacks living, or free to live, where they choose in every suburb to make it at once fruitless for the white to run to another suburb and impossible for him to improve his kid's school without at the same time improving the black kid's school, to build himself a park, without building one for the black down the block. And it means that gradually the outlook of suburbia toward the center city will become an interracial attitude, not an all-white one.

What remains is to suggest some method for bringing about this grand solution. And this is where I see the role of urban black power coming into play, provided it is not long delayed.

I see urban black power as an imposing weapon, but one that will paradoxically grow weaker as it appears to grow stronger until, at the moment of its triumph, it is completely impotent. Right now, the strength I see in urban black power derives from two sources. First, white urban leaders see the black take-over coming and don't like it. Second, many black problems are urban problems with which white establishment leaders and voters are concerned.

At the point where blacks, by sheer concentration of numbers, take over the cities, the strength that derives from the white leaders' fear is gone. At that point, urban problems become black problems, instead of the other way around. At that point, black power is reduced to the power possessed by a small minority isolated in a few emasculated and deteriorating central cities. Such power is no power.

Now is the time to use black urban power. It is powerful now because it has the leverage to engage white urban power as its ally— an unwilling ally though it may be. Right now, the white urban power structure could solve many of its problems if it could get state and federal resources to rebuild ghettos and if it could somehow remove the growing black pressure it feels by compelling the suburbs to absorb a larger share of the increasing metropolitan black population. Here, then, are two points of white self-interest which blacks can and must turn to their own advantage.

What is needed is a public instrument capable of exploiting this white self-interest to open up the suburbs. Let us start by openly acknowledging that there is *no* administrative or governmental system acceptable to American society that is certain to succeed. Neither the federal government nor the states, neither a regional special-purpose agency nor a loose confederation of well-meaning municipalities can offer any guarantees.

For my part, I would want a system to open up housing in the suburbs that has the following characteristics:

1. It is not exotic to most Americans.

2. It is capable of experimenting with various techniques both to adjust to special circumstances in each metropolitan area and to test out alternatives that may be usable elsewhere.

3. It has all the sovereign powers: to tax, to regulate, to condemn.

4. It has a broad enough geographic base to embrace competing white urban and suburban power structures.

5. It has a broad enough political base to permit it to make some locally unpopular decisions without being so distant that it appears to be dictating policy without a concern for local interests.

I suggest that of any plausible choices, only the states meet all these qualifications. They are a familiar entity; they have demonstrated a capacity to experiment and innovate; they have the sovereign authority; they are a forum where local interest brokering is routine; and the governor is once—but not twice—removed from local conflicts.

I know all the arguments against placing hope in the states . . . I've made many of them, myself. I remind the blacks, however, that a separatist solution that leaves the cities to the blacks will depend for its success upon a state legislature controlled by whites. The black separatists cannot scorn the state as an instrument to open up the suburbs to blacks and still assert that the state will help black cities.

I propose a state land-development agency appointed by the governor that would have the power to override local land-use decisions that operate to exclude housing for low- and moderate-income families. It could authorize private or public agencies to build housing for low- and moderate-income families. This idea is not new. Massachusetts is trying out a similar idea, right now. The Tentative Draft No. 3 of the American Law Institute's Model Land Development Code contains a system for state review of land development proposals involving housing. Senate Bill 992, the Nixon Administration's National Land Use Policy Act, contains the same concept, although the Administration is understandably reluctant to broadcast this feature of the bill.

The agency should be empowered to establish guidelines that would be applicable both to white areas of the central city and to the suburbs. These guidelines, while recognizing that no simple arithmetical ratios—or quotas, if you wish—will work, should emphasize:

1. The special obligation of a community that has industry to open up its housing
2. That some land is not suitable for *any* housing, high- or low-priced, and communities shall not offer marginal land next to the city dump for low-income housing
3. That if a community designates certain areas as suitable for any housing, the burden is on the community to prove that there are reasons, unique *to that community*, why such land should not be available for subsidized or public housing as well as market housing
4. That the communities which adopt a plan or policy, call it what you will, for a 5-year period of inducing such housing *and implement it,* will receive special consideration under other state programs or under federal programs administered by the state
5. That communities that do demonstrate their willingness to do more than mouth their dedication to open housing and do in fact get about the business of providing sites, will be protected from becoming the repository for all the low-income housing in the metropolitan region.

That list is not exhaustive; neither is it universal. Variations must occur from metropolis to metropolis. Where black power is stronger, the guidelines may be tougher; where it is weaker, less may have to do.

I do not regard such a system as pie in the sky, provided the blacks do not wait too long. Once the cities have become all-black, there is no longer the likelihood of using white society's self-interest. Right now, on issues concerning opening the suburbs, blacks can count on the self-interest of the Establishment in the city. Black urban power is at a critical point where it must be used or lost. Similarly, once the suburbs were opened, blacks could count on the self-interest of every suburb to be sure that every other suburb got its fair share of out-migration. A state agency would force these competing white interests into the ring where their combat must foster a type of integration not heretofore possible.

In short, I propose a solution which seeks to get the most leverage out of black urban power by using it to form uneasy, but nevertheless effective, coalitions with competing segments of white society—each pursuing its own particular self-interest. And I do not ask the voters to buy a strange governmental structure.

Obviously, such a solution is not going to insure overnight victory on every point for the black race. Indeed, some points may never be won. But to me it seems to offer hope of strength beyond that offered by separatist solutions, for it seeks to avoid the unavoidable reality of such separatist solutions—the black population of this country is only 10 to 12 percent of the whole, and its power as an isolated minority will be limited accordingly. And talk of a coalition of white, black, and brown poor is the most tragic romancing. The white middle class is more powerful than ever in this country, and any proposed solution to the social inequities of our society that ignores this fact is either dishonest or frivolous.

Thus far, I have addressed only the objections of those black separationists who propose concentrated black urban power as the solution to the insincerity of white racism. A few words are needed on the other black objections to integration which underlie opposition to open housing in the suburbs.

Black cultural nationalists advocate separation not so much in terms of black power, but in terms of black pride and the preservation of a distinct black culture. They may still say that, power or not, what is important is the preservation of that culture and that while my solution may effectively integrate them into American society, it will do so only at the expense of assimilating them to that society.

To this I say that the black race does not have to be unemployed together in order to work together for common black goals. Culture is not simply a matter of living next door to persons of common background. Perhaps black institutions, like Irish or Italian institutions, may not survive outside of black ghettos. I am not advocating a compulsory dispersal. I propose a system to break down barriers to allow freedom of choice. If the price is some loss of culture, ask the third-generation Poles and Greeks if they would trade equality for culture. In any case, I refuse to believe that black culture depends on the continuation of a black population condemned to exist in the squalor of forgotten urban ghettos.

I do not seek assimilation. I advocate only an open, pluralistic society where black men have freedom to be black, where black men can live in white neighborhoods without becoming white. The achievement of this goal requires a constant attack on municipal laws that impede mobility. It also requires strong black institutions and deep unity of black purpose, but I reject those purposes as ends in themselves. I see them only as means to a goal of true black freedom and equality.

Other blacks charge that suburban integration is just a new name for ignoring—or breaking up—the ghetto. Clearly, no matter what happens in the suburb, the ghetto will remain the home of many blacks for some time, some by choice, some by economic compulsion. For this reason, ghetto renewal is imperative, and there should and will be ghetto organizations with a large voice in the way that renewal proceeds. If anything, ghetto renewal will become more feasible once the pressure of increasing overcrowding is alleviated. Until then, land and relocation costs will consume disproportionate amounts of ghetto renewal funds leading to less than satisfactory renewal.

Finally, there is the charge that integration is not necessary to the improvement of the black race and that to suggest it is an insult. I take it this sentiment explains in part the opposition of CORE to busing and a similar initial reaction by the black caucus at Gary. While I understand this sentiment, it does not change my mind about the need for integration if the black lot is to be improved. What black people need are *better* schools, health care, housing, and jobs, not *integrated* schools, health care, housing and jobs. But I suggest that you cannot expect better without integration. The "no benefit from integration" argument assumes separate but equal facilities. We have tried that once in this country, and it did not work. Since then, blacks have acquired more power and some whites have acquired new outlooks, but I question whether either change has been enough to make a significant difference.

Of course, here some blacks will say that I am wrong in assuming that they want things "better." The goal, they say, is *free,* not *better,* in the sense that people in the white rat-race use the term. On one level, that is a philosophical choice that each person must make as to his own lifestyle. On another level, however, personal freedom in this country comes only with the end of economic dependence and so we are back where we started: You can never be personally free while compelled to exist in a forgotten ghetto, and in my view you cannot effectively avoid that compulsion by voluntarily isolating yourself.

In conclusion, it appears to me that black separatists have become so involved in forging tools that they have lost sight of the goal. The tool has become the goal. A united front in the black community and black urban power are tools to be used to obtain the goal of equal status in this society, not to obtain the status of some urban reservation dependent on handouts. If the black distrusts the white, he should place himself in a position where the white cannot help himself without helping the black. That is what some of us are trying to do in our attacks on "exclusionary" zoning. It is imperative to forge the tools with all the energy you possess; but unless you then use the tools, they become meaningless, and the work is wasted. I submit that one of the tools is a judicial crowbar (admittedly a clumsy instrument, at best) to pry open the suburban lockbox a crack and thereby inspire the legislators—by fear or good will—to design a more decent container for metropolitan housing.

REFERENCES

Allen, Charles.
    1971   "The View from the Black Community." *Planning Agency and the Black Community: A Workshop Report,* ASPO Planning Advisory Service Report No. 274 (November).

Friesema, Paul.
    1969   "Black Control of Central Cities: Hollow Prize." *Journal of the American Institute of Planners,* XXXV (March).

Glazer, Nathan, and Daniel P. Moynihan.
    1963   *Beyond the Melting Pot.* Cambridge: MIT Press.

Kristensen, Chris, *et al.*
    1971   "The Suburban Lock-Out Effect." *The Suburban Action Institute Research Report* No. 1 (March).

Moynihan, Daniel P.
    1970   "Moynihan: Architect of Dispersal." *CPR National Journal,* October 17.

The Suburbs:
A Necessary Alternative

RICHARD BABCOCK'S credentials are well known among all planners and lawyers who try to define and implement land-use policies through the crude instruments of zoning and subdivision control. Partly because I admire the contribution he has made in stimulating reform in the use of these instruments (reform directed to a large extent at breaking down the racial and economic exclusionary effect of these instruments) and partly because I agree with much that is said in his paper, there is a strong temptation to say, "me, too." But that would violate the charge given to me to make a critical analysis and respond in such a way as to foster significant discussion. The following comments are offered in that spirit. One general qualification: the lack of time available to develop a response results in the use of generalizations and assertions where documentation ought to be present. You will sense, therefore, that these comments have a tentative flavor.

We all have a tendency to build our arguments on easy assumptions, or at least to select those assumptions that fit our views. It has been suggested that the white exodus to the suburbs is a flight from the black. It is said to be fear of the black man that invariably drives the white out of the city and into the suburbs. If this is true, we should expect to find that white suburbanization rates correlate to the proportion of blacks in the city. I'll overstate to make the point: The greater the number of blacks, the greater whitey's fear and the more rapid his haste to the suburbs. In the absence of blacks, whites would have no motive to move, and suburbanization would not occur. But suburbanization is vigorous in some cities with small proportions of blacks. Gary, Indiana, and Salt Lake City have central cities nearly equal in size, but the black population in Gary is significantly greater. Yet suburban growth has been greater in Salt Lake in the last decade. This is too simplistic, but where we find white suburbanization in the absence of a strong black influence, we have evidence of other than racial motives at work and must consider the possibility that these same motives are also present in those communities where black pressure is influencing white suburbanization.

This is not to deny pervasive racial prejudice. But racism is too simple an answer. Dwelling on that alone encourages us to ignore other forces that must be understood in the development of strategies to open up the suburbs. We cannot ignore, for example, the changing economic functions of city and suburb and the effect of these forces on residential movement. David Birch (1970:6) argues that the older central cities are becoming specialists in service and government industries, with manufacturing and trade moving to the suburbs. As employment opportunities move, housing tends to follow. It is worthwhile to note that the strength of these employment movements varies with the age and size of cities. The older and larger cities tend to show greater specialization in the center than do smaller and younger cities. The effect of this specialization in service industries is to narrow the range of job opportunities available, even when the number of jobs remains constant. For those who would choose to remain in the central city, education for the available jobs is the most obvious alternative to unemployment. The employment situation relates to another assumption to be questioned.

It is said that the blacks will inherit the cities. This may be probable, but it is by no means certain. Consider these facts. Among the fifty central cities with the largest number of blacks, six have a black majority. Another seven have between 40 and 50 percent blacks. In more than half of these cities, blacks make up less than 20 percent of the central-city population.

The view that blacks will inherit the cities assumes a continuation of past trends. There are some indications of shifts in the trends but evidence checked in this cursory investigation is confusing.

The President's Report on National Growth sets forth the following:

During the 1960s the black population of central cities grew by 3.2 million, while the white population in these cities declined by 600 thousand. In contrast, the number of blacks in suburban areas grew by 800 thousand, while the white population showed a 15.5 million increase. Most of the increase in blacks outside central cities took place in a relatively small number of areas; two out of every three new black suburbanites were in one of the twelve largest Metropolitan areas, and more than one third of them were in just three areas—New York, Los Angeles, and Washington (1972:23).

The statistical breakdown in the President's report is between population "inside central cities" and population "outside central cities." Using slightly older data, David Birch makes a breakdown between population in "central cities" and population in "suburbs." He finds the percentage of black population in the rapidly growing suburbs holding steady at about 5 percent between 1960 and 1968. This means that a numerical increase of suburban blacks in the range of 2.4 million to 3.3 million occurred during eight years.

Even if these numbers prove to be of dubious merit, the analysis that accompanies them is of interest. Birch suggests that there is an increasing ability among blacks to pay their way in the suburbs and a tendency for suburban migration to be concentrated among young blacks. This leads him to the following conclusion:

It is not at all clear, therefore, that black concentrations in central cities will continue to rise. If we assume that retail and manufacturing jobs, on which blacks rely so heavily, will continue to be located outside the city, there is every reason to suppose that the growth of central-city black populations will taper off as the war babies reach their twenties and begin to move out in search of those jobs. . . . This process may already be at work. The central-city black growth rate has dropped from 3.4 percent per year to 1.0 percent per year. If this is coupled with the strong need of wealthy families—black and white—to live near the high-paying service jobs at the city's center, there is the real prospect of a declining black population in the central city and the substantial reuse of present ghetto areas.[1]

None of the above comments argues for a relaxation of efforts to break down the exclusionary walls of suburbia. If anything, they suggest that economic forces will increase the desires of black and poor people to move out. Out-migration will lessen pressures in the city and provide some flexibility for redevelopment. Failure of blacks to integrate the suburbs will indeed be a hollow victory.

There is another aspect of the move to suburbia that should be considered explicitly. Will blacks and the poor concentrate in a limited number of outlying areas, or will they disperse? Concentration will tend to contradict Babcock's suggested strategy of "insinuating society" to such an extent that any benefits will be shared. A

1. From David L. Birch, *The Economic Future of City and Suburb* (New York: Committee for Economic Development, 1970), p. 30. By permission of the publisher.

predominantly black suburb with limited tax resources could be even more helpless than the central cities in the future as aging public facilities need replacement. Most evidence shows a tendency for black suburbanization to concentrate in enclaves (Birch, 1970:34; Executive Office of the President, 1972:23). This raises a touchy subject: quotas.

Nobody likes to talk about quotas. They reflect prejudice and appear to condone it by clothing it in the garb of public or institutional policy. But, given the realities of present-day public attitudes, there may be good pragmatic reasons to consider quotas to assure a dispersal of housing opportunities for blacks and the poor.

About two years ago, the Miami Valley Regional Planning Commission initiated a plan for the dispersal of low- and moderate-income housing throughout the Dayton, Ohio, Metropolitan Area.[2] The five-county region was subdivided into fifty-three small areas. The number of housing units currently needed for low- and moderate-income people, about 16,000 units, was then assigned to the planning units on the basis of a formula that took into account such things as present population, existing housing, and adequacy of public facilities. All areas of the region will get some units, but extreme concentration is to be avoided. An extensive public information and selling job has been undertaken to sell the idea to developers, public officials, and citizens of the region. Persuasion has been supplemented by the planning agency's review powers on publicly assisted housing projects. It is too early to render a judgment on success. Some obstacles still exist in the suburbs, but progress has been made in getting several suburbs to lower barriers. One of the keys to success in the suburbs appears to be the assurance that no one area will be inundated with low-income housing. As communities reach their quotas, the regional agency will deny requests for additional projects in the same location and push for placement in other less affected areas.

This is a working example of some of what Babcock is recommending. We should learn from its failures and successes. It is operating on a metropolitan scale but without significant state involvement. Federal co-operation does seem to be crucial. Without the lever of federal funds, the regional agency would have to rely on persuasion.

2. This material was drawn from several sources: *A Housing Plan for the Miami Valley Region* (Dayton: The Miami Valley Regional Planning Commission, 1970); Dale F. Bertsch and Ann M. Shafor, "A Regional Housing Plan," *Planners Notebook* (Washington, D.C.: American Institute of Planners, 1971); and Lois Craig, "The Dayton Area's Fair-Share Housing Plan Enters the Implementation Phase," *City,* January 1972.

I see no reason why federal leverage and the state reforms Babcock requests have to conflict. Anthony Downs (1968:1331–1378) outlined a strategy for racial dispersal several years ago that would be highly compatible with Babcock's suggestions but would emphasize federal incentives for local government co-operation.

I wish I could be optimistic about the possibility of state-initiated reforms in land use. I am, if they continue to be pushed by environmentalists and reform-minded lawyers. Planners should be lending their support, also. The work of the American Law Institute in developing a new model enabling act for land-use controls can go a long way toward breaking down exclusionary barriers. Babcock's strategy is as good as any I've heard. But don't try to go it alone. Seek the support of lawyers, planners, environmentalists, and others who have an interest in land-use control reform. The direction of the reforms is spelled out in some detail in Babcock's *The Zoning Game.* Once the machinery Babcock advocates is set up, the attempts to manipulate land-use controls for exclusionary purposes will be more obvious and open to successful attack.

One final note on a planner's bias. Land-use controls don't have to be evil. Some court cases have not only uprooted the application of large-lot zoning for exclusionary purposes, but have cast doubt on any use of large-lot zoning.[3] Planners will argue that large lots can be justified in certain situations without exclusionary effects. They will probably oppose a pendulum swing from excessive and improper controls to little or no control. The idea is to provide opportunity and justice in the context of a livable environment.

These few comments are not equal to Mr. Babcock's thoughtful paper, but perhaps they cast it in a different light for purposes of examination.

REFERENCES

Birch, David L.
1970 *The Economic Future of City and Suburb.* New York: Committee for Economic Development.
Downs, Anthony.
1968 "Alternative Futures for the American Ghetto." *Daedalus* (Fall).
U.S. Executive Office of the President.
1972 *Report on National Growth, Domestic Council.* Washington, U.S. Government Printing Office.

3. Re Appeal of Kit-Mar Builders, Inc. (Pa.), see 22 Zoning Digest 110.

Building Viable Ghettos

T HE topic assigned for me to speak on today is "Building Viable Ghettos." For the past three years, a debate has been raging around the question of whether the ghetto should be developed— gilded is the poetic term which has seeped into the literature as a result of an article by Kain and Persky—or dispersed. To be sure, this debate has proceeded primarily in the white academic community rather than among blacks. Blacks apparently so clearly recognize and accept the reality that the black ghetto will be with us for quite some time, if not permanently, that prolonged discussion about dismantling the ghetto strikes them as pointless. The resistance to blacks moving into white suburbs, which is where the white urban population is currently headed, shows little signs of abating, and we are witnessing a backtracking even on the acceptance of integrating the public school system. In New Jersey, for example, which is where I live, the recent announcement that 2,000 units of integrated housing were to be built in the white suburban community of Readington Township, close to a rapidly industrializing area where jobs are expected to be plentiful, was immediately met by a chorus of opposition from the community, an opposition which will inevitably delay construction for a considerable period and which may well prevent the construction from ever taking place. East of the Hudson River, in Forest Hills (New York City), the opposition to erecting a major integrated housing development continues unabated and even became an issue in Mayor Lindsay's now abortive effort to win the presidential nomination. In the face of such resistance to black dispersal, it would appear that the black community is being realistic when it gives priority to ghetto development over ghetto dispersal. To the foregoing, of course, we can add, for preserving the ghetto, a rich variety of cultural arguments which I will not go into at this time.

Given that the ghetto needs to be and should be afforded special treatment to assist its development, in what context should this development take place? Is the rationale for ghetto development simply an outgrowth of the fact that vast numbers of black people live in the ghetto, that they live there under unacceptably low standards of living, that they are likely to be imprisoned there for quite some time, and that therefore their conditions should, for humanitarian reasons, be ameliorated? Are these the principal arguments for giving special attention to the ghetto?

I should think that these would constitute an inadequate rationale for black ghetto development, at least as viewed from a black perspective, although they might be a sufficient basis for winning the support of concerned whites. But in 1972, the black community is thinking beyond this evening's supper. It is thinking beyond merely convincing the local A & P to employ a black manager. It is even thinking beyond such limited objectives as the raising of black incomes to parity with whites, although that is a vital and still far-from-achieved objective.

Rather, the contemporary frame of reference for blacks is one conditioned by power. "Empowerment" is the term currently in vogue. Last month in Gary, the Black Convention platform was subdivided into sections entitled "political empowerment" and "economic empowerment," among others. A high percentage of the agendas of black conferences these days usually include panels on some aspect of black empowerment. Black scholars are attempting to analyze the true sources of power in America and to discover how the black community can best obtain a grip on one or more of the levers of power.

The question which arises then, is one of the degree to which development of the ghetto enhances the power of the black community. If development of the ghetto seems likely to bring a major accretion of power to blacks, then there may be good reason for blacks to afford such development a high priority. If not, then one may wish to channel available resources elsewhere. Of course, one cannot ignore the humanitarian considerations: Black people in the ghetto are in desperate need of help just to survive, so obviously they must be aided, regardless of whether or not such assistance really fits well into an over-all strategy for black empowerment. But succor for the poor should never be confused with development, nor can it ever be an integral part of planning. The black reality, of course, is that the number of black disadvantaged folk is so great that catering to their needs for survival absorbs virtually all of our energies and resources, leaving little for pursuing a significant development strategy. Given this disparity between needs and resources, our charitable instincts must be tempered by some realistic appraisal of over-all developmental requirements.

At the Black Economic Research Center we have made a few choices regarding our own priorities and they relate rather closely to our vision of what a strategy of black empowerment should look like, although we can justify it on other grounds, as well. Stated briefly, it is our belief that the long-term interests of the black community are best served by the achievement and consolidation of effective black political and economic control over a sizable piece of American territory. It is only through such an achievement, we feel, that the multiple black objectives of security, freedom, self-determination—that is to say, the real fruits of political and economic empowerment—can be approximated. I say "approximated" rather than "achieved," because a realistic appraisal of the black man's position in American society can lead one only to the most pessimistic of conclusions. As a 10-to-12-percent minority of the U.S. population, our security and status are permanently dependent upon the good will of the majority. By the judicious use of our numbers and our brains, we can strive to achieve the best possible accommodation with that majority; we can live in a comfortable or in an uneasy truce with them. But barring the two extremes—either of open warfare, which could lead to our annihilation, or of the disappearance of all vestiges of racial animosities, which seems highly improbable—the black man in North America will forever be vulnerable to the white majority which outnumbers him by better than five to one. Thus, we can strive to approximate a condition of security and of political, economic, and social well-being for our people. We cannot hope to achieve it in some absolute sense.

Recognizing and accepting this reality, then, we must attempt to discover the optimal strategy within these given parameters. At the Black Economic Research Center, this strategy leads us to stress the importance of utilizing a test of black political viability as the major criterion for focusing black economic resources. Given the severely limited magnitude of the resources available for black economic development, good judgment tells us that we should not scatter these resources widely, but rather should concentrate them in a few well-selected locations where it may be hoped that they can have maximum impact.

Since we are seeking empowerment, it seems logical to us that the places where the black political potential is greatest are the locations where a complementary economic thrust can have most significance.

Clearly, these are generally the areas where the black population is proportionately the greatest—a few cities, largely in the North, and a number of counties, entirely in the South. To be sure, submunicipal societal units such as neighborhoods offer even stronger black population concentrations—but the political advantages of this high black population density is counteracted by the very localized type of power which is wielded at the neighborhood level. At the other end of the spectrum, we have the state, which wields considerable power, but which in no case offers, with present population distribution, an opportunity for blacks to capture the machinery of government at the state level. Above the state, of course, sits national government, and at this level the potential for a black assumption of power is impossible in America unless the nation were somehow subdivided into units of more modest size.

Confronted with this array of vineyards in which to work, the Black Economic Research Center has chosen to select the black majority counties of the South as the "ghettos" in which it feels its resources can most effectively be channeled.

An urban neighborhood ghetto, such as Harlem, does not impress us as the most promising type of black framework within which to work. Inner-city ghettos tend to be geographically quite circumscribed, to occupy land which commands such a high economic rent as to render it noncompetitive for most types of industrial development, to be heavily burdened with bureaucratic restrictions of all sorts, to be hopelessly enmeshed in municipal politics often of the most corrupt type, to be held hostage by organized crime and/or organized labor, to be pockmarked by unorganized crime, and more often than not to be suffering from physical blight and decay. The major attraction of such ghettos, other than the potential political clout provided by the density of the black population, is their proximity to employment—an advantage which, incidentally, may be in the process of disappearing.

Black political take-overs of entire cities, however, offer a new and challenging opportunity to maximize black empowerment at a level which is far more meaningful than the development of neighborhood ghettos. Newark, New Jersey; Gary, Indiana; Compton, California; and numerous other cities in the 50,000-and-over class are beginning to come under black leadership as whites abandon the cities to the minority groups which continue to stream in from rural areas. To be sure, the economic strengthening of these black-run municipalities is not synonymous with black economic development. Most of these cities continue to have substantial white populations. In some cases, the cities are mere bedroom communities, with most of the population commuting to a nearby industrial or commercial center to earn its income (viz., Compton, California). And in almost every case, the economic base of the community lies with whites who have the option to move their capital elsewhere if they so desire. These cities, like most of the larger American cities, are in dire financial straits, oftentimes lacking even the constitutional authority to tax themselves, usually staggering under an excessive tax burden already and, in fact, deteriorating before our very eyes.

Despite these rather substantial handicaps, however, the city may be an excellent vehicle for assisting in the development process of black people. It does have some degree of sovereignty; it often has some taxing authority; and other public revenues come to it as a matter of right. The city spends substantial sums of money and, through its licensing power, can influence the expenditure of considerably more. Much the same can be said for many school districts, which sometimes raise and disburse hundreds of thousands, even millions of dollars. The power to control such expenditures is a significant power, and we are all aware of efforts being made to emasculate such power when it comes within the grasp of the black community. Metropolitan government is not the only culprit in this type of action. The recent Richmond school decision, so widely hailed by many liberals as the most important judicial decision in many years, may well prove to be a disaster from the point of view of what it costs the Richmond black community in lost economic development potential. (Whether the gains on the educational side somehow justify the losses elsewhere is hard to say, especially inasmuch as both the gains and the losses are largely hypothetical at this moment.) In sum, there can be no doubt that the city offers a significant avenue for black development.

But we at the Black Economic Research Center prefer to focus our sights on the next level of government, the county. The 1970 census listed 102 counties in the nation with at least 50 percent of their population black—all of the counties being located in eleven southern states. To be sure, these counties tend to be the poorest counties in the nation. The black majorities in them are not, for the most part, translated into black political control. The portion of these counties' assets which are in the hands of the black community tend to be negligible. And perhaps most significant of all the unpromising characteristics is the fact that the blacks are continuing to migrate out of these counties at a fairly high rate, although possibly less rapidly than in the recent past.

Nevertheless, in the face of these very discouraging characteristics, we have chosen to place our emphasis on assisting a selected few of these counties to become viable places for black people to live. The black counties of the South, or some few of them, strike us as being the ghettos which merit a major development effort. We feel that the pay-off, if such a thrust is successful, will be far greater than the returns on a comparable investment of resources made anywhere else.

To be sure, there is a high component of idealism in our decision, and the political factors weigh at least as heavily as the economic ones. But in our view, economics is inseparable from politics where black economic development is concerned, for we are beginning from a near-zero capital base and will perforce be obliged to pull ourselves up primarily by our political bootstraps. Even the 35 to 40 billion dollars of purchasing power attributed to blacks is of little collective value unless it can be harnessed and channeled, which is essentially a political activity.

For us, building viable ghettos means going into a southern county where blacks are beginning to assume some political control and assisting these blacks in planning an economic development strategy which can give their political leadership real meaning. A black county commissioner who earns his living as a porter at the local bank or as a tenant farmer is not likely to be a forceful member of the county board of supervisors. To say that he would be disadvantaged in dealing with the county's financial or its agricultural issues is to state the obvious. Yet, unless an independent economic base can be established for at least the leadership group in the black counties, political control will be virtually meaningless. Traditional small farming is no longer viable in many areas and the local white establishment may be opposed to new industry coming in for fear that industrial employment will provide greater independence to the black residents. Furthermore, the relative illiteracy and lack of industrial skills in these communities do not make them especially attractive locations for industry to settle, in any case.

Clearly, the obstacles to success in this approach are overwhelming. Nevertheless, we feel that there are some advantages, also. There is plenty of space. The people are trusting, reliable, eager, thereby permitting greater community co-operation. Some of the urban ills such as crime and narcotics, are not yet widespread. The cost of living is less expensive, so limited resources go much farther than they do in the urban North.

When we attempt to assess what types of industries are likely to be providing an expanding supply of jobs in the future, it is the service industries, including especially government, which seem to head the list—health services, education, housing. The South's needs for these sorts of programs is as great as the North's; and with proper political maneuvering, black people are likely to be able to fare at least as well, if not better, in exercising control over these vast spending programs in the South as in the North. This is due to the fact that the 25-to-35-percent leverage which blacks have on southern statewide elections can easily emerge as the balance of power as the two-party system begins to take hold. There are already indications that the South may well be the major growth area of the country in the coming decade; and where blacks are exercising political control either directly at the county level or indirectly at the state level, they will be able to help fashion this growth.

If we focus for a moment on the most recent census figures (1970), we note that the migration patterns of blacks are essentially unchanged from what they have been in the past several decades. According to the Census Bureau's report of June 28, 1971 (U.S.D.C., June 28, 1971:2–3):

The heavy out-migration of Negroes from the South during the 1960s remained at about the same level as in the previous two decades . . . Out-movement was principally felt by nonmetropolitan counties, although many metropolitan counties in the South showed net out-migration of Negroes . . . Movement of the Negro population to areas outside the South, although more widely scattered than in previous decades, was still heavily concentrated in a few large metropolitan areas . . . For the 29 metropolitan areas outside the South with 10,000 or more in-migration, the total net migration gain for Negro and other races was 1.7 million. Within the South, a few SMSAs showed substantial increases due to in-migration of Negro and other races, including Washington, D.C. (110,-000), Houston (52,000), Dallas (43,000), Atlanta (37,000), and Baltimore (34,000). Nearly two thirds of all Southern SMSAs had a net out-migration of Negro and other races, however.

It may seem foolhardy to attempt to swim against such a strong tide. In the face of so powerful an out-migration from the South and toward the largest cities, can an economic development thrust which runs diametrically counter to this trend be justified?

We think so. Indeed, we justify it for the very reason that it does flagrantly contradict current black migration patterns, for we do not feel that the existing migration pattern is the optimal one for the black community. We cannot accept the urbanization of the black community into a dozen overcrowded cities as the ideal population configuration for our people, as the population configuration which promises us most in terms either of security or of income maximization. We do not feel that it offers the greatest promise for the build-

ing of a genuine sense of black nationhood, although we do recognize
that a substantial sense of community can be built in each of these
separate areas. We are also unconvinced that the super-urban life
style is in some absolute sense preferable to that found in smaller
communities. That black Americans are more urbanized than whites
(74 percent versus 68 percent) is a fact (U.S. Department of Commerce, July 1971:13). That we should be so distributed is debatable.

In November, the nation elected its first black tax assessor in modern times, in a rural county of Mississippi. Not surprisingly, few if
any blacks had the slightest idea of what the precise duties of a tax
assessor were. Gradually, however, we are discovering how racial
discrimination has been reflected in this basic aspect of the economy.
One of the reasons behind the mass exodus of blacks from the South
may well have been the disadvantages which they suffered at the
hands of racist county tax officials.

We know that the decline in black land ownership in the South has
been precipitous in the past thirty years, a phenomenon which is not
unrelated to the heavy out-migration of blacks from the South. We
are only now beginning to examine not only the implications but also
the causes for these related phenomena. Although we tend to assume
that the land was lost largely because of migration, to an undeter-
mined extent it may be the case that migration took place because
title to land had been lost—i.e., the direction of the causality may be
the reverse of what it is generally assumed to be.

Because we feel that it is so important for blacks to continue to
own as much land as possible, we have organized an Emergency
Land Fund whose objective will be to stem the tide of loss of land
by blacks. This effort is part of a larger effort to halt the black migration out of the South. The most essential ingredient of any land or
population retention plan, however, will necessarily be to devise
means to enhance the economic development potential of the black
South. Southern black youth will not be tempted to remain at home
once they finish school unless they can see concrete employment opportunities awaiting them, opportunities which will compare favorably
with the rumored opportunities available in Detroit and Chicago.

Towns and counties which are coming under black political control
appear to us to offer the most promising areas in which to focus black
development efforts at this time. A plethora of public programs,
largely funded by Washington, are available to smaller political units
almost for the asking, if a modest local cash contribution is available.
These programs range from water and sewer programs to open spaces
and recreational facilities development projects. Roadbuilding, hous-

Stokes quotes p. 4, 10

'Counterbudget' p 28–29

Concentration p176
'good overview
   & issues – ch 11

Davidoff ch 12 p 155–206

Anti-dispersal arg. ch 13 p 207–
reviewed; use of
   power

Ch 15 – Dev. rt dispersal

Blumstein
Martin 70s

Dreaming he's falling, Jerry forgets the
well-known "always-wake-up-
before-you-land" rule.

ing, school lunches, health care are only a portion of the types of programs available which simultaneously provide a community benefit and also create employment. In some cases, ancillary enterprises are likely to spring up to service the main project. In the past, such programs have benefited whites in the South primarily, with only the laboring jobs being made available to the black community. With emergent black political control, a potential exists for a broad range of public employment and business opportunities of various sorts to be made available to blacks. An alternative to migration is beginning to emerge. We should set a high priority on creating the conditions which will permit maximum economic exploitation of this changing Southern political picture.

In sum, we do not feel that President Nixon should have a monopoly on the concept of a "Southern strategy." The South continues to constitute black America's most promising ghetto, and rendering viable its blackest enclaves should be the strategy of black America.

REFERENCE

U.S. Department of Commerce, Bureau of the Census.
  1971 *Population Estimates and Projections, Current Population Reports Series*. June 28. Series P-25, No. 461.

Planning for New Communities

PASSAGE of the Urban Growth and New Community Development Act of 1970—with many significant developer-oriented programs of grants, guarantees, loans and special assistance for new community development—enhanced the attractiveness of investment in new community development. The purpose of the act as stated in the preamble to Title VII is

to provide for the development of a national urban growth policy and to encourage the rational, orderly, efficient, and economic growth, development, and redevelopment of our states, metropolitan areas, cities, counties, towns, and communities in predominantly rural areas which demonstrate a special potential for accelerated growth; to encourage the prudent use and conservation of our natural resources; and to encourage and support development which will assure our communities of adequate tax bases, community services, job opportunities, and well-balanced neighborhoods in socially, economically, and physically attractive living environments (42 U.S.C. §4501).

So far this year, HUD has announced guarantees of developer debts in the amount of 124 million dollars for new communities. To secure such guarantees, developers must expend considerable amounts of land, make engineering studies and pay application fees. New community development not only ties up capital for a substantial period of time; it also necessitates harsh commitments of a developer's firm capabilities and limits maximum utilization of investment potential during the planning and development processes.

Prior to the passage of the act, only a few new communities—notably Columbia, Maryland, and Reston, Virginia—had progressed toward the goals expressed in the act. In both cases, considerable financial commitments were made by private industry.

Community development means developing for people. The systematic building of a satisfied community based on a perceptive design of neighborhoods in new town planning apparently is an area which has been grossly neglected by new town developers and planners. The production of an acceptable housing product (house or apartment) for the builder is certainly not a very difficult task. Units with the latest design in appliances, rooms, and finishes can be produced by the average tract or subdivision developer. But building communities and neighborhoods on which humans depend for survival extends to far greater considerations than appearance and design. The successful building of these environments depends on the ability of the planner and developer to be sensitive to human needs beyond the dwelling unit.

Jim Rouse, the developer of Columbia in Maryland, has apparently gone well beyond the usual development process. In the early stages of the Columbia process, he sponsored a series of research seminars where sociologists, educators, and social planners were interfaced with urban planners, financiers, mortgage specialists, and others to identify the human and social considerations needed to create "happy neighborhoods" and "community coherence" in a new community setting. The groups probed ways to create pride and a sense of belonging and responsibility for people in a new environment. The Columbia village and neighborhood concept is an outgrowth of that interchange between the soft and hard disciplines.

The Urban Growth and New Community Development Act of 1970 requires the Department of Housing and Urban Development to give special consideration to applications for loan guarantees for communities which effectively pursue social goals, such as opportunities for housing low-income families, racial and economic integration, and innovation in delivering educational and community services (social) to residents of the new environment. Experience, however, shows that a very special effort is needed to accomplish this goal. Generally, the planners and developers are not attuned to the human needs of people coming together in a new environment. They have fears that the financial investment may be jeopardized by the integration of racial and economic groups and have no experience in addressing these particular problems. A review of several statements of programs planned for new communities shows a lack of planning for the elderly, the nonworking family, the nuclear family, and families of low and moderate incomes. No new community has planned to house a population of more than ten percent of these special groups. In most cases, the developers address housing subsidized under Sections

235 and 236 of the 1968 Housing Act for this population with no public housing planned. No programs of social-service consequence are planned.

The investment in services to people by the new towns in England, Sweden, and other European countries shows that successes in these areas are achievable. The European experience shows the government insisting that the aforementioned services be provided or the government itself providing such services. New towns and communities have proven socially and financially successful despite the fact that they were undertaken to provide environments for people with overriding regard for profit to the developer. Family counseling, special adult education programs, homemaking, day care, community orientation, job counseling and placement, health care and education, services to the elderly, youth services including counseling, recreation and youth centers, and more, are provided with government assistance in the European new towns. The result is that, twenty-five years later, the new towns are socially, as well as economically, viable enterprises. This viability prevails despite the fact that, in some cases, a great majority of the inhabitants of the new environment come from economically and socially depressed areas (slums) as in England. The environment of the towns is well maintained by the residents, whose employment is supported to some degree in the towns and who take pride in "their" towns and in coping with life problems in the new environments.

The problems of the American suburbs are well known to all of us. These problems may be as bad as—or worse than—the problems of many inner-city areas: increasing incidence of vandalism; petty theft; destruction of public property; shoplifting; drugs at every age level; car theft; burglaries and every imaginable assault against humans and property. One reason for these increasing problems in our suburbs may be that the population is frequently highly transient—without roots—and simply does not care about the area in which it temporarily resides. Another reason may be that there is a total absence of an effort to create a community or neighborhood by the developers of suburbia. It seems that community and neighborhood spirit, social cohesion, and family identity with the community are essential to those who are new to suburban living.

Without a composite rationalization on the part of a new community developer and investor as to what human-oriented services he is willing to provide or offer at a cost to the residents of the new environment, the investment of capital and human resources traditionally expended in new community development may well be dissi-

pated in a sea of people problems. A high rate of turnover and dis-
content by the residents will not enhance the image of the new
community. Thus, there is a crying need for a rational evaluation of
the need for human services and how they may be delivered to the
new town/community. The problem may be addressed in terms of
new worth. What is it worth to the developer and his investment to
have co-operative, responsible, well-adjusted residents in the community? This worth has never been effectively discussed in a new town/
community proposal and has never been budgeted in a feasibility
study or rationalized in an economic "model."

To secure HUD loan guarantees for new community development,
the developer must show opportunities for low- and moderate-income
families and racial and ethnic integration of home buyers and tenants.
To provide for this diverse new group of constituents, the developer
must plan a diversified community, well-integrated socially and economically. The developer needs expert advice and counsel regarding
the social needs of humans and a thorough and professional understanding of what human problems are all about. To direct a salesman
to show or not to show a particular area or a particular house to this
or that consumer is counter-productive. The salesman, regardless of
his experience, is not a psychologist or a community-oriented sociologist. A developer needs people who know the social end of community
development to assure the success of the community for which he
will have responsibilities extending over long periods of time.

In the past, the average developer built and sold his subdivision,
putting all buyers into an area as neighbors, and left after a few years.
What happened to that area did not necessarily interest the builder,
once it was sold. In the building of a new community, the developer
probably will be on the receiving end of all the problems he creates
for a substantial period of time. The quarrels, complaints, and the
aforementioned problems will be the developer's to deal with. Dealing with the people's problems in the end is far more expensive and
aggravating than effectively planning and implementing community
and social programs, as programs of design, finance, and construction
are advanced.

The National Urban League and its development foundation recently established a committee to determine the extent and level of
soft planning required for successful new communities. Those groups
may well wish to engage in the development of certain new or expanding communities. Currently, we feel quite capable of offering
assistance to developers of new communities in the area of social
planning, substantive educational services, and community service

planning. This is evidenced by our development of a planned social system for new environments.

It behooves the "hardware" producers of new communities and the "software" planners to get together, so that our emerging new communities will not have the same problems as those designed in the past.

REFERENCE

U.S. Congress.
   1970   Urban Growth and New Community Development Act. 90th Congress, 2d session, 1970. 42 U.S.C. §4501.

AUTHORS

RICHARD F. BABCOCK
Ross, Hardies, O'Keefe, Babcock & Parsons
122 S. Michigan Avenue
Chicago, Illinois

ANDREW BILLINGSLEY
Vice-President for Academic Affairs
Howard University
Washington, D.C.

ROBERT S. BROWNE
Black Economic Research Center
112 West 120th Street
New York, New York

CARLOS C. CAMPBELL
11530 Links Drive
Reston, Virginia

GLENN A. CLAYTOR
National Urban League, Inc.
55 East 52nd Street
New York, New York

PAUL DAVIDOFF, Director
Suburban Action Institute
150 White Plains Road
Tarrytown, New York

H. JACK GEIGER, M.D.
Department of Community Medicine
School of Medicine
State University of New York
Stony Brook, Long Island, New York

MACK H. JONES, Chairman
Department of Political Science
Atlanta University
Atlanta, Georgia

MARK R. KILLINGSWORTH
Department of Economics & Business
  Administration
Fisk University
Nashville, Tennessee

JOHN KRAMER
Georgetown University Law Center
New Jersey Avenue
Washington, D.C.

R. GRANN LLOYD
Professor of Economics
Chairman of the Division of Studies in
  Economics and Business
College of Business Administration
University of North Florida
St. Johns Bluff Road, South
Jacksonville, Florida

DUNBAR S. McLAURIN
University National Bank
15 Park Row, Suite 434
New York, New York

WILLIAM A. ROSS
National Urban League Development
  Foundation
425 13th Street, N.W.
Washington, D.C.

HUGH J. SCOTT
Superintendent of Schools
Presidential Building
415 12th Street, N.W.
Washington, D.C.

JAMES A. SPENCER
University of Tennessee
Graduate School of Planning
Knoxville, Tennessee

CARL STOKES
NBC News
30 Rockefeller Plaza
New York, New York

CLIFFORD L. WEAVER
Ross, Hardies, O'Keefe, Babcock &
  Parsons
122 S. Michigan Avenue
Chicago, Illinois

PRESTON WILCOX
AFRAM Associates
6872 East 135th Street
New York, New York

Index

President's Committee on Urban Housing, 177
President's Council of Economic Advisers, 58
President's Report on National Growth, 224
Price controls, 28
Priorities. *See* National priorities
Professionalism, 69
Profit motive, 180
Proxmire, Senator William (D. Wisc.), 28
Pruitt Igoe, St. Louis, 183
Public education. *See* Education
Public forums, use of, to affect policy, 66
Public Health Goals, Mayor's Task Force on, 158
Public housing, 182–183
Puerto Ricans, 145, 147, 149, 152, 156, 158, 169, 170

Quality of living, 137
Quarles, Benjamin: quoted: on the Negro, 23

Racism, 20–28 *passim*, 68, 129, 152, 188, 215, 216, 220, 224
Radicals and radicalism, 150, 169
Radio Corporation of America, 205
Raleigh, N.C., 180
Rangell, Charles, 39
RCA. *See* Radio Corporation of America
Reading skills, 134
Readington Township, N.J., 229
Real estate dealers and developers, 152, 176, 188, 240, 242
Recreation: facilities, 182, 236; projects, 108, 111
Regional planning agencies, 215
Reich, Charles: *The Greening of America*, quoted, 67
Reid, Prof. Herbert O.: quoted: on blacks and law enforcement, 21
Republican governors, 110
Republican party, 103, 112
Reston, Va., 239
Revenue-sharing, 13
Revenue sources, 76
Revolutions, 11, 213, 216
Richmond, Va., 210, 233
Rights, human, 63, 131, 148–149, 214
Riots, 5, 150, 153
Riverdale (New York City), 158
Robert Walker Houses, Chicago, 183

Rockefeller, David, 71
Romanian Americans, 12
Romney, George, 196
Roosevelt, Franklin D., 12, 36, 57
Rouse, Jim, 240
Rural poor, 169
Rural redevelopment, 81
Ryan, William: *Blaming the Victim*, quoted, 154

St. Louis, Mo., 183
Salt Lake City, Utah, 223–224
San Antonio, Tex., 108
Sanitary reform movement, 146
Scandinavia, 146
Schaefer, Dr. Arnold, 104–105
School absenteeism, 159
School bond issue, 6
School drop-outs, 133
Schools: separate, 4, 5; lunch program in, 96, 100, 101, 105, 110–111, 113, 123, 237; nonpublic, 129; health facilities in, 167
Scott, Hugh, 139, 141, 142
Seattle, Wash., 112, 113
Segregation, residential, 180, 201, 204
Self-determination of blacks, 142, 150, 231
Senate of the U.S. *See* U.S. Senate
Sencer, Dr. David J., 104
Senior citizens, 12; *See also* Elderly
Separatism, 6, 7
Shreveport, La., 180
Sierra Club, 65
Slavery, 155
Slums, 8, 22, 70, 147, 150, 152, 158
SMSAs. *See* Standard Metropolitan Statistical Areas
Social protest, 154
Social reform, 131, 146, 151
Social security, 40, 63, 147
Social Security Administration. *See* U.S. Social Security Administration
Socioeconomic barriers to education, 131
South, The, 58, 62, 74, 151, 155, 169, 232, 234
South Africa, 6
South America, 39
South Carolina, 104, 116
Southeastern States, 60
Sowell, Prof. Thomas, 48
Spanish-speaking Americans, 12. *See also* Chicanos; Puerto Ricans
Special Risk Insurance Fund (FHA), 183